Essays on Fiscal Decentralisation to Local Governments in India

Essays on Fiscal Decentralisation to Local Governments in India

M.A. Oommen

Published on behalf of

KILA

GIFT GULATI INSTITUTE OF FINANCE AND TAXATION

Concept Since 1974

Series Editors

K.N. Harilal, K.J. Joseph and Joy Elamon

Book Design
Godfrey's Graphics

ISBN: 978-93-5439-772-1

First Published 2022

Published and Printed by

Concept Since 1974

Concept Publishing Company Pvt. Ltd.
A/15-16, Commercial Block, Mohan Garden,
New Delhi-110059 (INDIA)
T : +91 11 41101460
E : publishing@conceptpub.com; *W* : www.conceptpub.com

Cataloging in Publication Data--Courtesy: D.K. Agencies (P) Ltd. <docinfo@dkagencies.com>

Oommen, M. A., 1932- **author.**
Essays on fiscal decentralisation to local governments in India / M.A. Oommen.
pages cm -- (Series ; I)
Includes bibliographical references and index.
ISBN 9789354397721

1. Fiscal policy--India. 2. Decentralization in government--India. 3. Local government--India. 4. Federal government--India. I. Kerala Institute of Local Administration, issuing body. II. Gulati Institute of Finance and Taxation (Trivandrum, India), issuing body. III. Title. IV. Series: Series (Kerala Institute of Local Administration) ; I.

LCC HJ1334.O56 2022 | DDC 336.54 23

Contents

List of Tables

CHAPTER 9

CHAPTER 11

List of Figures

List of Appendices

Foreword by
Series Editors

We are in the Silver Jubilee year of the People's Campaign for Participatory Planning in Kerala. It is now widely recognized as the most enduring as well as one of the most successful experiments of its kind in the world. Even the much-celebrated governance experiments in different parts of the world, like the famous Participatory Budgeting (PB) of Brazil in Porto Alegre, have dried out or discontinued. Scholars identify multiple reasons for the success of the Kerala experiment, including the legacy of the larger democratic movement in the state, which the people's campaign had sought to take forward. In our opinion the single most reason for the success of the people's planning in the state has been the commitment to democracy not only for its intrinsic value but also for its obvious instrumental importance. The people's plan, no doubt had several other important goals, such as development of local infrastructure, enhancing efficiency in service delivery, improving local production and distribution, ensuring environmental harmony, extending social justice, augmenting welfare, and many more. But the over-arching goal has been deepening democracy. People's planning widened the scope for collective action. It is this extensive scope for citizen's participation and collective action, which worked as an inbuilt mechanism of self-learning and rectification from within, that made the Kerala experiment successful as well as enduring.

The epochal intervention would not have been possible without the inspiring guidance of E M S Namboodiripad. The programme took off at the instance of Chief Minister, E K Nayanar and the Minister for Local Administration Paloli Mohammed Kutty with the active involvement of Kerala State Planning Board led by I. S. Gulati. It was declared that 35 to 40 per cent of the ninth plan would be devolved to the local plans prepared and implemented from below. However, the key constraint was the widely prevalent capacity deficit for designing and implementing development projects/programmes at the local level. The answer to the issue, which made decentralized development in Kerala a unique experience, was the Peoples Planning Campaign (PPC) spearheaded by the Members of the State Planning Board T M Thomas Isaac and E M Sreedharan. The campaign aimed at a reorientation towards decentralized development along with the building of needed capacity to design and implement such a development strategy. This has been accomplished by harnessing the capabilities of different stakeholders that include but not limited to scholars of eminence, the elected representatives, officials in the various departments and the expertise of the non-officials and mass organizations.

People's planning generates informed deliberations involving people at all levels. Moreover, it has attracted large number of scholars from within as well as outside the state undertaking insightful studies on various aspects. This incessant process of learning from the experience of doing, especially self-critiquing, helped correcting the mistakes and strengthening the virtues. Undoubtedly the people and the local governments have evolved many successful development models. It is important to follow up such good work by undertaking research so that the lessons to be learnt are picked up and added to the body of existing knowledge in the relevant discipline. It is highly encouraging to note that there has been a number of Ph D dissertations that analysed the Kerala's People's Planning Campaign as well as the decentralization process and its outcome. This book series, jointly published by KILA and GIFT, as part of the 25th year celebration of People's Planning Campaign aims at highlighting the achievements and limitation of Kerala's decentralized development strategy. The series comprises mostly of Ph D dissertations that analysed the decentralized development. Our aim is to ensure that the continuity of 'doing and learning and doing' is sustained well.

We feel privileged that the opening volume of this series is by Professor M A Oommen, a renowned academician and a scholar known for his commitment for the upliftment of the less privileged. The first part of this work, consisting of five chapters, seeks to provide a theoretical foundation for evolving an institutional architecture that facilitates decentralized development. The second part, provides a highly perceptive analysis of the process of fiscal decentralization as it evolved over a quarter century in India and Kerala. Needless to say, this volume by Professor Oommen, who has been closely associated with the decentralized development process and having ringside view of the decentralization process in Kerala, will be welcomed by all interested in development in general and decentralized governance in particular as well endorsed by scholars of acknowledged eminence.

KN Harilal, K J Joseph, Joy Elamon

Foreword

Around the world, citizens rely on their governments to provide essential public services. The important question of which level of government should provide which services has been studied by many scholars and practitioners. However, few have focused their work on the importance of local governments in serving their populations. Of late, there has been a distinct swing of the pendulum towards democratic decentralization that could reflect the collective choice and priorities of the local people. Professor M.A. Oommen is one of those few, and perhaps, one who has done the most thorough and careful work on local governments in India. His experience as a teacher, researcher, and advisor comes together in this series of essays focused on the framework and experience of decentralization in India.

There are compelling reasons for Indian local democracy and the nuances of its fiscal decentralization dimensions to be studied in great depth. I fully endorse the definition of decentralization in this volume that in the federal context it is the empowerment of the local people (a non-entity for all practical purpose in India) through the empowerment of local government and that fiscal decentralization is fiscally empowering them. Indeed the 73rd/74th constitutional amendments were a radical departure from the colonial past which ostensibly inherited much from the government of Indian Act, 1935 and the quasi-centralized federal constitution. To be sure, the idea of gram sabha (direct democracy at the village level expressing people's preference), the finance commission at the sub-national level, and the institution of decentralized planning and so on are alien to the western fiscal federal principles.

The original tenets of decentralization are grounded in a landscape where the population can match their desired set of public services with the government that provides that set of public goods. Tiebout's theory (1956) is often summarized by the notion that citizens can vote "with their feet" under several heroic assumptions including costless mobility and complete information. Wallace Oates (1972, 1999), notes that decentralization can lead to welfare gains in the absence of such mobility when governments can match those demands. Critical components of decentralization would thus be the ability for governments to face hard budget constraints, raise revenue from own sources, and for officials to be held accountable. The traditional collection of thought on decentralization largely envisions two tiers of government with the prospect of resolving vertical and horizontal fiscal imbalances from revenue sharing as well as from the enhancement of own revenues. This is not the reality which faces decentralization among tiers of government in India. This collection of essays documents the reality of India's decentralization, which do not fit neatly into the traditional paradigm. To be sure, the global literature on fiscal decentralization and local democracy can benefit from the works of M A Oommen.

As an economist, Professor Oommen has a unique lens through which to study local governments. His work, reflected in this volume of essays, has a strong theoretical and empirical base. Unlike many economists, however, he also focuses on institutions and their role in the successes and failures in decentralization at the local level. Due to his expertise and experience with subnational finance, he was called upon to serve as the Chairman of the 4th State Finance Commission of Kerala (2011). The overriding mandate of the State Finance Commission (SFC) was to improve the efficacy of decentralization at the local level in Kerala. Under Professor Oommen's leadership, the recommendations of the SFC demonstrate the value and importance of bringing together theory, practice, and institutions to address that mandate.

As the chapters of this volume exemplify, the study of local government finance should not be a static or disparate exercise. Economic circumstances, regulations, central government policies, data development, and technology can contribute to improved public service delivery at the local level, but these factors can also hinder anticipated benefits. Changes in policy—especially decentralization—are a long game where success does not typically progress in a linear fashion. Instead, serious researchers lay out what a best-case scenario for decentralization reform would look like, and then investigate how the reform was implemented, find the best data to evaluate the impact, illuminate what is missing in the analysis, and use the information as a lesson to develop a new policy or tweaking an existing policy. This deep, thoughtful, and practical investigation of decentralization reform is Professor Oommen's hallmark and is reflected in this volume. A lesson learned is that one does not necessarily study for study's sake, but to make actual progress in decentralization. And that progress can take a long time.

The first part of this volume is dedicated to the important theoretical considerations for decentralization policy, including a summary in Chapter 2 of the principles of local taxation, intergovernmental transfers, and expenditure assignment. Case studies of Brazil, India, and Kerala provide insight into the impact of socioeconomic, demographic, and regional differences on the impact of decentralization. The message of this first group of essays is quite clear. Decentralization and democracy can improve the lives of individuals, and the architecture for doing so exists. This includes India's framework for decentralization as well as the potential to collect the data necessary to evaluate and respond to the needs of citizens.

The second part of the volume brings us experiences of the practice of fiscal decentralization in India with a focus on local (sub-state) governments. Professor Oommen's vast experiences with all aspects of decentralization allow him to concisely summarize the background and recommendations for five State Finance Commissions in Chapter 6. The detail provided in the chapter (and in Chapter 7) once again demonstrates that there is no one size fits all decentralization, and that local context and institutions are critically important to moving the needle. Additional detail and insights on some of the infrastructure for decentralization are highlighted in Chapters 9 and 10 and the volume concludes with a chapter that makes the case for expanded fiscal space for local governments in India. The entire volume is peppered with unique data and includes an expansive, well-documented literature. The essays serve as an enduring guide for developing and evaluating decentralization policy in India.

I have had the honor to work with Professor Oommen in Kerala with my colleague Dr. Abdu Muwonge. Together, we analyzed the sources and uses of the finances of the gram panchayats of Kerala and estimated their impact on overall local revenue while also looking for ways to improve the financial reporting system (Chapter 9). Sitting in Professor Oommen's study, we talked about how revenues should flow among the local governments and what impact they might have on collection of other revenues and expenditures at the local level. Just when I was about to throw away information due to an assumed error in the data, Professor Oommen would smile and tell us exactly why the data point was valid (or not), how it had likely changed over time, and how it compared to the situation in other localities. These discussions led us to much richer conclusions and better-informed policy advice. This volume's essays will take the reader through that process and enrich their ability to better understand the path of decentralization in India and make them a better policy-researcher.

In a recent interview by one of his colleagues, Professor Oommen mentioned that his choice of economics was made somewhat by mistake. The public finance world is thankful for such mistakes. With his vast knowledge and experience and generous nature for sharing the same, this volume of essays on fiscal decentralization by Professor Oommen helps us understand how all levels of government can work together to make the world better for their people.

Sally Wallace

Dean and Professor of Economics,
Andrew Young School of Policy Studies
Georgia State University

Introduction

This volume brings together eleven papers selected from a much larger number relating to the theme of democratic decentralization and its fiscal dimensions, written since Part IX and Part IXA became a part of the Indian Constitution in the early 1990s following the 73rd and 74th Constitutional Amendments (CAs) which accorded constitutional status to panchayats and municipalities once considered an appendage to rural and urban departments to function as a third stratum of government. The several institutions (e.g. state finance commission, district planning committee) and policy reforms introduced and the conformity legislation of states that ratified them were mandated to create 'institutions of self-government' at the local level tasked to prepare "plans for economic development and social justice". This was in a way a cross-section of democracy and federal principles which certainly demanded informed policy choices, reforms and research. Looking back the academic community, notably political scientists, economists, public finance pundits and policy-makers have failed to comprehend the transformative potential of this project. The purpose of this compendium is to bring together some papers on fiscal decentralization the most important component in making local democracy viable and vibrant. The papers are not chronologically sequenced but thematically and organically linked as far as possible. Some overlapping is but unavoidable.

The papers in part I captioned *theory and policy* tries to bring a theoretical perspective to bear on the fiscal dimensions of the decentralization reforms heralded by the two constitutional amendments. The constitutional mandates to create autonomous government and deliver economic development and social justice are quintessentially fiscal. The vast fiscal federalism literature is overwhelmingly western (Chapter 2). Public finance literature in India accepts them as universal models. To be sure, fiscal balance, vertical as well as horizontal are the essence of fiscal federalism. The assignments of expenditure and revenue-raising responsibilities along with intergovernmental transfers thus become critical in a multi-tiered governance system. Even so, the panchayats with their three-tier system of built-in imbalances and institutions like gram sabha, district planning committee and so on do not effortlessly fit into the fiscal federalism literature. In this context building theoretical perspectives is not easy (Chapters 1, 4 and 5).

The implications of the institutional innovations are sought to be crafted in a theoretical framework where the democratic principle of inclusion and federal principle of spatial equity are linked in a theoretical framework in chapter 1. Kerala's big bang approach with its momentous decision to devolve 35-40% of its additional investible resources to the local governments in July 1996 and the multi-stage process of development planning from below provide the empirical basis. In several chapters, I have drawn on the experience of Kerala, for two reasons: (i) the state more than most others threw away the age-long reluctance to devolve authority and power and launched into the deep of democratic decentralization called people's plan campaign and admittedly acquired considerable success relatively speaking and (ii) I was associated with decentralization reforms in the state in various capacities (Member of the Committee on Decentralization of Powers (1996-99); Chairman, Committee for Evaluation of Decentralised Planning and Development; Chairman, Fourth State Finance Commission, among several others) and acquired some field knowledge. Institution of self-government can happen only when the state parts with authority and responsibility and do a clear functional mapping and financial devolution.

The neoclassical paradigm of growth and the postulate that it can in the long run promote inclusiveness is untenable and unsustainable. Market mediated growth is inherently excluding. One important way to promote growth along with inclusion ensuring minimum basic services for all and that with dignity irrespective of the choice of their residential location is the panchayat system (Chapters 1, 4 and 5). If Union Finance Commission (UFC) works towards rectifying inter-state vertical imbalances and Sate Finance Commission (SFC) works to reduce intra-state horizontal disparities and vertical gaps to the extent possible, 73rd/74th CAs could be hailed as a feasible and certainly desirable proposition (Chapter 5). Chapter 2 serves as a fitting backdrop for two reasons. One, there is no contextual review of literature. Two the received fiscal federalism literature fit the market-mediated consumer choice rather than the development concept of the citizen around which 73rd/74th decentralization reforms revolve.

Chapter 3 comparing Brazil and India may appear somewhat odd. It certainly is not. India is placed in comparison and contrast with Brazil probably a well-designed three-tier system of the world. In presenting the salience of the two federations in a common framework, concerned readers can gain helpful insights about the working of multileveled federations.

Part II is a continuation of the earlier part and serves to highlight the progress and problems of fiscal decentralization with reference to the third stratum of government for over a quarter century. Although inaugurated with great hope, this reform with tremendous potential for transforming local governance and promoting federal principle was allowed to decay. Covid-19 pandemic has shown the cost of neglecting the third tier of government as the Fifteenth Union Finance Commission (UFC-15) has affirmed. India has a well-functioning budgeting and fiscal system and financial reporting arrangement at the union and state government levels. But, the 2.5 lakh rural and urban local governments comprising nearly 3.2 million elected representatives do not have a budget system or reliable financial reporting system. Two statements from chapter 10 are quoted here to show how shocking the ground realities even where decentralization has made respectable progress. "That the slipshod manner of budget-making can go to fictitious extreme is well-exemplified in the case of income from investments where the Annual Financial Statement actual diverges from the budget actuals by 10338.8%...." in a Corporation. "Budgeting is an exercise in self-deception". The frustrations faced by all the UFCs from FC-11 are not entirely insurmountable (Chapter 9). Any way things have been allowed to drift for years.

UFC whose duties and responsibilities have been broadened following the two constitutional amendments and the SFC its sub-state level counterpart are complementary institutions in working towards better fiscal balance in India. It is a moot question whether equalization of fiscal capacity to provide minimum basic services to all citizens irrespective of their choice of location of residence has been attempted and realized (Chapters 4,5,6,7, 8 and 11). Looking back one can say that the much-needed organic and strategic link between UFC and SFC seems to have been miserably missing in practice. Given the onerous task of the first and second generation SFCs to set norms, conventions and practices relating to fiscal federalism in the context of the 73rd/74th Amendments, they have done a creditable job (Chapter 6 and 7). Instead of handholding them such ill-informed general comments like 'sketchy', 'patchy', etc., by the UFCs were unprofessional indeed. Even so, it is worth noting the significant efforts made by the FC-13 to organically link local governments to the public finance of Indian federal polity. Most of these restructuring efforts were thoughtlessly discarded by the UFCs that followed.

The most compelling macro fiscal policy reform especially after the exit of the Planning Commission relates to the redesigning of the transfer arrangements. The growing presence of centrally sponsored schemes and strengthening of MPLAD, MLALAD etc., forget that the prime rationale for establishing local governments is that they reflect the preferences of the local people. All the chapters in this volume (in particular see chapters 4, 5, 6, 7 and 11) try to show that the progress of a well-functioning local democracy depends on sound fiscal decentralization coupled with promoting a substantial own revenue source.

We believe that this work will be a useful source of information for anyone who wants to understand what happened to financial decentralization to the third tier of government in India during the first quarter century of its existence.

Part I

Theory and Policy

CHAPTER 1

Social Inclusion and Institutional Innovations: Working Towards a Policy-Theoretical Framework with Reference to Local Governance

Social inclusion has occupied an important place in contemporary development discourse [see Rodgers Gerry et al. (ed) 1995); Kabeer Naila (2006) among others]. It is projected as the major development goal by the planners and policy makers of India. The three volume XIIth Five Year Plan (2012-17) draft with the sub-title 'Faster More Inclusive and Sustainable Growth' approved by the National Development Council on December 27 2012 has added a new chapter captioned social inclusion. This is expected to be different from "a purely corporate-led growth strategy" [Planning Commission (2012): 5]. Even so, the term is neither defined nor strategized. The underlying assumption of this paper is that the existing institutional architecture to be truly inclusive needs reform and that in any redesigning exercise decentralised democratic institutions has a place of significance. Ever since United Nations/CDS (1975) study identified the relatively high social achievements of the regional economy of Kerala, with low per capita income, Kerala has attracted considerable attention from development thinkers the world over. In the development literature, Kerala's development experience came to be widely characterized as a 'Model' (more as an expost facto generalization of an historically evolved experience than as an exemplar). A high human development without a sharp rural-urban divide or obvious gender disparity, an extremely respectable food and nutritional security, a wide social security system, a very high female-male ratio, fertility decline way below replacement rate achieved as a matter of choice, collapse of an oppressive caste structure (with not only untouchability, but with unapproachability and unseeability as its dominant character) and imparting self-respect to the 'lower' caste/strata people, abolition of feudal relations of production in the agrarian sector, a multi-religious, multi-cultural population living in symbiotic relationships and so on indeed are great social achievements in human history [See Robin Jeffrey (1992, 2001); Dreze and Sen (1995) and Oommen (1999); among others]. The 'big bang' people's plan campaign launched in August 1996 backed up by the decision to devolve 35-40 per cent of the state plan outlay was in the best traditions of Kerala's public action [See Isaac and Franke (2000)]. Besides the capability demonstrated in mobilizing people and resources for augmenting productive base and the great potential for improving the quality of public services, the most important contribution of the people's plan has been the introduction of a new methodology for decentralized planning which has widened the avenues of people's participation. Indeed, participating in social choice is a valued capability and freedom [See Sen (1999)]. The purpose of this chapter is to explore the possibilities of building the contours of a policy-theoretical frame for a meaningful social inclusion based on the institutional innovations in decentralized governance initiated by the Kerala state since mid-1990s.

Social Inclusion, Inclusive Growth, and Inclusive Development: Some Conceptual Issues

At the outset, it is important to clarify the concept of social inclusion, inclusive growth and inclusive development because of the confusing explanations centering around the terms. No theoretical postulate or policy option can be built on ambiguous concepts. We prefer the term social inclusion rather than inclusive growth which is used profusely in the XIth and XIIth plan documents. In 'inclusive growth' the major emphasis is on expanding the size of national income and is projected as a normative framework for development whereas a more fundamental and rational approach is to focus on the lives that people live and the freedom they enjoy. Economic growth is only a means, to improve the quality of human well-being. It is not an end in itself. Looking back the concept of Hind Swaraj of Mahatma Gandhi could be envisioned as a goal towards inclusive human development. But this is too idealistic with almost impossible demands on transforming human nature and values. The 'reverse engineering' involved is indeed too formidable.

We prefer to use the concept of social inclusion rather than inclusive growth and inclusive development where the context warrants the use. Social inclusion implies that no one should be left out or kept out including the social misfits. We may elaborate the concept more specifically. First, unless you have the exchange entitlements to participate in the market (e.g. income, employment, assets, social security, credit and so on), you will be keptout.

Charity can help, but that is antithetical to all genuine ideas of inclusion with dignity. Social arrangements for the public provision of education, health care, food entitlements, social net provision and so on assume significance here. They are the barometers of the progress and sincerity of a society. Second, social inclusion is not a binary model in which some are 'in' and others out. Inclusion has no meaning unless it is done to enhance human dignity and freedom. In other words Inclusion should be on equitable terms. The classic example of inequitable social inclusion is the caste system of India. Institutional architecture and social arrangements for provision of basic needs and all arrangements for building capabilities have to be suitably reformed and modified to promote social inclusion. It is assumed that Panchayati Raj Institutions (PRIs) following the 73rd Constitutional Amendment have a special role in promoting social inclusion as part of an integrated design. Third, growing economic inequalities is an expression of social exclusion. In a situation where growth keeps increasing and poverty is reduced, but at the same time faces widening inequalities, there can be no equitable social inclusion [Sen (2000)]. The opportunities offered by the market in the social production of goods and services should not be appropriated by a small minority. The institutional arrangements must provide equitable social and economic opportunities. Fourth, inclusive development should be participatory. This means increased efforts are needed to include the disadvantaged people in the process of decision-making (e.g. decentralised planning in Kerala) as well as in the process of social production. Fifth, relevant policy formulations related to social inclusion will have to recognize the diversity of exclusions which result in capability deprivations, that range from enforced exclusion like slavery and attached labour to credit market exclusion, gender-related exclusions, lack of educational facilities, health care and the like [See Sen (2000)].

Government of India (GoI) have never precisely defined or clearly and comprehensively strategized their policy regarding the provision of entitlements to include the excluded. Sen's capability and freedom perspective has great potential to be used as a normative framework to evaluate development practices. This is in sharp contrast to the unidimensional measure of growth of income or consumption or industrialization and the like even when they are declared to be pro-poor[1]. Without expanding the capabilities and freedom of individuals, there can be no social mobility and social inclusion. Bhagwati and Panagariya (2012) take a somewhat different view and argue that what is important for India is to promote economic growth through more and better economic reforms. They do not address the question of social inclusion as their argument is that more and rapid growth can take care of that. Sen in his various writings argues that people differ in their ability to convert goods into valuable achievements due to personal and locational factors, besides the social arrangements in the provision of education, health care, social security, democratic rights, participatory institutions, ruling central values such as the treatment of women and so on. Democratic decentralised governance if well-designed and strategised can help in the process of social inclusion considerably.

A fundamental flaw in the approach of the Government of India about inclusive growth has been their treatment of inclusiveness and growth as disparate entities. Presenting growth and inclusiveness as co-equal development objectives, M S Ahluwalia (2011) observes:

> "The Eleventh Plan aimed at delivering faster and more inclusive growth and it is logical to assess performance against this dual objectives"[p.88] and goes on to say that, "it is difficult to assess inclusiveness than performance on growth"[p. 89].

Treating inclusiveness and growth as separate entities and again maintaining that as "logical" policy choice rules out structural transformations, institutional reforms, market failures, redistribution strategies, envisioning sustained capability enhancing policies and so on, besides upholding the trickle down approach. By increasing the number of monitorable variables of inclusiveness to 27 (health, education, sanitation etc.) as is done by the Planning Commission, you cannot social inclusion meaningfully. Increasing the number of target variables to assess departmental progress cannot be inclusive growth or development by any reckoning.

Not only that, Ahluwalia (2011) also speaks of the 'systemic reforms' since 1991 based on a wider play of market forces, gradual liberalization of the financial sector and the opening up of the economy to world trade and capital flows. (*ibid*). But the moot question is whether 'the cumulative effect of the systemic reforms' has promoted social inclusion, in the sense in which we have postulated it. Presumably, the more important question is why the planners and policy makers of India have failed to think of corresponding systemic reforms for a growth process that includes those excluded or likely to be marginalized on the wayside of growth.

Logically and factually, rising inequalities is an inherent by-product of the growth process in any market–mediated economy particularly with deep disparities in initial endowments.[2] As Ifzal Ali (2007) argues, inequality has to be strongly contained through relevant policies to promote an inclusive democracy. The GoI do not have a deliberate inequality reduction strategy[3]. Besides the lack of positive redistributive strategies, the poor progress and appalling inequities in the access to health services and education are now very well-documented. [Rama Baru et al. (2010), William Joe et al. (2008), Sonalde

Desai and Amaresh Dubey (2011) among others]. That large inequities in health and access to health services continue to persist and have even widened across states, between rural and urban areas and within communities in the India of faster growth is well documented by five scholars (most of them health and community medicine experts) (Baru Rama et al. (2010)). This is powerful evidence to show that the goal of inclusive growth, leave alone social inclusion remains a far cry.

The approach of the Asian Development Bank to inclusive growth seems to be far more meaningful than that of the Government of India as is clear from the following definition:

> "Growth is inclusive when it allows all members of society to participate in, and contribute to the growth process on an equal footing regardless of their individual circumstances. (Ali and Zhuang (2007): 10).

This definition is positive and implicitly envisages a widespread employment pattern that grows faster than the rate of growth. However a growth process that works towards expanding equitable employment opportunities must spell out the technological paradigm underlying the growth process, define the policy choices relating to the composition of commodity flow, the structure and pattern of initial endowments, the social arrangements for enhancing the capabilities of individuals and the freedom needed to achieve the capabilities and so on. Apart from the protective support given to the traditional industries like khadi, handicrafts, coir, cashew and the like, India is for a capital–intensive technological paradigm. The latest numbers regarding employment from the 66th round NSS data (2009-10) reveal a "jobless growth" story as regards the rate of growth in employment which shows, a dramatic deceleration in the rate of employment generation to 0.8% per annum during the quinquennium ending 2009-10 as against 2.7% during the previous quinquennium. (See Chandrasekhar and Jayati Ghosh (2011)).

In sum, the concepts inclusive growth and inclusive development that frequently appear in GoIs policy documents and often used interchangeably needs precise definition and clear policy strategisation. It was because of this ambiguity that we have tried to broadly define social inclusion which envisages a democracy with an equitable and inclusive development.

Innovative Institutions as Change Agents

In this section we examine the potential and possibilities of institutional innovations. Long back John Rawls pointed out:

> "Justice is the first virtue of social institutions, as truth is of systems of thought. A theory however elegant and economical must be rejected or revised if it is untrue; likewise laws and institutions no matter how efficient and well-arranged must be reformed or abolished if they are unjust" [Rawls (1971): 3].

Many of India's political institutions were borrowed or adapted from the west and surely need reform to suit her growing needs and challenges. For example as Sen Amartya (1981) has demonstrated, it was not the lack of food availability or production, but institutional failure that caused the great famines of Bengal, Ethiopia, Sahel and so on in recent times (Sen (1981)). Relevant institutional innovation is continuously needed in strategizing development based on meaningful social inclusion. 73rd/74th Constitutional Amendments envisaged a welcome decentralization reform in Indian federal polity.

Innovation refers to the use of new ideas or new ways of doing things. Quite often innovation is associated with high-tech and is quite often considered to be motivated by profit. For such innovators, consumers and markets are the target field. The institutional innovations that we postulate, however, are social innovations motivated by the goal of social well-being. Innovations need not be about brand new ideas. It is as much about developing and adapting or refashioning existing ideas. But the application and adaption should yield enduring social value. The nature and quality of institutional architecture is crucial to any transformative project.

In socially oriented institutional innovations (e.g. the participatory mechanisms developed as part of the People's Plan and Panchayati Raj Institutions in Kerala), how challenges are framed is important in determining the kind of innovation one gets. When you formulate problems and challenges keeping the needs of the micro unit, individual, family, community and the like, the chances of making radical institutional innovations increase. Here people are not treated as consumers or customers, but as agents and participants. People are also not conceived as the recipients or beneficiaries of so-called development programmes but as agents enacting change as we have already noted. Capacity and motivation to act depend on relationships and mutual trust and support or what may be called social capital a la Robert Putnam[4]. Considerable personal relations, community networks and cooperation are fostered in a genuine democratic society. Individuals achieve additional functionings through a direct connection with another person and in recent literature referred to as "external capabilities"[5]. The range of external capabilities can be significantly widened by information and communications technology (ICT). Capabilities of individuals and groups are enhanced because of networks. Communication facilitated by ICTs (e.g. mobile phones) is an important instrument in building capabilities and expanding freedoms. Getting connected is a way of reducing the isolation of the poor people and fostering inclusiveness.

In what follows we try to explain the role and potential of the local governments in India with particular reference to the innovative practices Kerala has initiated since mid-1996.

PRIs' Claims for Social Inclusion

The institutional reforms following the 73rd/74th Constitutional Amendments which provide the legal framework for decentralisation in Indian federal polity bear tremendous potential for strategizing social inclusion . The Eleventh Plan noted that it is "absolutely critical for the inclusiveness of our growth process" that the 3.2 million elected representatives in the PRIs are "fully involved in planning, implementing and supervising the delivery of the essential public services" (Planning Commission (2007): 23). While involving people's representatives is important, empowering the PRIs to function as integral agencies of social inclusion however requires an altogether different approach and strategy.

The two Amendments seek to usher in 'Institutions of self-government' at the local level endowed with the tasks of 'planning for economic development and social justice' (Articles 243 G and 243 W). This mandate to deliver social justice is evidently a call to include the traditionally excluded, minorities as well as women and all marginalized in the scheme of planning for economic and human development. The institution of gram sabha, the assembly of voters mandated to deliberate on development priorities, budgets, audit reports etc., 50% reservation for women and representation for the historically marginalized communities on population basis, the establishment of the state election commission to ensure fair elections every five years, the creation of the state finance commission to rationalize state-sub-state level vertical and horizontal fiscal imbalances and so on are important steps towards enhancing the quality of participatory governance and inclusive development. A report of World Bank that critically studied the decentralisation process in India notes that PRIs as political institutions can play a critical role in strengthening voice and representation, access and inclusion of the marginalized, and that they can be effective only if they are able to broaden the democratic base by tackling political exclusion and strengthening the "synapse" between communities and governments for better local governance. (World Bank (2006): 78).

The institution of gram sabha[6] which is direct democracy par excellence has few parallels in the world. Equally important are the 50% reservation for women (although currently only a few states follow this, it is going to be mandatory following a Constitutional Amendment that is underway), representations to the traditionally marginalized classes and the various other reforms which were virtually efforts to create an inclusive, responsive and responsible democracy at the local level in India. These are somewhat different from the theory and practice of local democracy in the west. In the fiscal federalism literature produced and popularized mostly by the Western scholars[7] the role of local governments (municipalities alone matter for them) is confined to providing certain basic services to the residents (customers of these services) in a local jurisdiction at the cheapest possible price (taxes, user charges etc.) (See Oommen (2005)). This is far removed from the conceptualization underlying Part IX and Part IXA of the Indian Constitution. Poor performance of decentralization in some states does not deny the intrinsic value and instrumental role of decentralization reforms in enhancing human well-being and democratic practice.

In the contemporary world, the ruling political paradigm of state governance is representative democracy, characterized by balloting and majority rule. Strictly speaking, it has no compulsion to empower citizens, generate high or direct participation in government affairs or ensure social justice. The economic philosophy underlying representative democracy could be characterized as market-mediated economic growth (Dunn (1993)) which is the enemy of inclusive development as it believes in the natural trickling down of the benefits of growth. However meaningful democracy should contribute to real social choice (production process and distribution should also reflect this) of the people, by the people, for the people as we have been told for years now.

The Local Government Reform Initiatives of Kerala

While the 73rd/74th Constitutional Amendments provide for certain basic institutional reforms, the details of making them operational were left to the individual states. Kerala is one state that radically reformed the local governments. In this section we outline the salient features of these reforms that were made to widen the avenues of citizens' participation in formulating and implementing the local government plan especially at the panchayat levels.

Unlike other states, Kerala launched its decentralised planning and governance initiative in a campaign mode called 'People's Plan Campaign' (PPC) widely charactorised as a 'big bang' approach. The campaign mode was launched because it helped to facilitate people's involvement in the new process of local planning. The first major decision of the Left Democratic Front (LDF) Government that came to power in July 1996 was to transfer 35-40% of the state plan outlay to the local governments (LGs). This discretionary budgetary fund made available to LGs was a quantum jump compared to the past. Instead of the traditional wisdom to lay down the procedures and rules first and then create the structures and instruments, the PPC adopted a learning-by-doing approach. Although conceptually a bottom-up planning exercise, a lot of trial and error and guidelines from above was but inevitable and the State Planning Board (SPB) virtually acted as the nodal agency. However, it is important to note that to begin with, the setting out of state-wide theatrical processions on the theme of power to the people, called Janadhikara Kalajathas prepared the ground and created the ambience and awareness to launch and keep alive the campaign mode.

After the momentous decision to devolve a sizeable proportion of the state plan outlay to the local governments, almost immediately a Committee on Decentralisation of Powers (1996-99) (popularly called Sen Committee after the name of its first chairperson Sen Subrato) worked out the scheme of devolution of functions, funds and functionaries and the enabling legal framework for democratic decentralisation. Although subject to guidelines and accountability norms, there was considerable budgetary autonomy to these governments whose functional domains (broken up into activities and sub-activities) also have been mapped out in due course. More than a decade has passed since then and the institutionalization process is still underway.

The first step in the methodology of planning launched was the special gram sabha meet to identify the needs and priorities of the community. Each electoral ward presided over by the ward member (elected representative) constitutes a gram sabha in Kerala. There are as many gram sabhas as there are wards which number 16680 today. Besides that there are 5002 urban wards, making a total of 21682 wards all of which constitute the citizen assemblies. In fact, an important contribution of PPC was the convening of the special gram sabha, for ventilating the felt needs of local citizens and brings gram sabha into the centre-stage of decentralised planning. Under the PPC regime (circa 1996-2000) considerable preparation by way of elaborate publicity and pamphlet distribution was done to enlist more people's participation and to make it more inclusive and purposive. The special gram sabha is generally divided into subject-wise committees, to make the deliberative process more participatory. In the initial years during the 9th plan this was preceded by 'transect walks'[8], resource-mapping and similar such exercises, to make the gram sabha meetings fruitful and to prevent such meetings becoming a cataloguing of wish lists. Trained local facilitators helped to catalyse the process during the early periods. Direct beneficiaries of programme if any were selected by subsequent gram sabhas on the basis of well-defined criteria.

Once the 'felt needs' were identified and evaluated, the second stage was the preparation of a Development Report for each panchayat based on a scientific assessment of the human and material resources of the area, an exercise which was buttressed through several participatory mechanisms. This Development Report prepared for all village panchayats and municipalities under the Campaign dispensation was a basic document for local planning during the IXth Five year plan. Unfortunately so far it is not yet updated or revised. The Development Reports were discussed in what has come to be called Development Seminars which organise sectoral task forces (subsequently rechristened working groups), whose responsibility it was to prepare projects. In the words of Isaac and Franke, one important purpose was "to organise development seminars in every gram panchayat and municipality to discuss the (development) reports so that the ward-wise development dialogue initiated at the grama sabhas could be scaled up to a higher level of the village" (Isaac and Franke (2000):105). That under the PPC regime nearly 5 lakh people consisting of gram sabha members, political party leaders, civil servants, local experts and so on participated in the Development Seminars (See State Planning Board (SPB) (2000),) underscores the potential for deliberative problem-solving and participatory planning in a decentralised democratic setup. Needless to say this does not mean that all the development seminars were of uniform success.

The third is the projectisation stage which requires technical skill of a high order. This is the task of the working groups which were designed to be an ideal mix of stakeholders like people's representatives, bureaucrats and experts. Surely public participation does not automatically ensure the technical skill required. It is broadly understood that the projects should have both backward and forward linkages (Isaac and Franke (2000):128). During the PPC regime a 300 page Hand book on project preparation[9] was made available to all concerned not to let the project preparation a 'blind man's bluff'. More importantly special attention was given to the preparation of special plans for women (called Women Component Plan), for schedule caste (SC)/ and scheduled tribes (ST)[10] and that too by a Working Group presided over by a SC/ST member. Once a shelf of projects[11] was prepared the actual choice is constrained by the availability of resources.

The first three stages have meaning only when the proposals get concretized into a local plan. The fourth stage is related to the determination of the actual size of the annual plan. The state plan share is given as a grant-in-aid to LGs to meet the bottom-up plan they prepare. The plan grants (- subsequently called development funds) as designed during the PPC and continued later has three components: special component plan (SCP), or funds earmarked for the development of scheduled castes, tribal sub-plan (TSP) or funds for the development of scheduled tribes and the general sector funds. The horizontal distribution of the plan grant (development fund) till 2010-11 was on the basis of a composite formula based on population, area and backwardness with undue weight (ranging from 65% to 75%) on population. The fourth State Finance Commission (SFC-IV) changed this and recommended a formula which gives weight to population, area, tax effort and poverty measured in terms of five deprivation criteria viz., families living in huts, families without latrine, families whose access to drinking water is more than 300 metres away from residence, families without electricity and landless households (elaborated in the last section). This came into effect from April 1, 2011 and has imparted more equity into the scheme of devolution. Despite the best efforts even under the PPC, the plan preparation at the level of village panchayats and municipalities moved haltingly. While the responses of some of the elected representatives, chairpersons and mayors were positive that of several others were lukewarm although everybody had to fall in line. Actually, the transparent and participatory methodology was alien to the prevailing pattern of decision-making and definitely antithetical to the tradition of the contractor, politician, engineer, bureaucrat nexus that shaped the 'development culture' in the past. It was in this circumstance, several directives had to be given from above.

The task of integrating or rather meaningfully coordinating the village panchayat plan with that of the block and district panchayats, virtually a new dimension as far as Kerala was concerned, constitutes the fifth stage. A lot of duplication was inevitable especially because each tier had the freedom to plan for its functional domain. The multitude of centrally–sponsored schemes (CSSs) implemented through the local governments (LGs) in the past also had to be made a viable component of the three-tier system. For managing the system in such a circumstance, Kerala abolished the District Rural Development Agency (DRDA) created by the central government to implement the centrally-sponsored scheme and merged it with the district panchayats. The centrally-sponsored schemes were not only out of sync with the approach and strategies of the PPC but also seldom met the specific needs of a state that has made significant progress in education, health care, road connectivity and so on. To make the CSSs a viable and meaningful part of the State's decentralised planning the state government's matching contribution towards CSSs was routed through the block panchayat as against the prevailing DRDA in order to give them autonomy to use the state share as per the norms of PPC. Moreover, plan funds could be used to supplement CSSs where necessary. With the traditional block development officer acting as the block panchayat secretary the operational significance of many of the schemes was lost. The block plans, expected to avoid all duplications at the village level and dovetailing projects of inter-village panchayat relevance had to be discussed at development seminars before they could be approved.

It is the constitutionally mandated duty of district panchayats to have a consolidated plan for the district as a whole (See Article 243ZD). Despite the fact that urban areas do not come under the functional domain of district panchayats, as per constitutional mandate district planning will have to take into account the plans of municipalities and corporations. The overall planning as well as the consolidation as mandated by Article 243ZD of the Constitution is the responsibility of the constitutionally created institution of the District Planning Committee (DPC). The administrative sanction has to be given by the DPC. The technical support to the District Plan is made by the District level expert Committee (DLEC) and scrutiny of village panchayat schemes by the Block level expert committee (BLEC).

An important problem the PPC had to encounter in their quest for a methodology of local level planning which became most apparent almost at the last phase was the need to have a body that will evaluate the technical and financial feasibility of projects. The creation of the voluntary technical corps, (VTC), later on called Technical Advisory Groups (TAG) was in response to this need. Retired engineers, professionals, unemployed technical experts and so on were encouraged to register themselves as volunteers to appraise the projects of LGs and offer suggestions for improvement. The TAG in course of time became an appraisal team of officials and non-officials at the block and district levels. During the XIIth Plan the role of TAG is deliberately deemphasized. That during this time over 35000 persons, mostly retired persons registered as VTC members is a major indicator of popular participation, with no parallel elsewhere in the world.

The success of participatory planning is to be seen by its capacity to reduce (rooting out completely would be impossible) corruption and progressively clean the system at the local level. What has the decentralisation methodology done about corruption? The public works department (PWD) has been notorious for corruption. The growing construction activities on roads, buildings, irrigation and so on even at the local level-village, block and district – have been huge as more funds got devolved. This has further accelerated resulting in an unholy nexus between contractors, civil servants, technical personnel and politicians leading to huge leakage of funds which increase the cost of public services. In the words of Isaac and Franke:

> "Contractors made big profits, which were shared with politicians who connived to grant the work, engineers who gave technical sanction and monitored the work, as well as clerical staff who

> approved payment of bills. To contain corruption, innumerable checks and balances and ad hoc rules had been introduced over time. But these myriad rules and regulations trapped honest persons in a web of delays and approvals that discouraged them from participating" (Isaac and Franke (2000): 237].

The Beneficiary Committee (BC) system was PPC's answer to tide over this situation and introduce greater transparency and accountability in public works. If the beneficiaries come forward (the assumption was that they had the time, energy and expertise) to manage the projects that benefit them and the technical and administrative system lend them a supporting hand, ideally there is no better alternative. Although over 30,000 Beneficiary Committees were formed during the initial phase, most of them, succumbed before the continuing pressures and fights from the vested interests including engineers, officials and politicians. However, that nearly 25% cases successfully completed projects demonstrate the tremendous potential of BCs to function as a viable participatory mechanism (ARV Pillai (2000)). In course of time the BC system fell on the wayside and the contractor system has staged a comeback.

Another agency widely known as Kudumbashree (KDS) formally inaugurated in May 1998 and launched in April 1999, (fully operationalised by 2003), functions as a viable participatory structure in the decentralised governance of the state. It is 'a women-oriented anti-poverty programme' cast in a mission mode under the leadership and patronage of panchayats and municipalities. As the Mission statement puts it:

> "To eradicate absolute poverty in ten years through concerted community action under the leadership of Local Self Governments, by facilitating organisation of the poor combining self-help with demand led convergence of available services and resources to tackle the multiple dimensions and manifestations of poverty, holistically."

Kudumbashree through its micro-finance self-help group structure and through its many-faceted activities taken up through LGs over these years seeks to empower poor women who were identified using a nine-point criteria. The empowering process and activities of KDS are worked through a three-tiered community-based organization (CBO) referred to as community development society (CDS). The multi-pronged approach focuses on human resource development, community health, child welfare, basic human needs, re-habilitation of the destitute (The Ashraya Project of village panchayats), lease-land farming, housing and promotion of micro enterprises, besides its microfinance activities. The CDS which was functioning long before it was changed into KDS, continues to function as part of the participatory planning process. It is a fact that the KDS which has over these years functioned as a sub-system of the municipalities and panchayats, not only integrated the various anti-poverty programmes and functioned as their delivery system and participatory mechanism. The strength of the CDS system is largely because it was functionally linked to the LGs. (See Oommen (2007) for more details).

Towards More Institutional Effectiveness: Some Suggestions

The institutional reforms briefly outlined above and the actual practice yawn wide. In this section we present some suggestions or correctives in the light of what happened in the state.[12] Most importantly the three Fs, functions (broken-up into activities and sub-activities based on the principle of subsidiarity avoiding overlapping and concurrency), funds (which should match the functions transferred) and functionaries (adequate for the tasks assigned) should be properly aligned for any local governance apparatus that is responsive and accountable. This strategy implies considerable expenditure discretion, a large proportion of untied transfers along with own source revenue (the transfer system should incentivize revenue efforts) and the functionaries deployed should be answerable to the LGs. In many states this is not happening. Even in key sectors such as primary education, primary health, minor irrigation, crop production etc., which are the exclusive functional domain of PRIs the departments dominate. In Kerala also the system needs considerable improvement. The accounting and accountability arrangements in particular need drastic reform. Budget formulation and financial reporting in vogue despite ongoing reforms continues to be unreliable and irregular and needs to be radically improved to facilitate accountability, monitoring and evaluation. (See Chapter 10) Also, the pattern of spending should be evenly spread throughout the year. The prevailing pattern of spending in Kerala shows a heavy bunching of development expenditure during January to March.[13] Incidentally this is indicative of the extant corruption which has to be reduced if not rooted out. An increasingly corrupt system cannot be a model to follow, adapt or replicate.

Again the gram sabha should be made the kingpin of inclusive governance in the villages of India. Kerala's decentralised performance was at its best when citizen participation in gram sabhas and development seminars was high. However, as the GoK (2009) points out, when gram sabha

> "becomes a routine affair and a meeting place of beneficiaries or benefit seekers or when attendance gets fudged an important democratic tool stands discredited and the bureaucracy comes back with a vengeance. The gram sabha/ward sabha meetings

> which could have been developed into a forum for consensus building or throwing up constructive ideas for development purposes lose these significance" (GoK (2009): 45].

The failure of the beneficiary committee system and the continuation of the endemic leakage of public resources through artificial escalation of project estimates, total disregard to quality specification in the use of materials and so on are documented in the Report. In the words of the Committee, "Apparently nobody, seems to be worried about the continuation of the contract system and the archaic public works manual which have facilitated and legitimized corruption in the state" (GoK (2009): 46].

Certainly participatory methodology needs rethinking and refashioning. Making participatory institutions always answerable to bureaucracy (obeying the rules of game and rule of law notwithstanding) is permitting them to recapture power. Even so a mix-up of participation with administration has to be avoided. While participation of people has no direct role such as where a doctor, engineer, planner and other actors are directly involved, it is certainly for the people to design the destiny and direction of their future transformation.

This again drives home the need for strong systemic change and deep political commitment without which any worthwhile participating and inclusive governance can be made.

Sustainability of PRIs depends a great deal, surely not in romanticing their achievements but in fighting those vested interests that work against them, rallying forces that make democratic practice a way of life and above all in consistently building the capabilities of the citizens.

Inclusion of the Excluded: Towards Relevant Postulates

In sum, it is clear that the philosophy and institutional structures underlying the 73rd/74th Constitutional Amendments bear tremendous potential to promote inclusive development. The approach of GoI however, as explained in earlier sections envisages inclusiveness and growth/development as two disparate boxes and does not work towards social inclusion. Evidently this approach needs correction and the PRIs offer great possibilities. That policy choices for the inclusion of the excluded are very great in a decentralised regime is well exemplified in the design of the transfer of development funds from the state to the sub-state level in Kerala followed by the fourth state finance commission (SFC-IV) of the state.[14] An improved version of the SFC-IV recommendations are discussed below. (See also GoK (2011); chapter VIII).

(Generating relevant data is essential for inclusive policy initiatives). A comprehensive below poverty line (BPL) survey based on a Census of households in all village panchayats, municipalities and corporations of Kerala undertaken by the Commissionerate of Rural Development, Government of Kerala, in 2009 using school teachers as investigators, (to ensure quality of data) which SFC-IV processed yielded a wealth of information. From the BPL survey data SFC-IV constructed a deprivation index[15] and made use of it to identify the vulnerable communities viz., SC, ST, fisher-folk (admittedly a vulnerable group like SC, STs) and other categories in every gram panchayat (GP). Besides the deprivation index, a ratio index was also constructed to rank every village panchayat as regards the deprivation of these social groups compared to the total situation in the state as a whole. That this could be done for every local government holds out the possibilities for mapping out a strategy for the inclusion of the excluded.[16]

The demarcating deprivation line was drawn based on the data of the BPL survey, which used two schedules, form A and form B. Form A was used for every household. It contained questions related to eleven variables.[17] The social group classification of the household was also generated through this form. Form B was canvassed in a house only if all the eleven characteristics of form A are reported nil. This schedule contained information on the housing conditions, health status, land holdings, availability of other household basic amenities and so on. The main economic activity (occupation) of the families is also generated from this form. From this data four sets of information are obtained for SC, ST, fisherfolk and general population. The details of SC, ST and general population are obtained from the social groups in form A.[18]

From the data it is possible to generate eight to ten variables that can indicate human deprivations. Out of this SFC-IV used five equally important variables for constructing the deprivation index. They are given below:

a. Housing Status: Percentage of families living in huts and dilapidated houses;

b. Sanitation: Percentage of families reported as without latrine, kayal latrine, latrine without tank, pit latrine and common latrine;

c. Drinking Water: Percentage of families whose access to drinking water source is more than 300 meters away from dwelling place; and relying on pond, river and private distributors for drinking water;

d. Electricity: Percentage of families without electricity connection for household purpose.

e. Landholding: Percentage of landless families.

In order to compare different social groups under consideration, and also to identify the vulnerable GPs (gram panchayats), a composite index is constructed comprising all these five variables[19] and used them for the actual allocation of development funds as also for a definite resource allocation transfer arrangement to help the excluded viz., SC, ST, fisherfolk and the economically backward sections in the most vulnerable GPs identified on the Ratio Index basis.

The formula for calculating the index of deprivation used was similar to that of human poverty index employed by UNDP and is given below:

$$ID = [{}^{1}/_{5}\,(d_1^{\propto}+d_2^{\propto}+d_3^{\propto}+d_4^{\propto}+d_5^{\propto})]^{1/\propto} \quad \text{---------------- (1)}$$

Where ID is Index of deprivation, d1, d2, d3, d4 and d5 are the percentage of families who lack the five basic amenities in a given GP, $\propto$ is a weight parameter. If the $\propto = 1$, the index of deprivation is the average of its indicators. As the $\propto$ increases, greater weight is given to the indicators in which there is the most deprivation. Similar to the human poverty index used by UNDP and deprivation index used by Kerala HDR (2005), a value of $\propto = 3$ for computing the index of deprivation was used. Using this index, first all the GPs were ranked so as to identify the vulnerable Panchayats and then the relative position of SC, ST, and fisherfolk with that of the general population. Apart from the power weight of 3 for $\propto$, additional weights can be assigned to the variables. This enables one to give weights depending on the priority of the variables [On this see Oommen and Shyjan (2014)]. These illustrative cases actually employed by SFC-IV of Kerala are mentioned to show the potential of the tool in mapping out the excluded in the state (by each local government) which is a necessary condition for any strategy for social inclusion.

Conclusion

Innovative institutional architecture is a sine qua non for any sustainable transformative practice that works towards social inclusion. The 73rd/74th Constitutional Amendments have provided the necessary conditions for helping inclusive decentralised development process by creating a set of institutions such as the gram sabha, district planning committee, state finance commission, state election commission, reservations for women, and representation on population basis for the traditionally marginalised and so on in the local governments who are mandated to deliver 'economic development and social justice' and usher in 'institutions of self-government' at the local level. A lot of sufficient conditions also need to be fulfilled to put these into an integral part of the everyday practice of local democracy. The decentralised planning exercise of Kerala although launched on a campaign mode has been institutionalised through a multi-stage process of participatory structures that have demonstrated the possibilities of inclusive development. True, there is a yawning gap between theory and practice and has to be bridged. We have also shown that through a census of households in the village panchayats, municipalities and corporations it is possible to identify all the vulnerable households through universally valid deprivation criteria. That you can physically map out the socially and economically excluded is no pipe dream. Through continuing adaptations and innovative actions, it is possible to make local democracy a live instrument for local development. Probably there is no other institution that can be fashioned to increase the access and inclusion of the marginalized and strengthen the "synapse" between communities and governments for better local governance.

* Published in Lakhwinder Singh, K J Joseph, Daniel K N Johnson (2015) (ed); *Technology, Innovations and Economic Development, Essays in Honour of Robert E Evenson,* Sage, New Delhi. The help of D. Shyjan in the preparation of this paper is acknowledged.

Notes

1. Terms like pro-poor growth have very little in common with the inclusive development that strategises the inclusion of the excluded through relevant policy choices.
2. For an elaborate empirical evidence covering a period of nearly 300 years of economic growth one may read Piketty (2014). It is also useful to read Stiglitz (2012) and Wilkinson and Pickett (2010) in this context.
3. The following, observation of Ahluwalia, himself a leading policy strategist of India is indicative of the indifferent approach to inequality. "It is sometimes argued that inequality should not matter as long as the poor are getting better off and it is probably true that a rapid rate of improvement in incomes for the poor may make them willing to accept some increase in inequality. However, large increases in inequality accompanying only modest improvements in the levels of living of the poor are unlikely to be acceptable" (p.89). Are the poor to be treated as a distant somebody or cartoon characters to be commented upon by the elites and scholars?
4. See for e.g. Robert D. Putnam (1994; 2001)
5. More on this, see http://www.ophi.org.uk/pubs/OPHI.WP8.pdf.
6. It is interesting to recall that UPA (United Progressive Alliance) government in their National Common Minimum Programme declared (May 2004) that 'the Gram Sabha is empowered to emerge as the foundation of Panchayati Raj'. This is a major declaration of development goal.
7. For a review of literature on this see Oommen (2005) given in chapter 2.
8. Resource appraisal team consisting of experts in agriculture, soil and so on along with local people, local teachers etc. walk through the length and breadth of the village to gather basic data. This practice was done only during the initial process of the PPC although the special gram sabha has continued since then in the preparation of annual plans.
9. It is important to note that on almost every major aspect of decentralisation, there was a Handbook to help the planning process.

10. Scheduled castes refer to the so called low castes popularly called dalits and scheduled tribes refer to adivasis or tribal communities, both listed in separate schedules of the Indian Constitution.
11. Preparing a fewer number of sound projects could be a better alternative to multiplying projects that are an ensemble of good, bad and indifferent types.
12. For an elaborate critique of decentralised participatory governance and development in Kerala see Report of the Committee for Evaluation of Decentralised Planning and Development, 2009. (Government of Kerala (GoK) (2009))
13. It goes as high as 83.6% for Municipalities, 66% for gram panchayats 59.9% for block panchayats and 68.4% for district panchayats. (This is based on a survey conducted by the Fourth State Finance Commission and covers the period 2004-2009 and made available to the author.
14. The author of this paper was the Chairman of SFC-IV and wrote the chapter entitled, Devolution and the Inclusion of the excluded (chapter VIII).
15. For the devolution of plan grants to panchayats and municipalities also a formula with 30 per cent weightage to devolution index was followed (along with 50 per cent for population, 10 per cent for area and 10 per cent for tax effort).
16. This exercise is attempted in another paper by the author. (See Oommen and Shyjan (2014)).
17. Families with employees in government sector (Class I to Class IV); employees in private/quasi-government/aided sector; employees in co-operative sector; pensioners in government/service; pensioners in quasi-government/aided institutions; pensioners in co-operative institutions; regular salaried in public/private institutions; house structure higher than 1000 sqft; four wheeler motor vehicle for private purpose; NRIs; with land possession higher than one acre (except STs).
18. It may be noted that since the social groupings given in 'form A' are as SC, ST, Minorities and Others, it is difficult to get fisherfolk as a separate category from form A. Therefore, the fisherfolk group could be arrived at only by using form B, where the occupational details are furnished. The group 'fisherfolk' includes only those families whose main source of income is fishing either marine or inland. Hence the 'general' group includes fisherfolk and minorities also.
19. The extra variables left out are households with school dropouts, households with members above 65 years of age, households with disabled members, unmarried women with children etc.

References

Ahluwalia Montek S (2011), 'Prospects and Policy Challenges in the Twelfth Plan', *Economic and Political Weekly*, Vol. 46, No. 21 May 21 - May 27, 2011

Ali Ifzal (2007), 'Inequality and the imperative for inclusive growth in Asia', *ERD Working Paper*, Manila: Asian Development Bank.

Ali Ifzal and Zhuang Juzhong (2007), 'Inclusive Growth toward a prosperous Asia: Policy Implications', ERD *Working Paper Series No.97*, Asian Development Bank. (Downloaded from the website: http://www.adb.org/Documents/ERD/Working_Papers/WP097.pdf)

Baru Rama, Arnab Acharya, Sanghmitra Acharya, A K Shivakumar, K Nagarj (2010), 'Inequities in Access to Health Services in India: Caste, Class and Region, *Economic and Political Weekly,* Vol. XLV, No. 38, September 2010.

Bhagwati Jagdish and Arvind Panagariya (2012), *India's Tryst with Destiny Debunking Myths that undermine progress and addressing New Challenges,* HarperCollins Publishers, India

Chandrasekhar C.P., Jayati Ghosh (2011), 'Latest employment trends from the NSSO', *The Hindu, Business Line.*

Drèze, Jean, and Amartya Sen, (eds.) (1995), *India, Economic Development and Social Opportunity*, Oxford University Press, New Delhi.

Dunn John (1993), *Democracy: The Unfinished Journey, 508 BC to AD 1993*, New York: Oxford University Press.

Government of India (2011), *Mid Term Appraisal – Eleventh Five Year Plan 2007-2012,* Planning Commission, New Delhi: Oxford University Press.

Government of Kerala (GoK) (2005), *Human Development Report*, Thiruvananthapuram: State Planning Board.

------ **(2009),** *Report of the Committee for Evaluation of Decentralised Planning and Development,* Thiruvananthapuram: State Planning Board.

------ **(2011),** *Report of the Fourth State Finance Commission, Kerala,* Part I, Thiruvananthapuram: State Planning Board.

Isaac Thomas T M and Richard Franke (2000), *Local Democracy and Development: Peoples Campaign for Decentralised Planning in Kerala*, Left Word, New Delhi.

Jeffrey Robin (1992), *Politics, Women and Well-being. How Kerala Became: 'A Model',* Oxford University Press, New Delhi.

Joe William, U S Mishra, S Navaneetham (2008), 'Health inequality in India: Evidence From NFHS-3', *Economic and Political Weekly,* August 2.

Kabeer, Naila (2006), *Poverty, social exclusion and the MDGs: the challenge of 'durable inequalities' in the Asian context.* IDS Bulletin, 37 (3). pp. 64-78.

Oommen M. A. (1999), (ed.), *Kerala's Development Experience Vol. I & Vol. II,* Concept, New Delhi.

------ (2005), 'Rural fiscal decentralisation in India: A brief review of literature' in L.C. Jain ed, *Decentralisation and Local Governance,* New Delhi: Orient Longman.

------ **(2007),** *Report of Kudumbashree of Kerala: An Appraisal,* Thiruvananthapuram: State Planning Board.

Oommen and Shyjan (2014), Local Governments and the Inclusion of the Excluded: Towards A Strategic Methodology with Empirical Illustration (Working Paper, Centre for Development Studies, October.)

Pillai ARV (2000), *Beneficiary Committees: An Experiment under People's Planning,* Paper presented at the International Seminar on Democratic Decentralisation, Thiruvananthapuram, May 23-27.

Piketty Thoms (2014), *Capital in the Twenty-First Century*, translated by Arthur Goldhammer, Harvard University Press

Planning Commission (2007), *Eleventh Five Year Plan,* New Delhi: Government of India.

------ (2012); *Twelfth Five Year Plan,* New Delhi, Government of India

Rawls John (1971), *A Theory of Justice*, Clarendon Press, Oxford.

Robert D. Putnam (1994), *Making Democracy Work: Civic traditions in modern Italy*, Princeton: Princeton University Press.

------ **(2001),** *Bowling Alone: the collapse and revival of American community*, New York: Simon & Schuster, 2001.

Rodgers Gerry, Ronald D. Lee, W. Brian Arthur (ed) (1995), Economics of Changing Age Distributions in Developed Countries (International Studies in Demography).

Sen Amartya (1973, 1998), *On Economic Inequality,* Oxford: Oxford India Paperbacks, Oxford University Press.

------ **(1981, 1999),** *Poverty and Famines,* Oxford: Oxford University Press.

------ **(1999),** *Development as Freedom, New Delhi:* Oxford University Press.

------ **(2000),** 'Social Exclusion: Concept, Application, and Scrutiny', ADB Social Development Paper No. 1, *Asian Development Bank,* Manila, Philippines.

Stiglitz E Joseph (2012), *The Price of Inequality,* Allen Lane.

Sonalde Desai, Amaresh Dubey (2011), 'Caste in 21st Century India: Competing Narratives', *Economic and Political Weekly,* March 21.

State Planning Board (2000), *Economic Review,* Government of Kerala, Thiruvananthapuram

UN/CDS (1975), *Poverty, Unemployment and Development Policy, A case study of selected issues with reference to Kerala,* Centre for Development Studies, Trivandrum.

Wilkinson Richard and Kate Pickett (2010), *The Spirit Level – why equality is better for everyone,* Penguin books, London

World Bank (2006), *India: Inclusive Growth and Service Delivery: Building on India's Success: Development Policy Review,* Report No. 34580-IN, Washington: The World Bank.

CHAPTER 2

Fiscal Decentralisation to Rural Governments in India: A Brief Review of Literature

This review of literature seeks to understand and raise some issues relating to fiscal decentralisation in India in the context of the 73rd and 74th Constitution Amendments and the consequential mandate on the union and state governments to establish 'institution of self-government' in the Indian federal polity. The term 'institutions of self-government' (Article 243G) is not defined in the constitution. Even so, the broad task of fiscal decentralisation in India is to put public finance in order in the emerging federalism in the country. This review is done in the background of the received theories and is organized under two broad heads: (i) 'fiscal decentralisation: a theoretical resume', and (ii) fiscal decentralisation in India.

Fiscal Decentralisation: A Brief Theoretical Resume

Decentralisation is a concept that defies definition. Given the multiple ways it is interpreted and the vast diversity of experiences relating to decentralisation, the concept has to be contextually defined and understood [Bird and Vaillancourt (1998); Lister and Betley (1999)]. Roy Bahl's definition of decentralisation as 'the empowerment of local populations through the empowerment of local governments' (given in a personal communication) has a great appeal in the Indian federal context especially after the addition of Part IX and Part IXA to the Constitution in 1992 following the 73rd and 74th Amendments. Devolution, which denotes the transfer of power, specific functions and resources to subnational political entities is an evolved form of decentralisation and fits well with this definition [UNDP (1993); Litvack et al. (1998); Oommen (1998); Shahid et al. (1999); and Government of India (GoI) (2001)]. It is much broader than deconcentration and even delegation and generally has statutory backing. In the evolving multitier context of Indian federation, the concept 'devolution' has greater appeal and relevance. We may hasten to add that this observation does not mean that one can ignore the dangers and costs of decentralisation in terms of efficiency, equity, economic stability and so on [Prud'homme (1995); Tanzi (1996)]. Here it is not wide off the mark to cite a definition of devolution advanced by a Government of India task force as relevant to Indian rural decentralisation [GoI (2001): 5].

> Devolution in the context of the panchayats, means that when the authority in respect of a specific activity is transferred from the state to the local governments, the latter should have the prerogative of taking decisions in respect of planning and implementation of such activity. In fact functions, funds and functionaries are complementary to one another in the process of devolution of responsibilities and powers upon the panchayats.

This definition is cited for three important reasons: (i) it is comprehensive and has relevance for anyone studying the theory and practice of decentralisation in general and fiscal decentralisation in particular; (ii) it has been arrived at following a decade of experience in implementing rural decentralisation in India and can have lessons for other countries as well; (iii) local governance is seen as an integral part of the federal system.

Fiscal decentralisation is a subset of decentralisation. Fukasaku and De Mello Jr. (1999) define fiscal decentralisation as 'the devolutin of taxing and spending powers to lower levels of government' [Fukasaku amd De Mello (1999):9; see also V.Tanzi (1996)]. This is in line with the definition of devolution. Even so, we may note that it does not emphasis the process aspect of decentralisation and therefore we may broadly define fiscal decentralisation as fiscal empowerment of the lower tiers.

It may be noted that the literature on local-government economics (e.g. Hirsch (1970); King (1984); Bahl and Linn (1992); Bailey (1999)] as well as the extensive and vast fiscal-federal literature available has failed to recognize the institution of rural local governments called panchayats that have been evolving in the Indian federal system for quite some time now. Not only that, the defining characteristics of local government, as generally accepted in the fiscal literature, refer to democratically elected local bodies backed by some powers to levy local taxes by which to exercise genuine discretion over the provision of public services [Cole and Boyne (1995); Bailey (1999)]. Local government of this genre very rarely includes such functions as 'planning for economic development and social justice', or the several developmental and welfare responsibilities like rural electrification and distribution, nonconventional energy, public distribution system, operation and maintenance of community assets, etc., now falling within the functional domain of panchayats (Indian Constitution Article 243G and Schedule XI). Although several other developing countries have been taking to decentralisation of development programmes, projects, and administration (Cheema and Rondinelli (1983)], very few countries, at least in theory, have taken decentralisation to the level of rural local bodies in such greater magnitude and comprehensiveness as India did in the 1990s. Given the historical and social context of Indian decentralisation, theories of fiscal federalism that evolved under systems dominated by market allocations could not explain the behaviour of Indian local governments. This does not mean that general principles are not important. Indeed they are relevant.

There is a vast and growing literature relating to the theory and practice of fiscal decentralisation, which, broadly speaking, examines the fiscal autonomy of subnational governments. The theoretical literature has evolved from a quest to answer the basic question relating to the multitier system of government as in,'who could do What', in order to ensure the most efficient and equitable allocation and distribution of resources consistent with the preferences of people [Oates (1972); King (1984); Bird (2000); Shah (1994) and Litvack et al. (1998); see also Bahl and Linn (1992, Part IV)]. More specifically, fiscal decentralisation refers to the principles and practices concerning functional or expenditure responsibilities, revenue assignments, and rectification of vertical and horizontal imbalances. Vertical imbalance refers to the mismatches between levels of government in responsibilities and resources. Horizontal or interjurisdictional imbalances refers to the presence of geographical inequities. These fiscal balance questions have particular significance in a vast country like India with great regional disparities in resource endowment, level of income, level of development, fiscal disabilities, and even social deprivation. Seeking answers to the question, 'who could do what' thus turns out to be a continuing intellectual and policy pursuit.

A formal theory based on a demand-driven model of consumer choice goes back to Tiebout (1956), who postulates that individuals (households) 'shop' among a large local jurisdiction in an effort to balance marginal site costs (including all tax 'price') with the marginal evolution of public-services packages. This model involves a set of, assumptions so patently unrealistic as to verge on the outrageous [W.E. Oates (1981); 93]. Without laboring further on the merits of this model, it is important to note that such costless out-migration of 'consumers' in search of their preferred pubic-goods packages, or voting by feet as Tiebout puts it, is untenable in the context of a country such as India where over 70 per cent of the population (unlike hardly 2 per cent in the United States) depend on land. Probably it is more important to stress that the role of local governments in the democratic context of developing countries such as India is related to the developmental concept of the citizen in a wider community than the instrumental concept of the consumer whose voting is an expression of self-interest [Mulgan (1997); Council of Europe (1995). The concept of consumer choice is also not in sympathy with the concept of citizen's participatory rights (e.g., the institution of gram sabha where all voters in a village meet to discuss their development problems, the reservation of seats and posts for women and socially backward communities, etc., guaranteed as per the two Constitution Amendments in India). The traditional theory of fiscal federalism developed by Oates (1972) fails to note this difference in approach.

Oates (1972) outlines a 'decentralisation theorem' which argues for a geographical area that internalises the benefits and costs of a public good and should include precisely the set of individuals that consume it. It is asserted that welfare is maximized if each local government provides the Pareto-efficient output for its constituency [Oates (1972); 35—8]. While there is a case for internalising benefits to costs by way of taxes or fees, the ideal jurisdiction that it contemplates is a goal difficult to realise in practice [Shah (1994)]. A Pareto-efficient geographical jurisdiction is an El Dorado in poor countries and backward jurisdictions where many citizens simply cannot pay taxes or user charges.

The most important economic roles of government mentioned in the public finance literature are three: allocative (efficiency), distributive (equity), and stabilisation functions. To this may be added the regulatory role as well [Musgrave (1959); Musgrave and Musgrave (1989)]. It is argued by Oates (1972) and several others that 'stabilisation and distribution are primarily the concern of the federal government while resource-allocation functions, that is, decisions about how much to spend for each service and how to finance them belong properly to the lower tiers.' This is by and large true although considerable overlapping and intergovernmental coordination is required in regard to all these functions. To ensure effective redistribution of income and alleviation of poverty, the national government has a dominant role [Bird and Rodriguez (1995); W.E. Hirsch (1970); Raghbendra Jha (1998); W.E. Oates (1999)], although the local government also will have to work closely for effective implementation. Sometime a range of rewards and disincentives may have to be built into intergovernmental fiscal relations by the central government to achieve certain national goals and egalitarian objectives. Again, if more expenditure and resources are left to the control of local bodies, the stabilisation function cannot be handled effectively by the national government alone. Ensuring some degree of correspondence between the benefits obtained from public services in a particular jurisdiction with the revenue potential is important because it also promotes accountability [Litvack et al. (1998); Bird (2000)].

While we distinguish the economic role of governments at the various levels, the subsidiarity principle offers a good guideline for expenditure assignment. Each function assigned to a particular tier of government should conform to its most efficient performance. In other words what can be done best at a particular level should be done at that level and not at a higher level.

For categorisation of expenditure assignments as between different levels of government, it is instructive to refer to Shah (1994), Shah and Qureshi (1994), and Lister and Betley (1999). Even so, a watertight assignment of several services and functions would be difficult. This is particularly true as Bird (2000) rightly points out, when the relevant policy and regulatory framework and much of the financing may come from higher levels of government with the actual service delivery being done at a lower institutional level. Primary education statutorily 'assigned' to the village panchayat in Kerala but syllabus preparation, inspection, salary payment, etc., done by other levels of government is a classic illustration of this. Similarly, the public health services in Kerala although it is assigned to the lowest tier (gram panchayat), medicines and the consumables are purchased at the state level clearly because of the economies of bulk purchase.

The need for clarity in expenditure assignments brings home the equally important question of the channels of accountability. Bird (2000) outlines three major rules in this regard:

1. Subnational governments should, whenever possible, charge for the services they provide.
2. Where charging is impracticable, subnational governments should finance such services from taxes borne by local residents, except to the extent that the central government is, for whatever reasons, willing to pay for them through transfers.
3. Where the central government does pay, substate level governments should be accountable to the central government at least to some extent [Bird (2000); 3). This is one way to ensure accountability. But, in the context of decentralised democratic governance, it may be noted that the concept means much more than 'answerability'. Actually, democratic decentralisation is expected to correct not only the distortions caused by the abuse of power of public agencies (the answerability aspect), but also

to make them more responsive, participative and transparent. Transparency facilitates participation and participation makes a public agency really responsive to people's needs.

Democracy itself is the best basic means to ensure accountability. Even so, if it is not backed up by adequate, correct, and regular information there can be no effective accountability. This weakness of decentralised governments in developing countries has been pointed out in the literature [among others see Bird (2001)].

The Question of Revenue Assignments

Revenue assignments, basically is a question of who should tax where and what in a multitier government as Musgrave (1983) puts it. Broadly, revenue assignment refers to the division of revenue sources or fiscal instruments among the various levels of government in a federation. Several authors have advanced the principles underlying this. They range from broad principles to the rationale of specific taxes [Oates (1972); Musgrave (1983); McLure Jr. (1983); Bird and Wallich (1983); Stein (1998); Oates (1999); Bird (2000); Bahl (2001); among others). While the different authors stress different principles, there is consensus that taxes dealing with redistribution and stabilisation, taxes on mobile factors, taxes requiring national-level information and involving significant economies of scale in tax administration should be by the federal government. There is also no dispute on the question that the revenue instruments assigned to a tier of government should match as far as possible the expenditure requirements to induce 'fiscal responsibility' [Ter—Minassian (1997)]. That mismatches occur either deliberately (see India) or owing to practical difficulties is a major issue related to fiscal decentralisation. In the practical realm we have such cases as the district panchayats and block panchayats in India, which in most states do not enjoy any major revenue source except grants while their expenditure domain is pretty large (for a useful conceptual basis of tax assignment on a three-tier spectrum, federal, state or provincial and local, see Anwar Shah (1994)).

In the context of fiscal decentralisation in developing countries, it is important to identify those principles that are of particular relevance to local bodies. What is a local tax? What are the basic principles of taxation that are of particular relevance to local governments? A local tax is one where the local authority (i) determines the tax revenue by setting the tax rate and/or defining the tax base; and, (ii) retains the revenue collected for its Own Purposes [Bailey (1999); 152, Bird (2000): 78). Although basically the principles of local taxation are derived from the general principles, we may spell them out following largely Bailey (1999).

1. *Equity:* Usual notions of vertical and horizontal equity should apply as far as possible.
2. *Efficiency*: Local taxes should promote allocative efficiency.
3. *Transparency*: The accountability of service providers to tax payers depends on voters' knowing exactly how much they are paying in taxes.
4. *Local autonomy*: If the allocative-efficiency gains of Oate's decentralisation theorem are to be achieved, it is essential that local governments and their voters are free to determine the rates at which local rates are set.
5. *Economy*: From the local government's point of view, local taxes should be relatively cheaply collected. From the society's point of view, the tax should not create high default which will make tax realization expensive to enforce. From the taxpayer's point of view, the tax should be simple.
6. *Adequacy:* The tax yield should be as far as possible adequate to finance the levels of services for which people vote. The local tax should, therefore, have an easily adjustable and an elastic tax base, expanding as far as expenditure.
7. *Revenue Stability:* There should not be undue fluctuations in the flow of revenue.
8. *Immobile tax base:* Local taxes may do well to confine to immobile tax bases such as land, buildings, etc., besides levying user charges where relevant. This does not rule out imposing fees or other levies on business, trade and taxes on profession and so on.

Despite these widely stated principles, in reality the discussion on tax assignments remains inconclusive. The importance of the problem of tax assignments depends on the assignment of spending responsibilities. If local governments are responsible for expensive social services, the pressure on local revenues will be substantial. It is critical to note that meaningful tax assignment refers to the assignment of the ability (and responsibility) to determine own revenue (including the control over effective tax) (McLure (1999); and Bird (1999). It may be noted that as the value added tax (VAT) regime gets underway, the space for gloanl revenue assignment is likely to be reduced [Bahl (2002)].

Intergovernmental Transfers

The literature on intergovernmental transfer of resources is vast. Intergovernmental transfers arise largely out of vertical mismatches between functions and finance as well as out of the compulsions necessitated by the horizontal disparities between different jurisdictions. Inter-jurisdictional spillovers of costs and benefits also justify transfers. A higher-level government may also wish to compensate local governments because of fiscal disabilities like poor taxable capacity. As we have already noted it may be also because the national government may impose its preferences on the subnational governments in the national interest (e.g. eradicating poverty, ensuring a national minimum of public services of standard quality, reducing regional disparities, etc.) Here, broad national goals will rule over the so-called preferences of the median voter. The question is one of arriving at a rational size of a divisible pool by the higher government to the local government [Bahl (2000); Bird (2001)].

In the literature on transfers we see a broad typology of grants based on the prevailing practices. Grants are broadly grouped into conditional or specific and unconditional or general. The conditional categories are divided into matching and non-matching, the latter further into closed-ended or open-ended. There are also equalization grants largely governed by considerations of horizontal equity. Which of these and what combination of them is a policy decision largely governed by the objectives to be served by governments concerned [Bahl and Linn (1992)]. The design of transfers is critical here because whether a transfer is good or bad depends on the objectives to be served and the manner in which it is designed. The effects of the grants on the grant-receiving institutions and the economy are extensively discussed in the literature.

The intergovernmental grants, other things being equal, stimulate the provision of local government services, increase private-sector demand, and may even lead to the reduction of taxation. In theory, grant works by increasing the real income of the local citizens (the so-called income effects) and/or by reducing the relative price of the services in questions (substitution effects). The local voters' response will depend upon their respective income and price elasicities of demand. In all cases where the income effect is higher than the substitution effect there is potential for stimulating more demand for goods as well as services. Grants also open the option for reducing local taxation. Whether grants will stimulate more positive impact or reduce local taxation or produce other effects is an empirical question. While matching grants, particularly of the open-ended variety, have a greater stimulating effect on grant-receiving institutions because of both income and substitution effect, there are empirical studies that go to show that closed-ended grants stimulate expenditure than open-ended ones (e.g. Gramlich (1977); Shah (1979, 1989)]. The chief weakness of this type of grant is that it may distort local priorities besides widening spatial disparities as richer governments can attract more resources especially in an open-ended grant programme. This has very serious implications for countries such as India where reducing spatial disparities has been an avowed development objective of the country.

Another interesting issue of grants that has stimulated considerably discussion in the literature is the flypaper effect meaning money sticks where it hits. Extensively reviewing the literature on flypaper effects, Bailey (1999: 259) observes:

> The flypaper effect literature dates back to the early 1970s. It is overwhelmingly neoclassical in approach, attempting to improve the median-voter demand model and /or temper it with public choice supply-side perspectives. While this approach provided valuable early substantial analytical insights, more recent papers seem to have contributed only marginally to an understanding of the flypaper effect, if indeed it exists at all.

Successful fiscal decentralisation depends a great deal on designing intergovernmental transfers in a rational, equitable and accountable way. Given the wide institutional setup and socioeconomic factors governing countries, the transfer system has to be country specific and subjected to constant review depending on the changing demands of time. India is a country that has made constitutional provision for periodically evaluating and a recommending intergovernmental transfers with separate arrangements for union-state as well as state-local transfers.

From the vast literature on intergovernmental transfers, it may not be out of place, to distil out a few principles that will be relevant (Litvack et al. (1998); Bahl (1999); (2000); (2001); (2002); Bailey (1999); Bird (1993); (2000); (2001); Wildasin (1997); R Jha (1998); M N Murthy (2000); Shah (1994) among others) for federal systems like that of India's. They are:

1. Intergovernmental fiscal relations is a system and all of the pieces must fit together. Subnational governments must be made an integral part of the revenue mobilization as much as it has shared responsibilities.
2. Objectivity and transparency.
3. Needs, rights and desert are key criteria in intergovernmental transfers (Murthy 2000). A simple distributive formula that will give due weightage to needs, rights to minimum basic services, incentives to performance, inter-jurisdictional equity, etc., are important considerations relating to formal grants (among others Bahl (2000).
4. Predictability to ensure rational subnational budgeting.
5. Medium-term expenditure and revenue framework.

6. Transfers should not perform a 'gap-filling approach as far as possible. Any transfer from a higher to a lower government will help to close the fiscal gap and the objectives to be served therefore assume importance here.
7. Efficiency and inter-jurisdictional equity. Efficiency requires that those responsible for any service should have adequate resources (assuming the best own revenue effort) and sufficient flexibility to make decisions while being held accountable for results. 'Unless increased transfers are matched by a local contribution-however small that contribution may be in the poorest communities-the full efficiency benefits of decentralisation are unlikely to be realised' (Richard Bird (2001);19). To ensure inter-jurisdictional equity, the best way is to work towards what is called in theory the equalization grant, which is widely hailed as the 'glue' that has held the Canadian federation together [W.E. Oates (1999)]. If equalization objectives are abandoned, one is left to question why any grant should be paid at all [Bailey (1999); Bird (2001)].
8. Transfers should not bail out the incompetent and the irresponsible.
9. Fiscal autonomy and responsibility at all levels. Fiscal autonomy cannot be built in a regime of grants, but will have to progressively rely on tax effort and innovative revenue mobilization including project-tied loans, public donation, and the like.
10. Transfers should have clear lines of responsibility including expenditure and performance conditionalities and accountability.
11. There should be proper tax coordination and harmonisation.

In sum, it is important to note that democratic decentralisation is a new strategy of governance. It needs champions as well as close monitoring, constant correction and direction. Roy Bahl's ground rules on fiscal decentralisation is a good summary of guidelines in this regard [Bahl (1999); see also Rondinelli et al. (1983)].

Fiscal Decentralisation in India

We have given a brief outline of the theoretical literature as a backdrop to the study of fiscal decentralisation in India. This section is devoted to a short review of the scenario with focus on rural decentralisation in the 1990s. The 1990s witnessed a sharp paradigmatic shift towards a market-mediated economy starting from June 1991. The 73rd and 74th Constitution Amendments have virtually sought to make local governments a third stratum of local self-government. It may sound strange, but yet true that local governments had not been a part of Indian planning and development strategy. The rural local bodies called panchayats, which for all practical purpose had been an administrative appendage of the rural departments, have come to enjoy a constitutional status. With 532 panchayats at the district level and 5,912 at the intermediate level (block/taluk) and close to 3.4 million elected representatives (representing 742 million rural people) to govern these institutions. India has taken political decentralisation to great dimensions. Some of these local governments are very small in size. Their size as well as locations are the result of historical accidents, rather a matter governed dictated by allocation-efficiency, or scale-economy considerations. The economic liberalization and the economic decentralisation it implies and the political decentralisation that is taking democratic governance to the remotest parts of the country, can be seen as complementary events. Here is probably a meeting point of widening of choice and expansion of voice [Tiebout (1956); Oates (1972)]. Of course where the markets fail, governments intervene. In this respect, there is a compelling need to reexamine the design of the transfer system in Indian fiscal federalism. This section is organized under three broad heads: the historical setting, fiscal assignment, and the transfer system.

The Historical Setting

The Indian Constitution envisaged a two-tier system of federation. It was quasi-federal and biased towards the union. It draws heavily from the Government of India Act, 1935. The observation of B.R. Ambedkar, the chief architect of the Indian Constitution, in the Constituent Assembly that: 'I like a strong united centre, much stronger than the centre we had created under the Government of India Act of 1935', reflected the mood of the makers of the Indian Constitution [GoI (1946):78; for details of the debate see also AVARD (1962)]. No wonder in the first draft of the Constitution. 'Panchayat' was left out and when it was introduced under Gandhiji's intervention it found a place only under the Directive Principles of State Policy as Article 40, which 'casts a duty on the centre as well as the states to establish and nourish the village panchayats so as to make them effective self-governing institutions'. Actually, it took more than four decades to make this into a statutory reality and that too after two constitutional amendments. The road towards this goal was hard and difficult as the centripetal bias of the constitution was considerably accentuated particularly because one national party ruled over the union and states for a long period.

Indeed, India had a long legacy of village panchayats that goes back to Vedic times. The Village Panchayat Acts actually existed in all the British Indian provinces and in twenty native states long before independence. Coming to the post-independence times the three-tier panchayat raj institutions were introduced by the union government following the Balwantray Mehta

Committee's (1957) recommendations. When the community development and national extension service programme introduced from 1952 onwards for rural reconstruction by the Government of India it failed to enlist people's participation. PRIs and bureaucratic and democratic decentralisation were recommended by the Balwantray Report. For the first time, PRIs were made an integral component of India's development administration. The PRIs that came into existence following the Committees's recommendations went through a phase of ascendancy (1959-64), a phase of stagnation (1965-69), followed by a phase of decline (1969-77), [GoI (1978): 1-4). The progress made had been extremely tardy and uneven. It was at best, bureaucratic decentralisation. Democratic decentralisation remained a far distant goal.

Following the Report of the Committee on Panchayati Raj Institutions (1978) (also referred to as Asoka Mehta Committee) which argued for 'democratic local government' based on party-based elections, the state government of West Bengal, Karnataka, and Andhra Pradesh attempted their own models of PRIs. During the latter part of the eighties, the central government took several initiatives, and the 73rd and 74th Constitutional Amendments of 1992 could be considered as a sort of culmination of the efforts. This is an important landmark because a two-tier federation has virtually become a three-tier federal polity, the latter with several sub-systems. These amendments have made five-yearly elections, reservations for women and socially backward communities, provision for appointment of a state finance commission (analogous to the Union Finance Commission) to review and streamline state-sub-state level financial relations and transfers, the creation of a district-level apparatus for planning, and several such measures constitutionally mandatory. The organic federal link between the Union Finance Commission (UFC) and state finance commissions was sought to be established by amending clause 280 (3) of the Indian Constitution. We examine below the theory and practice of fiscal decentralisation that evolved.

In the backdrop of a review of the theories of multilevel finance, Rao and Chelliah (1991) have provided a brief survey of literature on fiscal federalism in India and raised several issues pertaining to fiscal decentralisation. They obviously could not have anticipated the isseus that emerged consequent to the constitutional amendments. Even so, it is important to note that they pointed out the 'glaring' absence of a reasonably developed independent institutional structure to provide public services at the local level [Rao and Chelliah (1990):18-19]. As Oommen (2000) elaborating the rationale of decentralised governance following the 73rd Amendment notes:

> Admittedly the most important rationale for decentralised governance is the provision of certain basic services and infrastructures of standard quality at the local level. To deprive a citizen of adequate level of schooling, drinking water, primary health care and other basic services because of her/his choice of location is an injustice. That even after more than fifty years of planning, the union and the state governments have woefully failed the people of India in this respect needs no documentation. At the same time the market mediated regime currently underway also cannot be trusted to promote territorial equity in access and quality of services. The need for local government involvement is greater now than ever before. (Oommen 2000 in D.K. Srivastava, ed. 2000, 412).

Although nearly a decade has passed since the 73rd Constitution Amendment Act, scholarly studies putting state-substate level fiscal relations in clear theoretical perspective are few and far between. Although the terms of reference of the Eleventh Finance Commission (FC-11) contained a clause for 'restructuring of the public finances' of the country, the task was limited to restoring of the budgetary balances of the union and state governments and the maintenance of macroeconomic stability. Neither the Government of India nor the FC-11 thought it fit and proper to include the local governments in this 'restructuring' exercise. No wonder most of the scholarly papers assembled by D K Srivastava in the context of the EFC's work [Srivastava (2001)] failed to take an integrated picture. The EFC, although it had collected and appended a wealth of fiscal data on local bodies for eight years for the first time in one place, did not care to use them (also because they were not sure of the quality of the data). In the body of the report, the data set hang like dead mutton in a butcher's shop.

Rao and Sen (1996) review the theory and practice of fiscal decentralisation within the framework of the received literature on fiscal federalism and make a strong plea for a reexamination of fiscal federalism in the context of the emerging economic reform in the country. This study, however, fails to include the third tier in its analytical framework. Several important suggestions for fiscal transfers (including a formula) that can help to reduce vertical and horizontal imbalances are presented in the study. Another study that actually reviews the changes in fiscal federalism including the state-local fiscal relations of India is that of Parthasarathi Shome (1999). This work stresses the need for fiscal consolidation in the interest of macroeconomic stability and the need for capacity building at the local level. While pleading for more taxing powers for local governments, Shome argues for restricting borrowing.

The World Bank's three-volume study on rural decentralisation probably the most comprehensive project undertaken so far in India in terms of reviewing of literature as well as in terms of the range of issues analysed in one place [World Bank (2000) Vols.I, II and III]. The finding of the study that political decentralisation in India has made considerable headway and taken root while administrative, fiscal and accountability mechanisms remain well below the desired levels is valid and well-grounded. The growing literature on rural decentralisation, both official and non-official keep emphasizing the goal of ushering in a more efficient, equitable, and accountable system of local governance as desirable for India.

As part of the World Bank study, Shikha Jha (2000) addresses directly the question of fiscal decentralisation in rural India following the 73rd Constitution Amendment and the conformity Acts passed by the state legislatures. Based on field studies and the state finance commission reports of seven states the author concludes that the progress made has been extremely uneven and halting. Lack of progress and the absence of administrative and technical capacity have weakened the process of fiscal decentralisation in many cases. The study notes that Kerala is a prominent exception. The basic dictum of devolution that functions, finance and functionaries should be devolved down in toto is observed in the breach. Kerala again is an exception. Although a formula-based devolution is welcomed by most state finance commissions, the criteria chosen by them relate largely to population and area.

In a recent work, M G Rao (2001) tries to analyse fiscal decentralisation in Indian federalism within the three-tier framework. He addresses the question of intergovernmental transfers and macroeconomic stability. Rao came to the disturbing finding that the aggregate fiscal deficit in 1997-98 works out to almost 15 per cent of GDP, of which 7 per cent is due to the local governments. This is patently unacceptable for a couple of reasons. First, except for the possibility of rolling over expenditure from one year to the other, local bodies do not have deficit-financing facilities that are available to the state and central governments. Local governments do not have ways and means accommodation from the Reserve Bank. For them, borrowing to finance revenue deficit would be an exception because loans are generally project-tied and not a regular tool of financing expenditures of local bodies. Second, the data used are of dubious quality. Consider the cases of Andhra Pradesh and Maharashtra, two states especially singled out by Rao (2001) as running heavy deficits at the local government level. In the 1997-98 revised estimates (RE), Andhra Pradesh has a total expenditure of Rs. 14,561.58 crore. But the expenditure of local bodies (as reported in the Eleventh Finance Commission data used by Rao) is Rs. 44,090.57 crore, that is more than three times the expenditure (revenue account) for 1997-98 (RE) is Rs. 22,390.69 crore and the total expenditure of local bodies is Rs. 1,05,224.65 crore which is 4.7 times that of the state. These are questionable figures. It is to be noted here that the Eleventh Finance Commission has neither used these data nor commented on them. If the local government could furnish such historical data so readily as they have done for the FC-11 (Annexure VIII), India has every reason to the future of decentralisation. Rao (2001) concludes that fiscal transfers done by the Union Finance Commissions have been more equitable than that done by the Planning Commission. But the unpleasant reality that remains is that regional imbalances in India reckoned in terms of a wide variety of economic and social variables have widened during the 1990s (Kurian (2000); Planning Commission (2002). The prime tasks of extending the coverage and improving the quality of core public services which is the foundational rationale of decentralisation still remains to be addressed [Oommen (2000); Choudhary and Sivasubramanyam (1999)].

Fiscal Assignments

Clarity in regard to the tax assignments and expenditure responsibilities of the various tiers is an essential prerequisite of any healthy federal system. Designed for a two-tier system, the Indian Constitution has specified the expenditure responsibilities as well as the resource-raising domains of the union and state through three lists given under Schedule VII. This schedule spells out the division of functions and finance into union list, state list, and a concurrent list where the state and the union have joint jurisdictions. In the concurrent areas, union law ultimately prevails. As per the 73rd and 74th Amendments, the Constitution now provides for an Eleventh Schedule for rural local bodies and a Twelfth Schedule for the urban local bodies to illustrate the respective areas of local jurisdictions. The two new schedules do not make any mention of resource-raising assignments, presumably leaving them to the concerned state legislatures. Compared to the UFC, the SFC has a more onerous task of rationalising state-local fiscal relations that are bedeviled by lack of proper fiscal assignments, a multiplicity of tiers, and the need to tackle a bewildering variety of new problems related to 'restructuring' sub-state level public finance. A few questions naturally arise at this point. Have these new arrangements provided for greater role clarity? How far do the functional and financial responsibilities of the various tiers match, and what transfer arrangements are envisaged to rectify the mismatches? How can we ensure and promote efficiency, equity, and macro-economic stability in the fiscal arrangements and transfer system? These questions need be examined under the new fiscal decentralisation that is underway in the country.

Apparently, the principle of legal separation of tax assignments is followed in India. It does not, however, square with the fiscal reality of India. There is considerable overlapping owing to the use of the same tax base (e.g. commodities) by various levels of government by way of excise duty, sales tax, and octroi [Rao and Chelliah (1991): 21]. As the Eleventh and Twelfth Schedules are silent on the question of tax assignments, the question of rationalizing substate level fiscal assignments, notably tax assignments, is left to the state legislatures and the newly created statutory body viz, the state finance commission (see Article 243J and 243Y). Only very few states attempted any significant change to strengthen the revenue base of PRIs. Almost every state continued the old pattern but in new statutory dress. Even so, there is considerable variation across the states in regard to tax and non-tax resources. Although there is a wide variety of taxes, by and large, the tax base covers property, business, and persons, with property tax dominating in almost every state. With a few exceptions the powers of taxation are confined to the lowest tier viz., gram panchayat and municipalities. The non-tax sources of the PRIs which too are concentrated at the gram panchayats level consist of a plethora of fees, fines and penalties, rents, receipts from remunerative enterprises, such as markets, cart stands, slaughter houses, and so on. In general few PRIs enjoy autonomy in imposing revenue, fixing rates etc., as they are generally done by the state government.

With the central government assigned more elastic and productive sources of revenue and the state governments left with substantial development functions, there is a built-in mismatch in the finances and expenditures of the states. This mismatch is sought to be resolved by the Union Finance Commission appointed every five years (actually, the SFC is its counterpart to periodically review and resolve state-local fiscal problems). The central government's almost unrestricted power to borrow along with its control over a substantial part of commercial bank resources has deepened the trend towards centralization of resources by the union. This trend has been strengthened, also, by two policy choices taken almost from the time of the inception of the constitutional process in the country. First is the creation of the Planning Commission under the union government which has been entrusted with the task of planning for the country as a whole, besides approving state plans which has a central assistance component with 70 per cent as loans and 30 per cent as grants. Second is the increasing entry of central ministries into the state government's assigned areas (now also of the local government) through what has come to be called centrally-sponsored schemes, often with some matching conditionality provisions. According to the Planning Commission, the share of the centrally-sponsored schemes in the Plan Budget of central ministers has currently increased to 70 per cent as against 30 per cent in the early 1980s (Planning Commission (2001): 49]. According to a Government of India paper, there are 26 schemes/programmes that come under the 29 subjects assigned to the PRIs (as per the Eleventh Schedule) that are now under the central government, which as per the 2000-01 budget costs a huge sum of Rs. 31,576 crore. This amount is equivalent to 42 per cent of the annual central plan outlay. A somewhat similar exercise for state plans for the same year (2000-01) shows that a sum of Rs. 40,819 crore was earmarked for programmes/schemes that strictly fall within the Eleventh Schedule and work out to about 74 per cent of the total states' plan outlay of that year [GoI (2001) for details.]. Because of the concurrent jurisdiction of states over local bodies as regards expenditure responsibilities, and because of centre-state concurrent jurisdictions over large areas, these inroads into the realm of local government the letter and spirit of the 73rd Amendment. The lack of role clarity in regard to expenditure responsibilities as between the different tiers comes out very conspicuously. Devolution remains a far distant goal under such a situation. How the trend towards centralization has affected the efficiency and equity of the intergovernmental transfer system in India both before and after the 73rd Amendment is well documented [Gulati and George (1995); Chelliah (1991); Oommen 1995 in Oommen and Datta (1995); Gulati (1987), Rao and Sen (1996), Rao (2001), see also in this context Planning Commision (2001): 40].

Part IX of the Indian Constitution mandates the state legislatures to endow the PRIs with adequate responsibilities, powers, and finances to enable them to function as 'institutions of self-government' (see Articles 243G and 243H in particular). As regards the expenditure responsibilities of the PRIs, there is much ambiguity in the conformity legislations enacted by the state governments, as the 29 subjects listed in the Elevenenth Schedule of the Constitution are not broken down into activities and sub-activities, and there is no clear allocation as between various tiers. This has created confusion and lack of role clarity not only between the state and the local bodies but also between the three tiers of the PRIs themselves. The subsidiarity principle has been routinely violated in almost all cases except Kerala [(for details see Oommen (1995); (1995)a; and Indira Rajaraman et al. (1996)]. When state-substate level fiscal relations are not backed by clear functional mapping and relevant laws and rules regarding revenue assignments, line departments will continue to pay crucial roles as under the pre-amendment regime. Indeed, when parallel mechanisms (e.g. District Rural Development Authority,

Janmabhoomi Programmes, MP/MLALAD funds etc.) thrive, functional assignments get blurred, and the PRIs are naturally weakened. The concept of devolution which involves the transfer of functions, funds, and functionaries remains a distant goal. It is important to take note, however, of the task force report of the Ministry of Rural Development which has drawn up a detailed functional mapping (as large as 200 development functions for the gram panchayat alone) along with an elaborate trajectory for ushering in financial and administrative autonomy (Government of India 2001). The principle of subsidiarity was kept very much in view in this exercise.

The Transfer System

While the conformity legislations by and large expanded the expenditure responsibilities of panchayats, very little adjustment in revenue assignments was made. This allowed the fiscal mismatches to continue because there was not much decentralisation of resources corresponding to the decentralisation of expenditures. The provision of the establishment of a state finance commission every five years analogous to the Union Finance Commission was an important step toward redressing this imbalance. The additional responsibility cast on the UFC to recommend measures needed to augment the consolidated funds of states is a clear acknowledgement of the mismatch between functions and finance at the various tiers of the Indian federal system on the one hand and the need for a dynamic reappraisal of the transfer system on the other (see Article 280 (3) (bb) and (c) of the Indian constitution). It also underlines the organic link between the various tiers and reaffirms the cooperative federal character of Indian polity.

The first generation SFCs have submitted their reports and in a few cases the second round of SFCs too have submitted reports. The tasks of the first SFCs were indeed huge as well as unconventional in the history of local fiscal relations anywhere in the world. Some comments based on a review of 13 SFC reports are given below. The approach, methodology, analysis, and recommendations of the SFCs differ significantly [Oommen (1998); O P Mathur (2000)]. We may begin with some positive and general aspects of these SFC reports, followed by certain comments on the transfer system recommended by them.

First, most SFC reports have affirmed directly or implicitly that the PRIs have an entitlement to state revenue under the post-73rd Amendment regime [See for example SFC reports of AP, MP, Tamil Nadu, Karnataka, Assam, Tripura, Rajasthan, UP and West Bengal). Some SFCs have argued for the creation of a divisible pool to local bodies and have specified a specific percentage of it [e.g. West Bengal, Karnataka, Tamil Nadu, Rajasthan, AP], while others recommended sharing of specific taxes. A few SFCs indicated the need to adjust transfers to inflation (Karnataka, Kerala). Second, while most SFCs have spelt out the known principles, Tamil Nadu has been innovative and pragmatic. Third, neglect of operation and maintenance of assets has been a bane of rural life in India. This has affected the quality of rural living. In fact in some states, as revealed in their SFC reports, maintenance expenditure has been declining (for example, Orissa and Maharashtra). It is heartening to note that most SFCs have recognized this problem. Some have recommended bold allocations for civic services such as public water taps, health centres, school buildings, and so on. The Himachal Pradesh SFC has recommended the creation of a Rural Infrastructure Maintenance Corpus to take care of the maintenance of already created rural assets. The Karnataka SFC has assumed 10 per cent of capital assets as the normative level of maintenance expenditure for the PRIs. The Kerala SFC has recommended that a maintenance grant should be based on the current cost of construction indexed for inflation and they even worked out the cost for schools, hospitals, health centres, street taps, street lighting, and so on. Uttar Pradesh has recommend, that 3 per cent of the net receipts of the state's tax revenue should be devolved to the PRIs for carrying out the important function of maintenance of capital assets and other essential services such as, roads, rural water-supply schemes, public lamp posts, and so on. Tamil Nadu has worked out a detailed norms-based maintenance cost estimate for 5 years for core civic services such as water supply, roads, street lights, and so on. The Maharashtra SFC has recommended a provision for depreciation on all capital assets and to invest the same in earmarked investments. Given the big backlog in maintenance and repair the allocation made could not be considered high. There remain a yawning gap in requirements and allocations made. Fourth probably the most important contribution is that several SFCs have brought home the need for objective criteria for transfer of resources from the state to local bodies. Population continues to be the dominant criterion. While population, particularly when disaggregated into SC/ST categories, agricultural workers, etc,. could be a good surrogate for demand for public services, a more relevant criterion reckoned in terms of equity, is backwardness and fiscal-equalisation measures that can remedy fiscal disadvantages.

Though large in number and constituting a potential bastion of democratic, governance in the country, the PRIs play an insignificant fiscal role in India. Based on the Eleventh Finance Commission's data (data given in Annexure VIII EFC is generally unreliable but revenue data are more reliable), we find that the tax-GDP ratio of the PRIs in 1997-98 was negligible at 0.025 per cent and that for urban local bodies (ULBs) it was 0.39 per cent, which is much better but still low. Unless the local bodies are fiscally empowered, there can be no meaningful decentralisation. Using four fiscal decentralisation ratios, Shikha Jha (2000) has studied six states (AP, Kerala, MP, Maharashtra, Rajasthan, and UP) and noted that Kerala is easily above all other States reckoned in terms of these ratios. The progress made by others has been generally poor (for details see Tables 12-15 in Jha 2000). It is significant that fiscal autonomy defined as share of local revenue from own sources in total income in the post-amendment regime is lower than the pre-amendment period for all the three tiers with the exception of the gram panchayats in AP and Zilla paishads in Rajasthan. Although, comparatively speaking, Kerala has a high fiscal autonomy ratio, it is significant to note that it declined from 61 per cent in 1995-96 to 15 per cent in 1999-2000. This is obviously because local government expenditure has made a quantum jump following the decentralised Planning process. In fact, the per capita expenditure of Kerala rose severalfold during this period because the government had chosen to devolve 35-40 per cent of plan fund to the PRIs as plan grants. For fiscal decentralisation to succeed there is need to set up expenditure decentralisation, viz., ratio of local expenditure by local, state, and central governments.

As the UFC after the 73rd and 74th Constitution Amendments is endowed with the specific task of recommending measures for augmenting the resources of the local bodies taking into account the SFC reports, the FC-11 had the historical task of reviewing federal finance *de novo*. Although the FC-11 had the backup of a wealth of data, it did not attempt a review of federal finance from the comprehensive perspective of fiscal decentralisation. They have not used decentralisation as a general principle of devolution of resources except in regard to the fund set apart for specific purposes like maintenance of accounts and creation of a data base for local bodies. For the distribution of taxes, they have used mostly conventional criteria such as population, income, area, tax effort and so on. FC-11 was critical of the SFC reports in general. The FC-11's criticism, that SFC reports did not follow any principle is not universally true as we have already noted. The EFC even went to the extent of recommending the abolition of the subclause which mandates the Union Finance Commission to base their recommendations, on the SFC reports. This is not correct as it takes away the opportunity for the federal commission to take a total view of public finance of the country (Oommen, 2000).

In critiquing the state-substate level transfer system, the first step is to seek a straight answer to the question whether the SFCs have promoted more vertical and horizontal equity. As regards the former, if the revenue and expenditure decentralisation ratios are any guide, the progress made to date leaves much to be desired (Shikha Jha: 2000; "Oommen: 2000a). Few SFCs recommended to the state legislatures new tax assignments, although almost all wanted streamlining of tax administration and radical restructuring of property tax which constitutes the single largest source of 'local revenue' in India. The Task Force Report on Devolution of Powers and Functions to PRIs (GOI, 2001) is not only a good guideline for the states on what should be done, it is also an acknowledgement of the general failure of states in pursuing clear functional mapping and financial autonomy.

In order to promote spatial equity, certain basic services of standard quality may have to be provided to all citizens. Several SFCs have addressed this question but with quite different emphasis. The Tamil Nadu SFC (1996) fixed expenditure norms for six core services and worked out the per capita unit cost for different areas and identified the gaps in resources required for a period of five years up to 2002 at the 1995-96 price level. Detailed rich and maintenance costs for each service were also worked out. It is argued that the resource gaps might be bridged from three sources: own revenue, revenue assignments, and grants from state and central government. Detailed proposals are outlined including a formula based on criteria such as revenue collection efficiency, population, expenditure needs, etc. The Commission notes the principle of equalisation in designing its transfer system, that is, 'the transfer should be made in such a way as to reduce the imbalances and equalise the financial status and service levels of the local bodies.' The divisible pools for rural and urban local bodies (60 : 40) are worked out after a detailed forecast of revenue generation of a state for five years from 1997-98 to 2001-02. The possibilities of privatisation or use of NGOs are also mentioned (the SFCs of Kerala and Punjab also made recommendations on these lines). The Tamil Nadu SFC in brief has recommended a normative factually based scheme of revenue assignments with suggestions for reducing vertical and horizontal imbalances.

Allowing local bodies to borrow except under restrictive conditions (as when you have a worthwhile project in which several panchayats have a real stake) can have dangerous consequences. Although several SFCs have permitted borrowing from financial institutions (e.g., Punjab, Kerala, Rajasthan, and Maharashtra), open-market borrowing is not widely favoured.

Some general criticisms of SFCs reports that will be helpful in redesigning state-substate level fiscal relations may also be mentioned.One, most SFCs failed to emphasise the link between revenue raising and expenditure responsibilities, a link that is needed to induce fiscal responsibility. Two, no SFC seems to be worried about fiscal management or the need to impose a hard budget constraint at the local level. The accounting and budgetary practices leave many things to be desired. Three, no suggestion is made by any SFC to reduce the multiple channels of devolution that exists at the local level, viz., line departments, state planning boards, SFC devolution, MP-MLA programmes, DRDA, and the like. This may not be their direct task, even so, there is need for suggestions to streamline state-local fiscal relations on a more rational footing. Four, although in the pre-amendment days the state-local grant system was unsystematic, adhoc, dependency promoting, and above all too many in number , many SFCs, have failed to fully address these shortcomings.

To conclude the theories and institutions evolved in the context of western market economies may not be strictly relevant or applicable to fiscal decentralisation in India. It is important also to note that several institutions and accountability mechanisms currently underway in India –the gram sabha, three-tier, substate-level rural institutions, State Finance Commissions, district planning committees, audit arrangements, and indeed the fiscal assignments and relations—are not all time tested. Some need nurturing, and others need radical modifications and corrections. For a country used to adhocism and hierarchy, concepts as autonomy, devolution, accountability, transparency, and the like may even appear alien rather than natural or normal.

The first-generation SFCs and the FC-11, which was expected to make its recommendations based on the SFC reports, could not be considered to have put fiscal decentralisation and transfer arrangements in proper perspective.

There is a vital need to redesign the transfer arrangements in India on a more rational, objective, and equitable basis. The functional domain of local governments, quality and adequacy of services they provide, the resources they raise, the autonomy they enjoy, and their accountability to the electorate are crucial aspects of fiscal decentralisation. At present, effective fiscal decentralisation remains a distant goal.

* Reprinted from L C Jain (2005) (ed), *Decentralisation and Local Governance,* Orient Longman.

Endnotes

1. The term union recognised in the Indian Constitution refers to the federal government and is used in the paper interchangeably with 'centre' which is widely used in India in lieu of union.
2. Two years after the 73rd Constituion Amendment, Anwar Shah (1994) treats India as a two-tiered federation, while Mexico, USA, Nigeria, and Brazil are classified as three-tiered fiscal federations.
3. The Union Finance Commissions of India have followed many of these principles with varying degrees of emphasis and success.
4. For historical accounts of Indian rural decentralisation [see G Mathew ed., (2000); SN Jha and P C Mathur (1999); and Oommen (1996); among others].

5 The Indian Constitution has borrowed approximately 250 articles 'Verbatim or with minor changes in phraseology from the 1935, Government of India Act', [B. Michael (1969); 207].

6 For example in 2001-02, states' own revenue receipts (tax and non-tax receipts) financed only 53 per cent of revenue expenditure and 44 per cent of total expenditure (Reserve Bank of India, 2002).

7. The SFC reports examined are that of AP, Assam, MP, Maharashtra, Karnataka, Kerala, Orissa, Punjab, Rajasthan, Tamil Nadu, Tripura, Uttar Pradesh and West Bengal.

References

AVARD (1962), *Panchayati Raj as the Basis of Indian Polity: An* Exploration into the proceedings of the Constituent Assembly. Association of Voluntary Agencies for Rural Development, New Delhi.

Bahl, Roy (1999), 'Implementation Rules for Fiscal Decentralisation', Working Paper 99-101. Georgia State University.

---- **(2000),** *Intergovernmental Transfer in Developing and Transition Countries: Principles and Practice*, World Bank.

---- **(2001),** *Fiscal Decentralisation, Revenue Assignments and the Case for the property Tax in South Africa*, Andrew Young School of Policy Studies, Georgia State University,

---- **(2002),** 'World Wide Trends in Fiscal Decentralisation'. Internet.

Bahl, Roy, and Johannes Linn (1992), *Urban Public Finance in Developing Countries*, Oxford University Press.

Bailey; Stephan J. (1999), *Local Government Economics: Principle and Practice*, MacMillan.

Bird, Richard (1993), 'Treading the Fiscal Labyrinth. Some Issues in Fiscal Decentralisation', *National Tax Journal* 46

Bird, Richard M. (1999), 'Rethinking Sub-national Taxes: A New Look at Tax Assignment', IMF Working Paper WP/99/165.

---- **(2000),** *Intergovernmental Fiscal Relations: Universal Principles, Local Applications*. Andrew Young School, Georgia State University.

---- **(2001),** *Intergovernmental Fiscal Transfers: Some Lessons from International Experience.* University of Toronto.

Bird, Richard M., and Francois Vaillancourt, eds. (1998), *Fiscal Decentraisation in Developing Countries*, Cambridge University Press.

Bird, R. and C. Wallich (1993), 'Fiscal Decentralisation and Inter-Governmental Relations in Transition Economies: Towards a Systemic Framework of Analysis'. Policy Research Working Papers. Washington -D.C., World Bank.

Cheema, G. Shabbir, and Dennis A. Rondinelli (1983), *Decentralisation and Development: Policy Implementation in Developing Countries*, London: Sage Publications.

Chelliah, Raja J. (1991), *Towards a Decentralised Polity: Outline of a Proposal*, Fourth L.K. Jha Memorial Lecture, New Delhi.

Choudhary, R.C. and K. Sivasubramanyam (1999), *Functional and Financial Decentralisation on PRIs: A Study Across Select States* (Mimeo), NIRD, Hyderabad.

Cole, M., and G. Boyne (1995), 'So You Think You Know What Local Government is for' *Local Government Studies* 21. No. 2.

Council of Europe (1995), *The Size of Municipalities, Efficiency and Citizen participation,* Strasbourg: Council of Europe.

Fukasaku, Kiichiro, and LR. De Mello Jr. (1999), *Fiscal Decentralisation-in Emerging Economies.* Development Centre, OECD, Paris.

Government of India (1946), *Constituent Assembly Debates,* New Delhi.

Government of India (1978), *Report of the Committee on Panchayati Raj Institutions,* Ministry of Agriculture and Irrigation, New Delhi.

Government of India (2001), *Report of the Task force on Decentralisation of powers and Functions upon Panchayati Raj Institutions,* Krishi Bhavan, New Delhi.

Gramlich, E. (1577), 'Intergovernmental Grants: A Review of the Empirical Literature' In *The Political Economy of Fiscal Federation* edited by W.E. Oates, Lexington. Mass: Heath

Gulati, 1.S., K.K. George (1985), 'Central Inroads into State Subjects' *Economic and Political Weekly,* (6 April).

---- **Ed. (1987),** *Centre-State Budgetary Transfers,* New Delhi: Oxford University Press.

Hirsch, Werner Z. (1970), *The Economics of State and Local Governments,* McGraw Hill Book Company.

Jha, Raghbendra (1998), *Modern Public Economics,* London: Routledge.

Jha, Shikha (2000), *Fiscal Decentralisation in India in World Bank (2000).* Vol. III.

King, David (1984), *Fiscal Tiers—The Economics of Multi-level Governments,* George Allen and Unwin.

Kurian, NJ. (2000), 'Widening Regional Disparities in India: Some Indicators', *Economic and Political Weekly,* (12 February).

Lister, Stephan, and Mary Betley (1999), 'Approaches to Decentralisation in Developing Countries'. *Background Paper for the DFID Workshop on Good Research in Public Expenditure Management.* Cape Town.

Litvack, Jennie, Junaid Ahmed, Richard Bird (1998), *Rethinking Decentralisation in Developing Countries,* World Bank, Washingon

Mclure Jr., Charles (1999), 'The Tax Assignment Problem: Conceptual and Administrative Considerations in Achieving Autonomy'. Paper presented at the seminar on Inter-governmental Fiscal Relation and Local Financial Management organised by the National Economic and Social Economic Development Board of Government of Thailand and World Bank, Chiang Mai (Thailand (February 24, march 5).

Mulgan, Richard (1997), "The Process of Accountability'. *Australian Journal of Public Administration 56,* No.1 March.

Murry, M N (2000), 'Tax Devolution in Corporative Federalism: Indian Experience' in D.K.Srivastava ed.

Musgrave, Richard (1959), *The Theory of Public Finance,* New York, McGraw-Hill.

---- **(1983),** 'Who should Tax Where and What', In *Tax Assignment in Federal Countries.* Edited by Charles Mclure Jr. Canberra: Australia University Press.

Musgrave, Richard, and Peggy Musgrave (1989), *Public Finance in Theory and Practice,* New York,:McGraw-Hill.

Oates Wallace E. (1972), *Fiscal Federalism,* Harcourt Brace Jovanovich Inc.

---- **(1981),** 'On Local Finance and the Tiebeout Model', AEA papers and proceedings, May 1981.

---- **(1999),** 'An Essay on Fiscal Federalism', *Journal of Economic Literature*, 37 (September).

Oommen, M.A (1995a), *Decentralisation of Resources from the State to the Panchayati Raj Institutions*, Occasional paper No. 18. Institute of Social Sciences, New Delhi.

---- **(1995),** 'Panchayat Finance and Issues Relating to Intergovernmental Transfers', in Oommen and Datta. 1995.

---- **(1998),** *Devolution of Resources to Local Bodies.* ISS Occasional Paper series 21, New Delhi.

---- **(2000),** 'Eleventh Finance Commission's Transfer System and the Local Bodies: A Critique'. ISS Discussion paper series no. 6. Institute of Social Sciences, New Delhi.

---- **(2000a),** 'Panchayat Raj Institutions, Eleventh Finance Commission and Working Towards a New Fiscal Federalism', in D.K Srivastava ed.

Oommen M.A., and Abhijit Datta (1995), *Panchayats and Their Finance*, New Delhi: Concept Publishing Co..

Planning Commission (2001), *Approach Paper to the Tenth Five Year Plan*, Government of India, New Delhi.

Planning Commission (2002), *National Human Development Report 2001*, Government of India, New Delhi.

Prud'homme, Remy (1995), 'On the Dangers of Decentralisation'. *World Bank Economic Review* 9.

Rajaraman, Indira, O.P. Bohra and V.S. Renganathan (1996), 'Augmentation of Panchayat Resources'. *Economic and Political Weekly*, (4 May)

Rao, M G. (2001), *Fiscal Decentralisation in Indian Federalism.* Working Paper No. 98. Institute of Social and Economic Change, Bangalore.

Rao, M G and RJ Chelliah (1991), *Survey of Research on Fiscal Defederalism in India,* National Institute of Public Finance and Policy, New Delhi.

Rao, M G and Tapas Sen (1996), Fiscal Federalism in India: Theory and Practice, MacMillan: India Ltd.

Rondinelli, Dennis, J.R. Nellis, G.S. Cheema (1983), *Decentralisation in Developing Countries: A Review of Recent Experience*, World Bank.

Shah, Anwar (1979), *Provincial Transportation Grants to Alberta Cities Structure, Evaluation and a Proposal for an Alternative Design*, Alberea Transportation, Edmonton..

---- **(1989),** 'A Linear Expenditure System Estimation of Local Fiscal Response to Provincial Transportation Grants'. *Kentucky Journal of Economics and Business* 9, no. 1. '

---- **(1994),** *The Reform of Intergovernmental Fiscal Relations in Developing and Emerging Market Economies*, World Bank, Washington D.C.

Shah, Anwar, and Zia Qureshi (1994), Intergovernmental Fiscal Relations in Indonesia. World Bank Discussion Paper, Washington, D.C.

Shahid, Javed Burki, Guillermo E. Perry, and William R. Dillinger (1999), *Beyond the Centre: Decentralising the State*, World Bank, Washington.

Shome, Parthasarathi (1999), 'Fiscal Federalism in India: Experience and Future Directions'. In Fukasaku and De Melo Jr., ed.

Srivastava D.K., ed. **(2000),** *Fiscal Federalism in India: Contemporary Challenges.* National Institute of Public Finance and Policy, New Delhi.

Stein, E. (1998), 'Fiscal Decentralisation and Government Size in Latin America'. *In Democracy, Decentralisation and Deficit in Latin – America* Edited by K. Fukasaku and R. Hausmann. OECD, Paris..

Tanzi Vito (1996), 'Fiscal Federalism and Decentralisation: A Review of Some Efficiency and Macro-economic Aspects', Annual World Bank Conference on Development Economics: 1995. World 'Bank.

Ter-Minassian, Teresa (1997), 'Inter-governmental Fiscal Relations in Macro-economic Perspective'. In *Fiscal Federalism in Theory and Practice,* edited by Teresa Ter-Minassian. IMF, Washington.

Tiebout, Charles (1956), 'A Pure Theory of Local Expenditure', *Journal of Political Economy,* (October).

UNDP (1993), *Human Development Report 1993.* Oxford University Press.

Wildasin, David (1997), 'Externalities and Bail Outs: Hard and Soft Budget Constrains in Intergovernmental Fiscal Relation, *Research Working Paper 1843.* World Bank, Washington._

World Bank (2000), *Overview of Rural Decentralisation in India.* Vols. I, II and III, World Bank, New Delhi.

CHAPTER 3

Federalism in Brazil and India: Locating the Local Governments

The widely acknowledged failure of the centralized state has led to a distinct swing of the pendulum towards decentralised systems considered more responsive to the people and offering more avenues of people's participation. Federalism and decentralisation are interlinked concepts. Federalism refers to a multi-level system of government in which different layers of governments exist, each with a defined jurisdiction with some measure of autonomy. Depending on the extent of decentralisation the degree of autonomy and importance of local governments in the federal setup, the nature of fiscal decentralisation varies. While in countries like India, Brazil and Denmark, local governments are constitutionally recognized institutions, in Canada and Pakistan it is created by state legislation and in extreme cases like China it is established by executive fiat. The purpose of this paper is to highlight briefly the place and significance of local governments in the federal structure of Brazil and India acknowledged to be two major federations.

Brazil and India: Some Comparative Magnitudes

Brazil and India stand way apart in terms of size of population, area and GDP as is evident from Appendix A. The working of democracy that we try to locate and compare is indeed happening in a wide and sprawling spectrum of space and different social, economic and cultural context. India's population is nearly six times that of Brazil, but in terms of area way below that (See Appendix A). Brazil's density of population is only 24 per sq. km. as against India's 368 which is over 15 times higher. The large rural population which is the defining character of India is not very significant in Brazil. Again in terms of income Brazil's per capita income is $10,900 which is 3.2 times higher than that of India's $3,400. India continues to be a predominantly agricultural country with 17.2% of GDP contribution as against 5.5% for Brazil. Reckoned in terms of the share in worlds GDP, India's share currently is only 5.4% as against a population share of 17.8% while that of Brazil is 2.9% which is precisely its population share (2.9%). But both are counted among the four rapidly advancing countries of the world, the others being China and Russia and they are along with South Africa are collectively referred to as the BRICS, a group of emerging markets. Besides being members of such a nebulous grouping the two countries present an extremely contrasting polity. Given this wide spectrum, it is important to locate the local governments in the federal structure of these countries to facilitate meaningful comparative perspectives. In both cases we use more or less the same framework.

Salience of Brazilian Federalism

The Brazilian constitution inaugurated in October 1988 provides for a three tier federal system: the central government (called the Union and also refered to as federal government); the intermediate tier (called states which are 27 in number); and the local governments (called municipalities (*municipios*) which consist of 5564 units). This marks a watershed in the history of Brazil which for long had been accustomed to a series of cyclical alterations between centralization and decentralisation including a series of military governments (See Appendix B). From 1964 to 1985, a period of military government which witnessed strong centralizing tendencies emerged. Under the military regime the forms of federalism were maintained with some sort of elections held for the Congress (union level), state level and the municipalities. Electoral rules down to the local level were manipulated by the national government to manufacture majorities in the National Congress for the pro-government party in spite of declining voter support[1]. Popular forces resisted the military dictatorship which finally led to the new era of democratic regime.

Under the 1988 Constitution, the federal executive branch is headed by a President who is directly elected for a four year term. The legislative branch consists of two houses: (1) Chamber of Deputies consisting of 513 members, with the number of representatives per state determined on the basis of population and (2) Senate comprising three members from each state. State governments are headed by directly-elected governors. States have unicameral legislatures, whose members are elected at large by proportional representation.

The 1988 Constitution, as we have already mentioned establishes municipal government as a third tier of the federation with almost the same status as that of the states. Unless their counterparts in India, the third tier of Brazil enjoys a higher constitutional status. For locating and identifying the place of local governments, we may do well to examine the expenditure responsibilities, revenue assignments and intergovernmental transfer arrangements. Also it is important to note what borrowing powers they have *vis-a-vis* their higher level counterparts.

Expenditure Assignment

As in most other federations, certain responsibilities (e.g., defence, control of public debt, regulation of inter-state and foreign trade) are exclusively assigned to the federal government. States are granted a wide range of responsibilities except those restricted by the Constitution. Unlike in most other federal countries, *municipios* of Brazil are assigned "the power to legislate over subjects of local public interests" and to provide "services of local public interest" (Article 30). They are not the creatures of state governments or state legislatures. States cannot compel or restrict actions by the *municipios* within their jurisdictions. While education, housing, urbanization and the like are municipal functions, public security is a state function and social insurance, energy, environment etc., are mainly federal functions.

Revenue Assignments

The Brazilian Constitution is very clear in regard to its tax and non-tax revenue assignments and follows the principle of separation. It assigns specific tax bases to each level of government with nearly 2/3rd going to the federal government with taxing powers on income (both personal and corporate), profit, customs, financial transactions, rural property etc. While value added taxes belong to the states, gross value of services, urban property and transfers of estates are the tax domain of municipalities. Brazil has a stable system of revenue sharing arrangements that redistribute vertically and horizontally their revenues. Nearly half of federal tax revenues are explicitly earmarked for social security.

Transfer System

Brazil has an elaborate system of intergovernmental transfer arrangements. They are mostly in the nature of revenue sharing of the federal income and industrial product taxes. Municipios whose tax revenue is less than 10% of the total tax revenue of the country receive transfers both from the federal and from the state governments. *Fundo de Participacao dos Municipios* (FPM) formed out of federal income and industrial product taxes are the principal federal fund transfer to municipalities. Population is the major criterion for *interse* distribution.

The state's share about 25% of their value added tax to the municipios. As per the Constitution 75% of this will have to be distributed on the basis of the origin of the tax receipts and the balance on the basis of formula designed by each state legislature.

Apart from these revenue sharing by the higher governments there are specific grants earmarked for specific services such as education and health. This is an important means to reduce interregional inequalities in the provision of basic services. Brazil's federal fund for primary education (FUNDEF) which began operating in 1998 and the state participation fund which supplements this are important transfer mechanisms to ensure equity in basic services such as education as between regions. Equally important is the unified health system (SUS), the basic health care grant on a per capita basis (TFG) and funding for family health programme given to the *municipios*. Thus, we find some efforts to ensure inter-regional equity in the delivery of core services like education and health through municipalities.

In Brazil intergovernmental transfers play an important role in rectifying vertical and horizontal imbalances. In 2004, 67% of all municipal expenditure which were equivalent to 7.3% of GDP were financed by transfers from federal and state governments. Budgets per capita in small municipalities have reached levels three times higher than corresponding figures for densely populated urban areas and densely populated metropolitan cities. Another feature of Brazil that also needs to be mentioned is the discretionary transfers which are one-off transfers generally meant to finance small scale investment and activities at the local level. [For details on transfers see Afonso and Araujo (2006)].

Borrowing Powers: The sub-national governments have substantial borrowing powers. This has landed them in great financial crisis in the past. Since 2000, Brazil has launched a more fiscally responsible regime. The Law of Fiscal Responsibility (LRF), 2000, requires sub-national governments (states and municipalities) to fix targets for revenues, expenditure, stock of debt and fiscal balances in the preparation of annual budgets[2]. The local governments have to work closely with the higher order governments as per the budget laws of the country. The LRF imposes controls on both the existing stock and new borrowing operations. States and *municipios* are required to maintain debt stocks below ceilings established by the Senate. If, at the end of any four month period, a state or municipality exceeds its ceiling, it is bound to reduce the excess within one year. More over, they are mandated to provide periodic reports about the financial position and cash flow to the public. Such transparency provisions are conspicuously missing in India.

Apart from these fiscal federal features of the Brazilian Constitution, there are certain participatory structures, called *Orcamento Participativo* (OP) or the Participatory Budget (PB) for which the country has now become world famous. OP started in the municipal city of Porto Alegre, the capital of the state of Rio Grande de Sul in 1989 and slowly spread to other municipalities in Brazil and to several other Latin American countries as well. A snapshot picture of the year-round process of participatory budget making is given in the figure (3.1) under Appendix C that explains the chronological cycle. The process starts exactly a year before the Budget year in March/April when the municipal office provides information, technical assistance and the needed infrastructure to facilitate the debate and decision-making people's participation is done at two levels–thematically and spatially.

Salient Features of the Indian Constitution

India which was under British colonial regime for over a century became independent in 1947, but became a federal republic in 1950. The Government of India Act, 1935 passed by the British regime was the earliest attempt to make a "Federation of India". It was made up of both British Indian provinces and the states ruled by native rulers called 'princely states' who functioned under the British, but with some autonomy in assigned areas. The Act made certain tax assignments and introduced a scheme of revenue sharing that in many respects laid the foundations of fiscal federalism in India. The Constitution of India borrowed heavily from the Government of India Acts 1935.

Although originally as per the Constitution of India, India was a dual federation comprising only the union and the states, following the 73rd/74th Constitutional Amendments, the Constitution has accorded a separate status to the Local Governments (LGs) making Indian federalism a multilevel system of governance (See Figure 1 for an illustrative outline). The main objective of these Amendments was to create 'institutions of self-government' at the local level. This is important because prior to the amendments the panchayats were an appendage of the rural department and municipalities that of the department of urban affairs. Based on these two amendments part IX and part IXA were added to the Constitution. Because local governments come under the state list, every state had to pass a conformity legislation incorporating the basic changes mandated in the Constitution by the Amendments such as the establishment of the gram sabha or assembly of citizen voters at the village level, one-third reservation to women, representation to scheduled castes and scheduled tribes[3] in proportion to their population, appointment of a State Finance Commission (SFC) every five years to rationalize state sub-state fiscal relations and so on. This exercise was completed by April 1993. Unlike Brazil which is a Presidential form of government, India is a parliamentary model with a bicameral system (Lok Sabha consisting of 552 members directly elected and Rajya Sabha consisting of 250 members indirectly elected and nominated) at the union level and unicameral legislatures at the state level. The local governments are divided into rural and urban, the former consisting of a three-tier system called Panchayati Raj Institutions (PRIs) and the latter in the major city bodies called corporations and others municipalities and those in transition naġar panchayats. The structure of this multi-level system of federation with the details of the local governments which constitute the third stratum is given in Fig.1. Rural local governments which number over 2.5 lakhs far outnumber the urban governments. Evidently the structure and pattern of the LGs in the federations of India and Brazil are of a different genre. The Brazilian federal polity does not envisage a rural local government structure as in India. They simply are insignificant.

Figure 1
Structure of Multilevel Governments in Indian Federalism

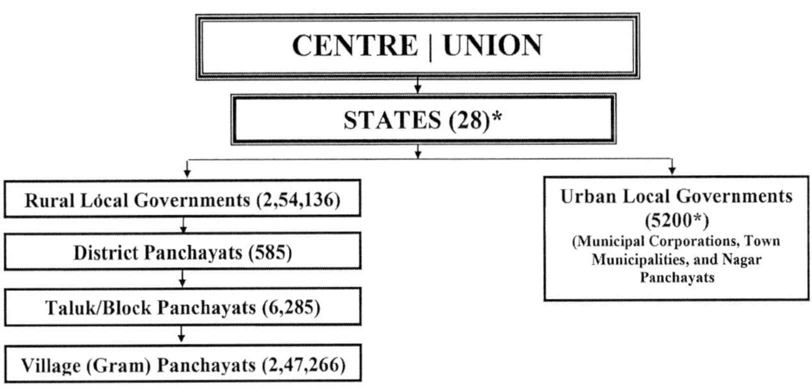

* Besides these there are 7 union territories directly administered by the federal government
(The data are as at the time of writing in 2012)

Indian federation has a built-in unitary bias. A constitution established in the backdrop of the partition of the country and facing internal threats of disintegration, this was probably inevitable. In terms of fiscal assignments, it borrowed heavily from the Government of India Act, 1935. The Constitution of India in its seventh schedule, assigns the powers of the centre and the states. The schedule specifies the exclusive powers of the federal government in the Union List; exclusive powers of the states in the State List and those under joint jurisdiction are placed in the Concurrent List. Originally local government functions formed part of the State List. Under the pre-reform regime the local government functions were mostly confined to civic duties. Following reforms of the 73rd/74th Constitutional Amendments, an eleventh schedule listing out the illustrative functions of the PRIs and a twelfth schedule specifying the functions of urban local governments were added to map out the functional domain of the third tier. Although it was left to the state legislatures to determine the actual expenditure responsibilities all of them stayed within the subject lists of the eleventh and twelfth schedules. However it became abundantly clear over the years that a mere listing of functions will not ensure role clarity and that division into activities and sub-activities assigning the specific functions of each government of the three tiers and urban local governments on the one hand and that of the states on the other is what is required. Many states have done this activity-mapping of local governments. Kerala is one State that has demonstrated considerable role clarity in the activity mapping it has undertaken.

Expenditure Assignments

Besides national defence, foreign relations and the like, the functions of the central government can be classified as those required to maintain macro-economic stability (e.g., issuing currency and coinage, foreign. exchange, foreign loans, banking, insurance etc.), international trade and relations and those having inter-state implications (e.g. railways, posts, telephones, highways, atomic energy and so on). The power of the central government has been considerably strengthened over the years by continuously adding items in the concurrent list through constitutional amendments and vesting it with overriding powers in regard to these subjects. The important items added to the Concurrent List are very large and include economic and social planning (which is virtually a hold-all), trade unions, social security, employment and unemployment, education and so on. In India most local government functions are concurrent with the state and the centre. Because the residuary powers are with the centre the controlling levers are practically vested in it.

The major subjects that fall in the state domain are public order, police, public health, agriculture, irrigation, fisheries, industries and minor mineral. In regard to the subjects in the Concurrent List like education, transport, social security and so on, the states would be compelled to assume a significant role because of their proximity to the people. Besides the overall task of 'Planning for economic development and social justice' and implementing them (Articles 243G and W) which every LG is mandated to do, Schedule XI of the Constitution mentions 29 subjects (individual states are free to expand the list) for the PRIs and 18 subjects for the urban local governments. Several subjects like agriculture, irrigation, animal husbandry, fisheries, small-scale industries which are of a productive nature, and welfare activities like housing, cultural activities, family welfare, social welfare, welfare of weaker sections and so on cover a wide range of activities which are invariably concurrent with the State and Union governments. Unless there is pronounced role clarity with autonomous space to act, the wide array of list does not necessarily mean that an autonomous third tier has arrived in India. The much needed activity mapping to ensure role clarity, first started in Kerala in the late 1990s remains a non-starter in several states.

Tax Assignments

Unlike the dominant area of concurrent jurisdictions, Indian constitution largely follows the principle of 'separation' as far as tax assignments are concerned. Tax handles are exclusively assigned either to the centre or to the states. Most of the taxes that have broad or national base and are productive such as income tax, corporate tax, customs, excise, taxes on wealth and so on are with the centre. Taxes on agricultural income and wealth, land revenue, taxes on motor vehicles, taxes on transfer of property (stamp duties), taxes on transportation of food and services, sales tax on goods etc., belong to the states. Though no separate tax handles are exclusively assigned to the local governments in the Constitution, taxes on professions, trades, property tax, entertainment tax, octroi etc., have been assigned by states to the LGs. The tax handles of LGs are those that have been traditionally assigned to them by the State and in several cases some of the assigned taxes are collected by the States and shared with the LGs. If we survey the conformity legislations, (which only copied the old lists in traditional panchayat and municipality Acts) of the various state governments, we can trace out as many as 28 items of taxes and their number in individual States ranges from 4 in Haryana to 12 in Gujarat in the case of LGs. [See Oommen (2004)]. The 73rd/74th Constitutional Amendments do not make any separate tax assignments to the LGs. This significantly affects the autonomy of LGs.

Inter-governmental Transfers

There is no federation where resources and responsibilities neatly match. This leads to considerable vertical imbalance which necessitates inter-governmental transfers to reduce these imbalances. The problem however is very much confounded in India because it has a built-in imbalance in resources and functional assignments. Moreover, given the tremendous inter-regional disparities in fiscal capabilities of sub-national governments, rectifying horizontal imbalances assumes significance. The Indian Constitution addresses this problem through the institution of Union Finance Commission to make inter-governmental transfers to rectify the vertical and horizontal imbalances. The Finance Commissions appointed every five years is a quasi-judicial authority and can determine its own procedures of business. India had the benefit of thirteen finance commissions since the appointment of the first commission in 1951. Although initially the divisible pool consisted only of income tax and union excises from the tenth finance commission onwards, all union taxes are made divisible. Before the 73rd/74th Constitutional Amendments the transfers were only between the union and states. But the amendments provide for the establishment of a State Finance Commission (SFC) at the state level to rationalize the state sub-state level fiscal relations. It is virtually a counterpart of the union finance commission at the state sub-state level. The SFCs' task is to rationalise the financial flow to the rural and urban local governments by quinquennial reviews and help them through revenue sharing and grants-in-aid. Most states have had three SFCs and quite a few like Bihar and Kerala had their fourth generation SFCs. By the two Amendments even the Union Finance Commission is mandated to augment the consolidated fund of a state to supplement the resources of PRIs and ULGs through appropriate measures. Thus, the Indian Constitution provides for considerable fiscal empowerment of the LGs.

Besides the UFC, India through an Act of Parliament has created another institution called Planning Commission which gives guidelines, grants and loans to the states (of late the latter is seriously restricted) in regard to the overall development of the country. Over the years the Planning Commission has emerged as a crucial agency in determining the development resource allocations in the country. After the BJP government came to power in 2014 the planning commission was abolished and an advisory body called NITI Ayog has taken its place. But it has no resource allocation power. Local governments do not figure prominently in this scheme of allocation. Although India since 1991 has taken to a market mediated growth regime, the overall indicative planning and sharing of public resources in investment and development continues. The country will be ushering in its twelfth five year plan from 2012 onwards.

Democratisation in Brazil and India

Alexis Tocqueville famously said that democracy has to be rooted in the 'habits and hearts' of the citizens. In other words the democratisation process should be part of the everyday life of the people and should be meaningful to them. In this context the idea of constructing a democratic public space which we have already outlined assumes significance for the practice of politics and economics in any democracy notably that of developing countries like

India and Brazil. While the world owes the West a great deal for providing the institutional forms of democracy, the latter surely does not ensure a growing and dynamic democratisation outcome notably social justice. While all Latin American Countries (LACs) that got freedom from the colonial powers, adopted liberal federal type constitutions, all of them relapsed into centralized and personalistic power systems at some time or other. In Brazil military dictatorship lasted for 25 years from 1964-1989. Even after democracy was formally introduced the transition was a long and arduous process. Authoritarian governments, clientelism and patronage have become endemic. Under such a situation the process of democratisation has to take a long and hard journey.

Leonardo Avritzer (2002) advances the concept of 'participatory publics' which is a variant of Habermas' idea of public sphere. He discusses the tension between democratic institutions and the culture that accommodates centralized power, clientelism and patronage in Brazil. The democratisation process by widening the public sphere is a means to fight this through expanding the public space. Social movements in the 1970s and 1980s in LACs like Brazil which coincided with liberalisation considerably helped the process of transformation to democracy and expansion of public sphere. Quite often fair election was difficult during the transition period because those who failed appealed to the military to intervene. To a great extent the moral values were kept alive by the Catholic Church and of course by the family. In Brazil the authoritarian regime conducted a process of transition lasting 11 years (1974-1985). Brazil could be considered as a typical case in which political society strengthened clientelism. Political competition renewed clientelism with democratically elected presidents in the early episodes of the so-called democracy promoted patronage of the worst type possible[4]. In spite of the impeachment of the second civilian President Collor de Mello, clientelism continued and is a major stumbling block to the democratisation process in Brazil. Unless and until the deliberative capacities at the public level are strengthened democratic elitism and structures could not be countered and weakened.

As regards democratic governance and progress India stands differently from Brazil. Hailed as the largest democracy in the world, India has a track record of democratic rule for nearly 70 years of continuous (two years of Emergency rule during 1975-77 being an aberration) history. The long standing struggle for independence from British colonialism was a mass movement led by the Indian National Congress which after independence under Jawaharlal Nehru its first Prime Minister took care to build this multi-religious, multi-lingual and multi-cultural country on democratic foundations.

India has a well-functioning electoral system. The electorate is highly politicized and has been generally speaking increasingly becoming participative. Quite often it has surprised the world through its discerning electoral verdicts. The question of those failing in the election appealing to the military to intervene is clearly unthinkable in India. It has a constitution which is highly respected and flexible enough to accommodate the growing needs of an expanding economy and society. Through its constitution, Indian democracy promises rights, justice, equality and freedom. Although caste continues to be a powerful factor it is being confronted through a series of affirmative actions like reservation of seats in legislature, for admissions and public jobs. *The Directive Principles of State Policy* (part IV of the Constitution) lay down the national goals of establishing a social order based on social and economic justice and outline measures and targets to secure these ends. It has a civil society that is democratic, a media that is alert and a judiciary that is active and dynamic. Innumerable movements since Independence such as peasant movements, environmental movements, land rights movements, women's organizations, dalits[5] movements, movements against displacement due to large scale projects, the naxalite[6] movements, labour movements, and so on keep alive forces of democracy in India. India has passed several progressive legislations guaranteeing human rights, rights to food security, education and information which in many countries is a great divide between the citizens and the government. Reckoned in terms of democratisation the most crowning achievement is the 73rd/74th Amendments to the Indian Constitution that accords constitutional status to the local governments and the three million strong elected representatives who are mandated to consult the gram sabha the assembly of voters and deliver "economic development and social justice" at the cutting edge level of governance. These Amendments have set the agenda for local peoples ownership in local governance.

In spite of the stability and progress of Indian democracy, its achievements are bedeviled by serious drawbacks. Constitutional provision notwithstanding, and the acknowledged progress of Indian democracy, caste discrimination and caste-based disparities and even atrocities continue to afflict the everyday life of the lower castes, tribes, women and several other deprived sections of society [See Shah et al. (2006) for an agonising account]. That more than one fourth of world's poor live in India is a dismal story that needs to be corrected. India is among those countries with the highest rates of inequality measured in terms of per capita income and per capita consumption [see World Bank

(2011) and the Annual studies by Oxfam]. The project of Indian democracy like that of Brazil has miles to go to build a truly inclusive society. As Atul Kohli (2001) points out the interests of the powerful in society are served without fully excluding the weak. The salience of democracy in these two democracies continues to be one of democratic elitism. In both countries, the political parties are oligarchical who know only to rule or command rather than govern democratically and efficiently. How soon and how far democracy will move forward depends the way the democratic institutions and the public seek to shape it.

To be sure, a well-functioning local democracy can transform the everyday practice of democracy.

Locating the LGs: A Comparative Perspective

In the light of the features of the two federal systems, we shall in this section focus on the place and significance of LGs more specifically. The two countries have a three-tier federal system. Brazil has a better and stable local government system than India in terms of fiscal decentralisation in respect of expenditure and revenue responsibilities and statutory support. The very fact that the municipalities in Brazil can make their own laws in regard to subjects of local interests makes a big difference between the two federations as regards their effective autonomy and power. Both federations acknowledge that most core services can be efficiently and equitably served only through the institutional framework of fiscal federalism. Surely there is no other way for participatory local democracy for big countries like India and Brazil with diverse preferences and sharp information asymmetry. Diversity in resource endowments, significant disparity in the pattern of development reached over time, wide disparities in the unit cost of providing different services and so on make fiscal capabilities highly diverse and skewed. The problem is considerably confounded by the built-in mismatch in expenditure responsibilities and revenue-raising powers. The institution of union finance commission at the federal level and its counterpart at the state level viz., the state finance commission are created to periodically rectify the vertical and horizontal fiscal imbalances on the basis of recommendations valid for every five years Brazil does not have such constitutional provisions and rely primarily on revenue sharing of specific federal government taxes or sharing of funds created for specific purposes.

Democracy is what democracy does to the people. One important area in which both the federations lay emphasis is on people's participation. The Constitution of India has created the institution of gram sabha/ward sabha, assembly of voters which has the power to decide on the size, scope and priorities of their local development plan, ratify budget proposal, receive audited statements and so on. It may be noted that statutory provisions for direct democracy does not mean that they are actually translated into a living reality[7]. Although Brazil does not have such counterpart institutions, they have initiated what has been famously referred to as participatory budgeting which we have already referred Participatory budgeting started in Porto Alegre in the State of Rio-Grande-De-Sul in 1989 is practised in several municipalities in Brazil. The gram sabha meetings called by the elected local government (Gram panchayat) insofar as they discuss resource allocation decisions in the village in a way has a sort of participatory budgeting exercise started in Porto Alegre.

The most striking contrast between Brazil and India is with reference to the institution of decentralised planning. Constitutionally LGs in India, both rural and urban are required 'to plan for economic development and social justice' and implement them. All the local governments in the rural and urban areas have to prepare plans (annual, medium and perspective) for their jurisdiction. Further Article 243 ZD mandates every state in India to constitute at the district level a District Planning Committee "to consolidate the plans prepared by the panchayats and the municipalities in the district and to prepare a draft development plan for the district as a whole". While the Planning Commission of India (abolished in 2014) was not a constitutionally created body, the District Planning committee mandated to consolidate at the district level the plans of all local governments at the rural and urban level is a constitutionally created institution. Such provisions and planning practices are conspicuous by their absence in Brazil[8] although the participatory budgeting exercise may be considered as a structure and a process of community participation that sustain popular participation in the decision-making process of investment priorities and budget allocation of municipalities.

Despite the large number of LGs (as high as 2,50,000), and the bigger geographical coverage, the economic size and power of Indian LGs is comparatively weak. In 2007-08, the share of LGs in the total public sector expenditure of India (comprising the centre, states and LGs) is 6.7% which is only marginally higher than what it was in 2002-03. But the share of LGs in the total own source revenue is still smaller and showed a decline from 3.6% in 2002-03 to 2.8% in 2007-08 (See Chapter 8) Although as a share of GDP, the local government expenditure increased from 2.13% in 2002-03 to 2.42% in 2007-08, it is way below Brazil's corresponding share of 7.26% for 2004. Even this is not very high compared to the OECD average of 14% of GDP. As a share of total public sector expenditure, local government expenditure is generally around 15% and the tax share well above 2% of GDP in Brazil in recent times. The contrast becomes very striking when we note that the own source revenue of PRIs in India is a negligible 0.03% of GDP and including urban local governments it becomes only 0.38% in 2007-08 and does not signify a respectable number.

It is abundantly clear from all these numbers and discussions that the political power and economic size and significance of the *municipios* of Brazil is far greater than that of India. This does not in any way underestimate the tremendous potential that lies ahead for India particularly for the expansion of participatory democracy, local development and decentralised governance India has built a lot of necessary conditions. But the, progress of building the needed sufficient condition is missing. The rural-urban divide that characterize India is conspicuously absent in Brazil and that is probably the striking contrast in the practice of local democracy between the two countries.

Appendix A
Brazil and India: Some Broad Magnitudes

Coun-try	Population	Area sq km	Density of population per km.	GDP$ (2010.) trillion	Per capita income (2010)	GDP Sectoral Distribution* (2011)		
						Agricul-ture (%)	Industry (%)	Service (%)
Brazil	201,103,330	8,514,877	24	$2.194	$10,900	5.5	27.5	67
India	1210193422	3,287,263	368	$4.046	$3,400	17.2	26.4	56.4
World	6,768,181,146	13494000	51	$74.43	$11,100	6	30.7	63.4

https://www.cia.gov/library/publications/the-world-factbook/geos/br.html
* Ref: http://www.indexmundi.com/brazil/gdp_composition_by_sector.html

Appendix B
The Centralisation/Decentralisation Cycle in Brazil

Landmark date of Regime	Regime Character
Post 1981: First Republican Constitution	Decentralisation
Post 1936: Vargas Dictatorship	Centralisation

Landmark date of Regime	Regime Character
Post 1946: Democratic Constitution	Decentralisation
Post 1964: Military Regime	Centralisation
Post 1988: Back to Democracy	Decentralisation

Appendix C
Figure 3.1 Participatory Budgeting Chronological Cycle in Porto Alegre

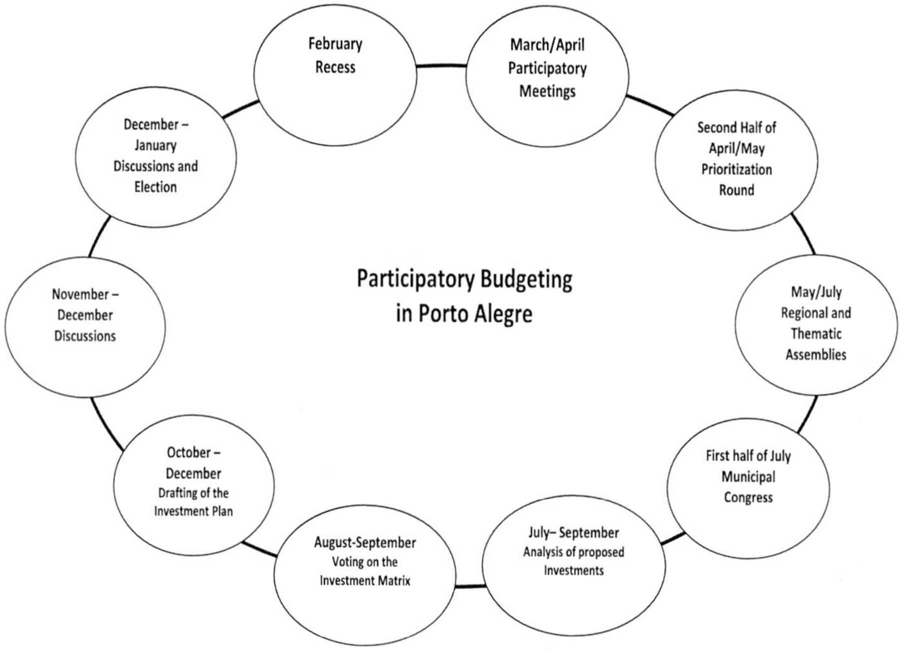

Fig 3.1. and 3.1. (a) Ref: 'Brazil Toward a More Inclusive and Effective Participatory Budget in Porto Alegre', (In Two Volumes) Volume I: Main Report, Report No. 40144-BR, Brazil - Country Management Unit, Sustainable Development Unit, Latin America and Caribbean Region, The International Bank for Reconstruction and Development/The World Bank (p. 15)

* Published in B.S. Baviskar Ash Narain Roy (edited) (2012). Publication Division, Government of India.

End Notes

1 For details See David V. Fleischer (1984).

2 This has some resemblance to the Fiscal Responsibility and Budget Management Act, 2003 of India.

3 Scheduled Castes refer to the former untouchables occupying the lowest position in the traditional caste hierarchy but as provided for in the Constitution. Scheduled tribes are original inhabitants mostly living in hill areas and listed in the Indian Constitution.

4 For a graphic account of this see Avritzer (2002).

5 Dalit is a designation for a group of people traditionally regarded as untouchable. By and large they are the scheduled castes.

6 The word Naxal, Naxalite or Naksalvadi is a generic term used to refer to various militant Communist groups operating in different parts of India under different organizational envelopes.

7 While holding Gram Sabha / Ward Sabha meetings is mandatory their frequency, agenda and quality of performance owe a great deal to the discretion and attitude of the elected representatives notably that of the village panchayat president.

8 Even so it is important to report that the municipality of Caxias Do Sul, Rio Grande Do Sul practice participatory planning (See Iain Bruce (2004), pp 85-99].

References

Afonso Jose Roberto Rodrigues and Erika Amorim Araujo (2006), 'Local Government Organization and Finance: Brazil', in Anwar Shah (ed.) *Local Governance in Developing Countries,* The World Bank, Washington DC.

Avritzer Leonardo (2002), *Democracy and Public Space in Latin America*, Princeton University Press, New Jersey.

Baiocchi, Gianpaolo (2003), 'Participation, Activism, and Politics: The Porto Alegre Experiment' in Archon Fung and Erik Olin Wright, ed., *Deepening Democracy,* Verso, London.

Fleischer V. David (1984), "Constitutional and electoral engineering in Brazil: A double-edged sword (1964-1982)", *Inter-American Economic Affairs* 37.

Iain Bruce (2004), 'The Participatory Budget in two other cities', in Iain Bruce (edited and translated), *The Porto Alegre Alternative,* Pluto Press, London.

Oommen M.A. (2004), *Basic Services, Functional Assignments and Own Revenue of Panchayats,* Institute of Social Sciences Occasional paper series-33, New Delhi.

CHAPTER 4

Towards A Conceptual Framework for Fiscal Decentralisation to Sub-State Level Governments: Kerala as an Illustrative Case*

This paper tries to present a conceptual framework for fiscal decentralisation with an illustrative underpinning based mostly on the experience of Kerala which has a respectable track record in implementing the 73rd Amendment. It is important to note here that the received theoretical literature evolved in the West under systems dominated by market allocations cannot fully explain the reality and responses of Indian local governments notably that of panchayats which have few parallels in the rest of the world[1].

What is Fiscal Decentralization?

We may first clarify what decentralization means? Planners, politicians, bureaucrats and many others tend to treat decentralization even today as either deconcentration which means reducing the work load or as delegation which is essentially a principal-agency relationship with well defined discretion to the lower tier. Decentralisation is truly devolution or autonomy in the assigned functional domain. Keeping the letter and spirit of the 73rd/74th Amendments we may define democratic decentralization as the empowerment of the people through the empowerment of the local governments which in our case primarily means panchayats. It follows that fiscal decentralization means fiscal empowerment of the panchayats. Operationally this is not an easy task. Giving greater functional responsibilities along with better taxing or broadly revenue-raising responsibilities is a necessary condition of the empowering process. While revenue-raising assignments are vital, local governments in most parts of the world depend a great deal on transfers from higher level governments especially in a multi-level federal system. This is more so in India with widely differing fiscal capabilities, resource endowments, development history, besides extreme disparities in infrastructural facilities. The vertical and horizontal imbalances yawn wide. The problem has to be addressed through an efficient, equitable, transparent, adequate and predictable transfer system. This is the key to fiscal empowerment which should be envisaged as part of a wider process of strengthening democratic decentralization.

Unlike in the case of the urban local government, taxing powers of Panchayati Raj Institutions (PRIs) are largely assigned to the gram panchayats (that tradition has been carried into the Post-Amendment regime via the conformity legislations of the states) with important exceptions. Presumably for enhancing responsibilities as well as for promoting greater autonomy, the block and district panchayats also should have greater revenue - raising powers. This is a matter of policy choice of individual states. The primacy of gram panchayats in the delivery of services and in implementing certain developmental responsibilities now vested in them as per Schedule XI has to be acknowledged. The GPs are important also because they are at the cutting edge level and have to interact with the gram sabha which is the bed-rock of decentralised democracy in the country. The emerging reality in India does not seem to empower them. Generally speaking gram panchayats (GPs) often with inadequate personnel and poor resource base have been over-burdened by centrally sponsored schemes (CSSs) and over-dependent on central transfers. Gram Panchayats in Indian rural setting have to be made the critical tier of fiscal decentralization, because they alone bear the real potential to emerge as 'institutions of self-government', and the kingpin of local democracy.

Decentralisation as Devolution

Decentralisation in India has to work towards the creation of 'institutions of self-government' at the local level as enjoined in Articles 243 G and 243 W of the constitution. It implies devolution where real power and authority are transferred to enable autonomous functioning within the legally assigned areas. In the words of Kerala's Committee on Decentralisation (1996) (popularly called Sen Committee after its first Chairman Subrata Sen) which contributed significantly to lay the legal and institutional foundation of Kerala's decentralised governance:

"Local Self-Government is essentially the empowerment of the people by giving them not only the voice, but the power of choice as well, in order to shape the development which they feel is appropriate to their situation. It implies maximum decentralization of powers to enable the elected bodies to function as autonomous units with adequate power, authority and resources to discharge the basic responsibility of bringing about "economic development and social justice". [Sen Committee (1996): 2].

In short autonomy is the basis of devolution. In this section, I stress on three dimensions of autonomy that are germane to decentralized governance: viz. functional autonomy, fiscal autonomy and administrative autonomy. This is what has come to be referred to as the transfer of the three 'Fs".functions, funds and functionaries to the local levels. All these have to be transferred simultaneously and any piece-meal transfer or even sequential transfer will have no meaning in practice[2]. Kerala attempted an almost simultaneous transfer as part of what has famously come to be called the 'Big Bang' approach to devolution. We may briefly illustrate how these have been devolved and operationalised in Kerala.

Functional Devolution

Devolution of the 29 subjects under Schedule XI of the constitution to panchayats has no operational significance unless they are disaggregated into activities and sub-activities. The Sen Committee (1996-98) was the first to do this in the country and the Government of Kerala (GoK) passed the amended Kerala Panchayat Act in February 1999. By this Act the functions of village panchayat were divided into 116 activities, block panchayats to 31 activities and district panchayat to 70 activities. This division was governed by the principles of subsidiarity, role-clarity and complementarity. Subsidiarity principle means, what can be done best at a particular level should be done at that level and not at a higher level. While role-clarity seeks to avoid overlapping and repetitive functions, complementarity insists that functions should merge into an overall unity through a process of horizontal integration. Activity mapping in Kerala is an operational reality and not something that rests in the statute book. Kerala currently is heading towards what is called Responsibility mapping that maps out a detailed operational division of labour between gram panchayats, block panchayats, district panchayats, municipalities and state.

A significant aspect of Kerala's functional devolution is that the institutions relevant to most of the devolved functions are transferred to the relevant tier of panchayats in an 'as is where is condition'. Important institutions of public services like public health centres, hospitals, schools, krishi bhavans, veterinary institutions, ICDS (anganwadis), and so on are transferred to local bodies. This institutional decentralisation has not happened elsewhere in India. Without institutional decentralisation functional devolution will be an incomplete exercise.

Financial Devolution

Functional devolution has no meaning unless it is backed up by financial devolution. What matters is the transfer of untied funds and not schematic transfers which basically is a negation of the spirit of decentralization. Scheme-specific transfers reflect the priorities of the Union and the state governments and not of the local governments. It is important to make changes in the Budget heads and allocations of the state for each one of the transferred functions to the extent possible. Even so I do not subscribe to the view that funds transfer which corresponds to the functions transferred is fiscally neutral. While changes in the budgetary allocations in the heads and subheads are important, democratic decentralization is not a zero sum game in this fashion. Actually ushering in a third tier in the rural areas quite often without even proper offices and elected representatives facing an electorate with rising expectations and growing demand, a strict fiscal neutral approach is untenable.

Transfers have to be formula-based. Room for discretion should be next to nil.[3] Emergence of transfers not based on any formula has been an important development in Indian fiscal federalism. The MPLAD[4], MLALAD, JNNURM etc. are classic cases of such transfers. Kerala created history by making the momentous decision in mid-1996 to devolve 35-40 per cent of state plan funds to local bodies on the basis of a formula [See Appendix A]. Although this order of devolution has not happened, 30 per cent has been the general pattern. Appendix IV of the State Budget of Kerala introduced since 1997-98 which shows all the funds allocations to each local body by name is a unique innovation that ensures considerable autonomy, transparency and predictability. As far as efficiency is concerned, one has to go beyond narrow cost benefit considerations. Service efficiency has a bearing on the own source revenue (OSR) base and the nature of transferred funds, i.e. whether it is project specific or untied which determines the flexibility of local bodies. OSR depends on revenue empowerment and collection efficiency. As already noted the plan allocations have been formula-based with focus on population, area and backwardness as appropriate to the various tiers to ensure equity [See Appendix A for more details]. In sum, efforts have been made to ensure transparency, equity, efficiency and adequacy.

Table 1 gives the trend in the magnitude of release to sub-state level governments from 1996-97 through 2007-08. The release to local governments which was only Rs. 616 crore in 1996-97 doubled in the next year which was obviously due to the momentous decision to devolve a part of plan grant to them. More than 60 per cent of the total release was because of plan grants.

Table 1
Structure and Pattern of State Sub-State Level Transfers (1996-97 – 2007-08)

(Rs. in Crore)

Year	States Own Revenue	Share of central Taxes and Grants	Total revenue	Release to LSGIs	Growth Rate	Percentage to States own Revenue	Release Percentage to GSDP	Percentage to Total Revenue	Per capita Release	Deflated value of per capita release
1996-97	4412.3	1732.78	6145.08	616.15	-	13.96	1.28	10.03	201.05	139.69
1997-98	5053.16	2065.06	7118.22	1243.97	101.89	24.62	2.31	17.48	402.50	258.53
1998-99	5207.22	1990.90	7198.12	1431.04	15.04	27.48	2.34	19.88	459.14	277.96
1999-00	5724.22	2217.53	7941.75	1400.32	-2.15	24.46	2.04	17.63	445.51	260.27
2000-01	6529.35	2201.51	8730.86	1238.62	-11.55	18.97	1.72	14.19	390.74	213.11
2001-02	6466.80	2589.59	9056.39	1100.41	-11.16	17.02	1.42	12.15	344.22	185.88
2002-03	7983.80	2653.58	10637.38	1647.33	49.70	20.63	1.91	15.49	509.11	264.89
2003-04	8895.76	2919.61	11815.37	1912.25	16.08	21.50	1.99	16.18	584.59	290.25
2004-05	9782.73	3717.75	13500.48	1703.18	-10.93	17.41	1.59	12.62	522.00	249.10
2005-06	10716.41	4578.11	15294.52	1991.56	16.93	18.58	1.67	13.02	603.17	278.06
2006-07	12879.39	5307.23	18186.62	2571.75	29.13	19.97	1.94	14.14	771.81	347.55
2007-08	15081.26	6415.72	21496.98	3071.47	19.43	20.37	2.08	14.29	909.71	400.27
Growth Rate									**9.81**	**5.50**

Data collected from Budget documents

Although the Table shows year to year fluctuations largely due to pruning of Annual Plans the magnitude of devolution has been significant. The total release (which comprises maintenance grants), which was 14 per cent of State's own revenue in 1996-97 nearly doubled to reach 27.4 per cent in 1998-99. Since then, it fluctuated between 17.02 per cent in 2001-02 to 24.46 per cent in 1999-2000. As a percentage of GSDP, release was above 2 per cent during the earlier period. This declined slightly during most of the subsequent years. Except for a significant fall in 2000-01 and 2001-02, the per capita transfers released have been steadily growing as is well exemplified in the graph given as Fig.1. The per capita release in 1996-97 which was only Rs. 201 rose to nearly Rs. 910 in 2007-08. It grew at the rate of 9.81 per cent per annum and in real terms (when deflated by GDP deflator) at the rate of 5.5 per cent. This progressive growth is due to the plan grants devolved. Indeed plan grants have significantly altered the financial base of local governments in Kerala.

Figure 1
Structure and Pattern of State Sub-State Level Transfers (1996-97-2007-08)

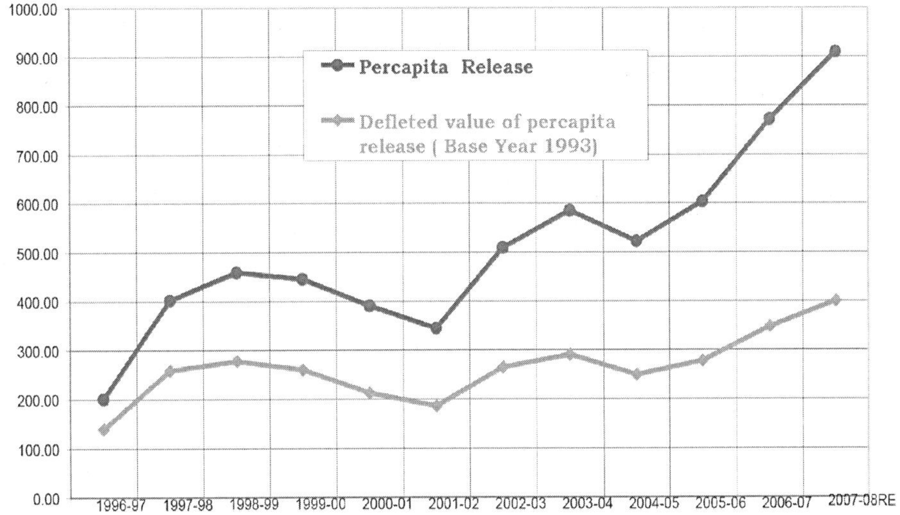

Year

Administrative Autonomy

Administrative autonomy which is closely linked to the devolution of functions and finance is best secured through creating an independent cadre specifically trained for dencentralised governance. This is but a distant goal but a necessary condition for effective decentralisation. What is needed is an immediate deployment of functionaries who can manage the functions devolved and the institutions transferred to the local bodies. Kerala is the only state that has made significant progress in this regard. Seventeen departments have transferred relevant functionaries to panchayats fully or in part. The panchayats have been given disciplinary control over the staff and have been declared as executive authorities and the transferred officers function under them. A virtual technical cadre has been set up for the local governments by deploying engineers from public works and irrigation departments. Technical committees consisting of engineers from Government, academic institutions and NGOs have been set up at the block and district levels for according technical sanction. This set up is part of the process of decentralized planning.

Devolution and the Transfer System

As we have already noted local bodies in India especially the panchayats cannot raise adequate resources to meet their functional responsibilities. So transfer of resources to panchayats is but inevitable. Moreover as the Tenth UFC (FC-10) rightly observe: "The Panchayats/Municipalities are late entrants in our federal democratic structure but their action or inaction is likely to affect the welfare of the people and area under their jurisdiction more directly than either the actions of the State or the Union" [Report of the Tenth Commission, p. 47]. While transfers to the panchayats is important and unavoidable, the real problem is to make the sub-state transfer and the mechanisms designed for them truly rational in terms of efficiency, equity, predictability, transparency and adequacy. The first step in designing proper transfer system is to spell out the objectives to be achieved and then examine how far the existing arrangements are adequate to meet them.

Objectives of the Transfer System

The following objectives are critical to a devolution package and transfer system in the Indian context.

(1) Reducing vertical and horizontal imbalances and working towards equalizing the financial capabilities and basic service levels at the level of gram panchayats. The realization of these objectives depends on the entire devolution package by the various agencies (e.g. Planning Commission, Central Ministries, State Government, besides the UFCs and SFCs). But here we are primarily concerned with the sub-state level transfers only.

(2) Facilitating local planning for economic development and social justice.

(3) Promoting and deepening participatory democracy.

The latter two objectives are somewhat unique for India. The received literature on fiscal decentralization treats the relations of local government with the local community as one that of a client, customer or consumer rather than as citizen concerned about shaping the development destinies of the local community. The gram sabha, the assembly of local citizen voters is assigned a critical consultative role in India's good governance. Good governance is not providing an immediate service. Quint-essentially it is local democracy in action.

I may mention here that Kerala has implemented a multi-stage process of decentralized planning, as part of its efforts to implement the vital Articles 243 G, 243 W and 243 ZD. The process starts with the special gram sabha/ ward sabha meeting to identify the felt needs of the people, then preparation of a development report, formulation of priorities at the development seminar, sectoral projectisation (12 working groups generally do the job), vetting by a voluntary technical group and finally approval by the District Planning Committee. This multi-stage process opens wide the avenues of people's participation and surely has an instrumental value in enhancing the quality of citizenship and governance.

Towards a More Rational Devolution Package

Once the objectives are clear, it is important to work out the approximate size and broad structure of the devolution package. In this section we mention certain important issues that will have to be addressed in evolving a rational devolution at the sub-state level.

At the state sub-state level the reality is that a comprehensive devolution package is missing. The SFCs and UFCs together could have altered substantially the fiscal landscape at the sub-state level. This great opportunity seems to have been missed. While the UFC has to make recommendations relating to local governments based on the recommendations of the SFCs, this has not happened. The timings of the Reports of the various SFCs and that of the UFC have never been co-terminus. The methodology and the analytical basis adopted by them varied so widely that it was difficult for the two Commissions (UFC and SFC) to collaborate to work out a rational devolution package. Most SFCs have failed to work out a scientifically valid resource gap estimate (based on relevant norms) which the UFC could consider or even the state could accept. The challenge before the Thirteenth Finance Commission and probably for others to come in the future is to take steps towards designing a rational transfer system taking local governments fully in view.

The 73rd/74th Amendments provided a historic opportunity to restructure the Indian public finance which still retains the basic financial structure handed over from the days of the government of India Act, 1935. Although the TOR of the Eleventh Finance Commission (FC-11) and that of the Twelfth Finance Commission (FC-12) had mandated them to restructure public finance, they chose to stay within the boundaries of fiscal responsibility and fiscal balance which in an integrated fiscal system should have included all the tiers of the federal polity. The FC-11 and FC-12 have failed to recognize the organic link between the union, state and local governments. All of them have treated local governments as eligible only for a grant-in-aid. Here too, for *interse* distribution of the grants to states FC-11 used a five point criteria, with a 20 per cent weightage to what they called 'Index of decentralisation'. In choosing the variables it is clear that the commission did not go deep into the idea or process of decentralisation. Andhra Pradesh, Bihar, Madhya Pradesh, Maharashtra, Rajasthan and UP were rated way above that of Kerala. FC-12, of course, abandoned the Index, but on the specious ground that "almost all states have by now taken effective steps for the implementation of the 73rd and 74th amendment" (p. 155). I do not think that any one, most of all the Union Ministry of Panchayati Raj (MOPR) would agree to this. The Seven Round Table Conferences of the Panchayati Raj Ministers sponsored by the MOPR during 2004 and the three volume reports produced by them support this. We hope that the FC-13 will not be guilty of such indifference.

The best measure to augment the consolidated fund of the state to supplement the resources of the panchayats and municipalities is to earmark a respectable share of the union tax revenue to the local bodies. *Interse* share to states can be worked out through a devolution index that measures the real magnitude of functional, financial and administrative devolution. The formula for the distribution of the share within a state should be left to the respective SFCs. This is one way, to integrate the local governments into the federal polity with an automatic claim on the gains of tax buoyancy and economic growth. Not only that the FC-13 will have to examine the possibility of taking local governments in their analytical framework of Indian public finance. Of course this depends a great deal on the strength and quality of data they have gathered.

The issue of maintenance of assets has to be taken seriously in any effort to build a rational transfer system at the state sub-state level. The fact that maintenance of assets appeared in the TOR of all UFCs in recent times shows that this vital issue is not addressed. All the governments, union, state and local have accumulated huge maintenance deficits leading to poor delivery of services and even collapse of assets resulting in waste of resources. There is a clear case for a planned methodology which takes into account a renewal strategy for assets and build that into the budgetary process. In order to ensure quality of services the FC-13 may create an Asset Renewal Fund that will ensure the maintenance of core services like public health centres, primary schools, anganwadis, krishi bhavans, panchayat offices and so on, so that the poor do not suffer due to breakdown or poor delivery. The union, state and local governments should be involved in the creation and operation of the Asset Renewal Fund.

The future of the third tier is heading towards a crisis unless timely action is taken at least in regard to two aspects. One relates to the proliferation of parallel bodies and diversion of panchayat funds. If an independent research agency prepares a Functions Funds flow matrix at the village and block levels the distorted picture of inroads into the functional domain of panchayats will be evident. The Union and the States are equally guilty of this. When it comes to panchayats most activities are state or union concurrent. Ultimately this can reduce panchayat to a non-entity or weak agent of the higher level governments. For example, Andhra Pradesh has "systematically disempowered PRIs in the recent past", through diversion of funds to parallel bodies, creation of Mandal Development Fund at the rate of Rs. 9 million per mandal to be administered by a special Minister (not even PRI minister), "to be distributed on party considerations", the distribution of MPLAD and MLALAD on party basis so that "the contractors and party workers are benefited", appointment of village workers (placed outside the PRIs) on adhoc basis for activities such as Andhrash Rythula for agriculture, arogya mithra for health, gram deepikalu for formation of SHGs, vidya volunteers for education and so on. [See Bala Ramalu (2008)].

Another important aspect is the poor resource base of the panchayats which is in contrast to the urban local bodies. The own source revenue (OSR) of panchayats as a proportion of the combined tax and non-tax revenue of the union, states and panchayats which was only around 0.40 per cent in 1998-99 declined to 0.36 per cent in 2002-03 and definitely much lower today. The reason for this poor share is partly because of state inaction in regard to the revenue raising statutes and rules and in most cases due to the panchayats themselves. While there are states like Bihar which have made no tax effort, a good many have made only an indifferent approach. The two quotes given below, one from Madhya Pradesh second SFC report and the other from Second Orissa SFC Report are illustrative of the general trend.

- "55.21% of the GPs in the state are not raising any tax revenue, 70% not raising any non-tax revenue and 45.46% not raising any amount of own resources.... There are 10 districts where 75% and more GPs are not raising any tax revenue, 16 districts not raising non-tax revenues" [Report of MP Second SFC, p.95].

- "The average tax revenue per GP varies between Rs. 935 to Rs. 1190 from 1999-2000, to 2001-02 which is quite low; while that for the year 2002-03 is at a nadir of Rs.336 only.... There has been no collection in respect of Registration Fees in any of the GP of Boudh, Bhadrak, Jagatisinghpur, Kendrabara, Nawarangpur and Puri districts during the period 1999-2000 to 2002-03.... There was no collection of Licence Fee or Latrine Tax or Street Lighting Rate or Drainage Tax in any of the GPs of the district. These bear testimony to weak financial position of the GPs in the Panchayati Raj Structure" [Report of the Second SFC Orissa, p. 287].

Kerala is one state that has a respectable record of tax mobilization among the India states. The per capita tax revenue of panchayats which was Rs. 51 in 2002-03 has more than doubled in 2007-08. Even so, I have a hunch that there is tremendous tax potential to be tapped. Not only that for 1998-99 a year that saw the people's plan campaign at its best, while in the scheme of actual financing of Annual Plan of the year balance from current revenue was only 5.54 per cent, beneficiary contribution accounted for 13.63 per cent. [This is based on a study of 654 GPs For details See Oommen (2003)] Today after a decade all circumstantial evidences show that these practices have vanished.

Finally the changes in the methodology of central funds transfer with direct grants to local bodies by the central governments bypassing the state governments also needs mention in the context of addressing the issue of better devolution. This has important consequences. One, it affects the state's fiscal autonomy and priorities. Two, states tend to lose interest in the projects which are not in their scheme of priorities. Three, it is very difficult to get comprehensive information about public spending on different services. This is vital for local planning. Four, states are confronted with multiple agencies, each with its own agenda and priorities.

To conclude, the local governments, notably the panchayats should be given a respectable place in the scheme of Indian public finance and planning. An integrated view of public finance and planning is missing. The constitutional goal of creating 'institutions of self government' and planning for economic development and social justice' seems to recede like the horizon even 15 years after the 73rd /74th Amendment. A well designed devolution package that helps to usher in a responsive and responsible local democracy is a crying need, but a difficult and demanding task.

Appendix A
The Criteria for the Distribution of Plan Grant-in-Aid for different Tiers

Indicators	Weightage (Percentage)			
	Gram Pancha-yat	**Block Pancha-yat**	**District Pancha-yat**	**Municipalities /Corporations**
1. Population	60	60	50	70
2. SC/ST Population	5	5	5	5
3. Area under Paddy	5	-	-	-
4. Geographical area excluding area under forest	5	10	15	5
5. Own income of Gram Panchayat	10	-	-	-
6. Composite index of Agriculture Labourers, Persons engaged in Livestock, Fisheries, etc. and Marginal Workers	15	25	20	-
7. Composite index of backwardness/houses without latrine and houses without electricity.	-	-	10	20

* Paper presented at the Conference on **'Issues before the Finance Commission: Empowering the PRIs'** sponsored by the Finance Commission-13 held at IRMA, Anand Gujarat December 22-23, 2008.

Endnotes

1 For a review of literature, see chapter 2

2 It is not wide of the mark to quote from the Report of the Government of India (GOI) *Task Force on Decentralisation (2001)* which has provided the guide lines for the Ministry of Panchayati Raj (MOPR) to push forward decentralization subsequently:"In fact functions, funds and functionaries are complementary to one another in the process of devolution and responsibilities and powers upon the panchayats".[GOI (2001): 5].

3 The Tamil Nadu Second SFC report gives 20 per cent discretion to the State Government.

4 The MPLAD fund introduced in 1993 almost co-terminus with the 73rd/74th Amendments although started with Rs. 5 lakhs, was raised to Rs.1 crore, 2 crore and now proposed to be raised to Rs.10 crore. Imagine what will happen to decentralized governance if all the 3.6 million local body representatives also demand a LAD (Local Area Development) Fund.

References

Bala Ramalu C H (2008), 'Five decades of decentralization process in AP', paper presented at the *National Seminar on State and Society in South India*, organized by the National Institute of Parliamentary Affairs, Thiruvananthapuram.

Oommen M A (2003), *Fiscal Decentralisation to Rural Local bodies: A Case study of Kerala*, World Bank, Washington.

--- **(2005),** 'Rural Fiscal Decentralisation in India: A brief review of literature' in L C Jain, ed., (2005), *Decentralisation and Local Governance,* Orient Longman, New Delhi.

Report of the Committee on Decentralisation (SB Sen Committee) (1996), *Interim Report,* Government of Kerala, Thiruvananthapuram.

Report of the Tenth Finance Commission (1994), Government of India, New Delhi.

Report of the Madhya Pradesh State Second Finance Commission.

Report of the Orissa State Second Finance Commission.

CHAPTER 5

Sub-state Level Fiscal Decentralisation in India: Theoretical Issues and Empirical Approaches

India's fiscal decentralisation, now a quarter century old is part of the larger process of democratic decentralisation reforms heralded through the 73rd/74th Constitutional Amendments (CAs). Decentralisation is defined as empowerment of the people by strengthening local governments. Obviously it is more than a governance reform[1]. Fiscal decentralisation may be defined as restructuring fiscal balance in a federation by fiscally empowering the local governments. It is a way of deepening democracy and fiscal decentralisation is to be seen as part of this substantive goal. For the first time in the history of fiscal federalism, India through the two CAs has created a state level institution called State Finance Commission (SFC) to rationalize and systematize state sub-state level fiscal relations. SFC is the real agent and instrument of fiscal decentralisation in India. The purpose of this chapter is:

(i) To postulate a conceptual framework for State sub-state fiscal relations in India;

(ii) To empirically verify the cases of three SFCs (latest available) in the light of that; and

(iii) To indicate the policy options for improving the fiscal decentralisation as it unfolds in India.

Towards a Theoretical Framework

There is no theory on fiscal federalism that can naturally accommodate the democratic decentralisation that India has initiated following the 73rd/74th Constitutional Amendments. To be sure, issues in decentralised public finance and governance can be understood only contextually. Indian fiscal decentralisation can be understood only from the larger political and administrative dimensions launched in the 1990s. Panchayats and municipalities, once appendages of rural and urban departments have now become a third stratum of government in Indian federalism. This calls for a radical reordering of fiscal balances, both vertical and horizontal at all levels, certainly at the state sub-state levels of governance. The state finance commission (see Articles 243I and 243Y) whose primary concern is to rectify the fiscal imbalances has to play a critical role.

The task of SFC is extremely onerous because of two important reasons. One, there was no reordering of fiscal powers and fiscal balance. Nobody ever asked the question *denovo* who should do what? and who should tax what and where? Two, the CAs did not provide for a local list, but added much confusion providing for an eleventh schedule for panchayats with 29 broad subjects and a twelfth schedule for urban local governments with 18 subjects which overlap with Schedule VII. Fine-tuning of functional mapping and ensuring role clarity was left to each state and its legislature. Therefore no uniform pattern could emerge. Actually simultaneous devolution of functions, funds and functionaries is needed to facilitate orderly fiscal balance. This amorphous situation can considerably complicate the tasks of SFC and consequently decision-making vis-à-vis Indian federal finance.

At this stage it is instructive to distinguish the salience of the decentralized reforms in Indian fiscal federalism from their Western counterparts. The basics of fiscal federalism theory be they classical or second generation variety [see (Oates (2005); Weingast (2009)] differ from India's fiscal federalism especially as modified by the 73rd/74th CAs.

For one, the fiscal decentralisation in India can be understood only from the larger political and administrative dimensions of decentralisation reforms introduced through the 73rd/74th CAs which try to create an autonomous space for local governments (LGs). The term local self-government repeatedly appearing in the official documents since the Mayo Resolution of 1870 has taken statutory significance only when the CAs specify the goal of creating 'institutions of self-government' at the local level (Article 243G and 243W)[2]. The local bodies[3] (panchayats in rural areas and municipalities in urban areas) are given constitutional status as a regularly elected government with powers, authority and responsibilities in defined areas. Logically, the CAs necessitate a reordering of the fiscal balances at the various level with focus on the local governments. Reordering of fiscal balance has both a vertical and horizontal component. Vertical imbalance refers to the mismatches between levels of government in responsibilities and resources. Horizontal or inter-jurisdictional imbalance refers to the presence of geographical and fiscal inequities. The fiscal balance questions have particular significance in a vast country such as India with great regional disparities in resource endowment, level of income, level of development, fiscal disabilities and even social deprivation. In brief the prime rationale of SFC in India can be traced to the rectification of imbalances at a sub-national level. In the case of sub-national governments, the resource pool would consist of both inter-governmental transfers and own source revenue (OSR) of the local government, besides borrowings.

Second, historically the sub-state level governance were departmentally administered. Bringing clarity in the functional and financial responsibilities of local governments has therefore become a demanding task and require tremendous skill. Given the adhocism and lot of ambiguities in the state local functional responsibilities, there is a need for a simultaneous devolution of functions, funds and functionaries. As the Government of India Report (2001) rightly puts it:

> "In fact functions, funds and functionaries are complementary to one another in the process of devolution of responsibilities and powers upon the panchayats." [GoI (2001): p.5]

Third, the tripartite framework formulated by the great public finance 'guru' Musgrave (1959) viz macro-economic stabilization, income distribution and resource allocation, although very popular in Western theories of public finance (and faithfully followed in Indian University syllabus) does not seem to be relevant to explain the decentralized realities of Indian pubic finance.

Fourth, it is important to recognise that the micro economic theory of consumer choice is inapplicable to the social and fiscal realities of Indian federalism. The formal theory based on a demand-driven model of consumer choice goes back to Tiebout (1956) who postulates that individuals (households) 'shop' among a large local jurisdiction in an effort to balance marginal site costs (including all tax price) with the marginal evolution of public-services packages. Such costless mobility of 'consumers' in search of their preferred public goods or 'voting by feet' in Tiebout's words in a federation like India where the majority of the population live on land and the mobility envisaged is inapplicable to the ground realities of India. Also it is important to stress that the role of local governments in democratic countries like India is related to the development concept of citizen than the institutional concept of the consumer whose voting is an expression of self-interest [Mulgan (1997); Council of Europe (1995)].

Oates dismisses this model "as a set of assumptions so patently unrealistic as to verge on the outrageous"[W E Oates (1981): 93]. He and most others of his persuasion follow the analytical framework of neoclassical economics and explain the economic rationale of multi-level governments on the ground that they would provide optimal public goods in accordance with voter preferences and choices. Oates (1972) outlines a 'decentralisation theorem' which argues for a geographical area that internalizes the benefits and costs of a public good. India's rural local governments with their three-tier system do not easily fit into a model of jurisdictions that would internalize costs and benefits. Such a theory virtually rules out intergovernmental transfer arrangements.

Fifth, the institutions, goals and strategies envisaged in the CAs such as the gram sabha (the voters' assembly that is mandated to articulate the preferences of the citizen, determine the priorities of budget, respond to the audited accounts and so on) the bottom up planning process consolidated by the institution of District Planning Committee which not only has to integrate sectoral and spatial planning, but also has to plan for economic development and social justice, etc., and most importantly the SFC which is mandated to carry forward the process of fiscal decentralisation are far from the institutional structures which western fiscal federalism literature postulates in designing its theoretical framework. Besides designing an intergovernmental transfer system at sub-state level , the SFC has to make recommendations regarding the principles which should govern the determination of the taxes, duties, tolls and fees which may be assigned to, or appropriated by the panchayats. In brief, the tasks of fiscal decentralisation cannot be performed independent of the constitutional responsibilities implicit in all these institutions especially in the SFC.

Given the fact that SFC is the critical factor in the state sub-state level fiscal relations some prevailing misconceptions on its role need be clarified. The political class, policy makers and even experts seem to harbor the notion that SFC and the local governments they deal with have only a subordinate constitutional status. This is totally incorrect. SFC is modeled on the union finance commission (UFC) created under Article 280 as is well exemplified in the language of Articles 243I and 243Y which establish the SFC. Almost the same wording is repeated. While the UFC is mandated to rectify or reduce the vertical and horizontal imbalances at the Union-state levels[4], SFC has to perform the same tasks with regard to state sub-state level local institutions. Evidently the constitution treats LGs on par with the state government, certainly when it comes to sharing of financial resources.

It is also inadequately appreciated that the task of addressing the question of horizontal equity by the SFC is much more onerous and to be sure instrumentally more significant. This is so for three reasons. One, SFCs as an institution in the aggregate have to consider a larger number of rural and urban entities and collectively speaking nearly 2.5 lakh local governments. The UFC has to consider only 29 states. Two, although implicitly, SFC is the institutional agency which has the responsibility to facilitate and promote the golden rule of cooperative federalism viz., that every citizen should be assured a minimum of public services irrespective of his/her choice of residential location. The XIth and XIIth schedules include most primary public services within the domain of local governments although the manner of financing them is left unspecified. Indeed to ensure intra-state equity in providing minimum essential services of standard quality to all places is no sinecure task particularly if the state government concerned is indifferent to the recommendation of the SFC or when SFC itself is silent on this responsibility. Three, Article 280 (3) was amended as part of the two CAs to add clauses (bb) and (c) in order to take measures to augment the resources of panchayats and municipalities on the basis of the recommendations "made by the finance commission of the state". These sub-clauses affirm the organic link between UFC, LGs and SFCs in Indian fiscal federalism. It is only when interstate disparities are reduced by the UFCs through their inter-se distribution criteria and intra-state disparities are reduced by SFCs through the horizontal distribution criteria, Indian federation becomes a sustainable and inclusive nation-state. To get the nation move in sync to ensure territorial equity is a collective goal, indeed a desirable one at that the issue of fiscal balance assumes considerable significance at the sub-state level in view of the need to provide a minimum level of public services of standard quality at the local level and determining the cost of such services. While one may raise the problem of affordability, in the cooperative federal context of India the SFC's role becomes very important in determining the vertical share as well as in the choice of criteria for horizontal distribution.

While the two CAs made provisions for the creation of necessary institutions and conditions, the major task of carrying forward the process of decentralized governance are left to the states. Public finance experts concur on the question that expenditure assignment is the first crucial step and all others including funds and functionaries follow from this. As already mentioned no such effort was made as part of the two CAs. There was no local list by way of assignment of expenditure responsibilities or revenue raising powers making it easy for states especially those who are reluctant to part with power to continue with the *status quo* and stick to the absolute minimum mandates warranted by the CAs. Whether done deliberately or inadvertently the retention of item no. 5[5] in the state list is an affront on the third tier of governments and the 73rd/74th Constitutional Amendments. The list of 29 subjects given in schedule XI and 18 subjects given in schedule XII have no operational significance unless they are broken up into activities and sub-activities and the functional domain of the Panchayati Raj Institutions and municipalities are clearly specified. Only the state of Kerala did it and incorporated it into the statute books. Several other states followed much later and particularly after the formation of Ministry of Panchayati Raj in 2004 which purposefully promoted activity mapping. The cherished goal of creating autonomous government (Articles 243G, 243W) which will deliver 'economic development and social justice' at the local level through a process of functional autonomy, financial support and functionary support to maintain this remains far away from reality. In other words, there is lack of clarity and ostensibly much over assignment including much unfunded expenditure. This creates problems of growing gaps in meeting the primary needs of the citizens at the local level.

Another important component relating to the state sub-state fiscal relations is the design of an efficient and equitable transfer system. In the Oatsian scheme which seeks internalizing costs and benefits, the design of transfer is unimportant. The two CAs have left this to the institution of SFC as we have already noted. It is also important to note that the objectives and tasks of the transfer system which SFC has to take into account are broadly indicated in the Constitution (Article 243I and 243Y). We have already noted that the real problem is the issues related to assignment of functions and working out an equalizing transfer system. True, this is considerably complicated by the fact that Indian federation never had a scientific assignment of functional responsibilities and revenue sources. At no stage did Indian Constitution makers raised the principle of subsidiarity or any other principles in drawing up the VIIth Schedule that listed out the union list, state list and concurrent list. The Constitution borrowed heavily from the Government of India Act, 1935[6]. Indeed the most redeeming feature is the creation of the UFC which has to review the finances of union and states and then design a proper transfer system. The two CAs faithfully followed the tradition and provided for a SFC modeled on the UFC to rationalize the fiscal relations at the state and local government levels.

The problems of assignment and intergovernmental transfer arrangements are considerably confounded by the lack of a system of financial accountability along with the absence of a systematic budgetary procedures and practices[7]. The union and state governments follow systematic budgetary procedures which the LGs may do well to emulate.

To sum up this section, fiscal decentralisation in the Indian federal context is the delivery of economic development and social justice, most conspicuously a set of public services through institutions like gram sabha, gram panchayats, district planning process and sound budgetary practices. I think it is appropriate to quote what Roy Bahl said a decade ago:

> "The key to structuring a workable system of fiscal decentralization is for government to decide how much expenditure autonomy they want to devolve to subnational governments and then to put in place a supporting system of vertical and horizontal fiscal balance"[Roy Bahl (2008)].

In the context of this paper we may substitute the term government by State Finance Commission on the assumption that the state government will implement the needed reforms.

Approach of Three SFCs – Karnataka, Kerala and Tamil Nadu

Article 243I (and also 243Y) mandate the Governor to constitute a SFC within one year of the CAs (24th April 1994) and thereafter every five years. At least 140 SFC reports should have been submitted by now. Actually only four states (Assam, Himachal Pradesh, Kerala and Tamil Nadu) have submitted the fifth SFC reports. All others are at different stages of submission from the second to the fifth. Evidently the large majority of states have violated the mandates of the Constitution with impunity.

This section examines the SFC report of Karnataka, Kerala and Tamil Nadu with reference to three issues germane to honouring the constitutional tasks:

(1) the effort to build a package of essential public goods;

(2) the formula for horizontal distribution and

(3) the progress towards building an autonomous fiscal space.

These are examined from an intrastate basis. The comparison over time helps to evaluate the trend in continuity and change.

Providing Essential Public Services

It is important to recall here that the Resource Group constituted in 1995 under the Chairmanship of Raja Chelliah by the Planning Commission[8] to provide assistance to the SFC recommended that water supply, sanitation/ sewage, solid waste collection, primary education and primary health as core services of local governments and even worked out normative standards for them. The task of providing essential services assumes significance only if SFCs follow the path of continuity of course on the assumption that the states accept the recommendations. Only the first Karnataka SFC took this seriously (see Chapter 6).

KSFC-I (Karnataka SFC-I), laid the foundations of sub-state level fiscal relations "a launching pad and bench-mark" as the KSFC-III correctly recalls. Among the first generation reports in India KSFC-I needs to be recognized for its contribution. KSFC-I avoided the gap-filling approach and chose what it calls "a pragmatic normative approach" in identifying the vertical share and in determining the shares of panchayats and municipalities. The well-known federal principle that every citizen should be ensured a minimum level of basic services irrespective of her choice of residence is firmly acknowledged and proceeded to operationalise that. All the SFCs of Karnataka followed this approach but differed in regard to details.

KSFC-I recommends earmarked or block grants as part of the total devolution to LGs for upgrading certain essential services in the rural and urban areas. KSFC–I has identified safe-drinking water, primary health, primary education and street lights for rural areas and safe drinking water, urban roads, street lights and sanitation for urban areas and compared their actual availability in relation to feasible normative level and worked out the additional expenditure involved for such upgradation. The competent institutions are identified (e.g. streetlight to gram panchayats, primary education to Zilla panchayats etc.) and the horizontal distribution details are also given. KSFC II introduced more concrete improvements and took up the question of normatively assessing capital investments. This is something which the so-called gap-filling approach does not entertain. As KSFC-II points out there was need to have a constant endeavor to achieve normative standards to improve the quality of essential public services. KSFC-III does not strictly follow a normative approach. It recommended the creation of a Rural Infrastructure Development and Finance Corporation for mobilizing capital for the development of rural roads, drinking water, street lights etc.

The Tamil Nadu first SFC or for that matter others did not follow a normative approach No SFC of Tamil Nadu so far did take up the task of provision of essential services seriously.

The first SFC of Kerala (KESFC-I) was well aware of Chelliah Committee Report (1995) and even worked out standards in regard to five core responsibilities viz., provision of street taps, provision of street lighting, collection and disposal of solid waste surface drainage, and upgradation of road on the basis of a sample survey it conducted. But KESFC-I did not make this useful information an essential component of its recommendations. No other Commission considered this. However, it is important to note that

KESFC-II and KESFC-IV devolved a share of state plan as part of the divisible pool to the LGs in the form of a development grant to be utilized on projects as prioritized by them. But this surely is not a substitute for what Karnataka SFC-I did or the Chelliah Resource Group recommended. This deficit continues to remain unattended.

The Horizontal Distribution Criteria

In this section we may compare how far the intra state equity especially in regard to the provision of essential public services is ensured. SFC surely is not an implementing agency or department. So what we examine are confined to the criteria followed with reference to the interse distribution in ensuring minimum services.

The Karnataka first SFC (KSFCI) which firmly underscored the need for territorial equity in the provision of basic public services first divided the total divisible pool [36% of the total non-loan gross own revenue (NLGOR)] among urban and rural bodies on the basis of three criteria. They are (a) proportion of population living in urban and rural areas, (b) proportion of rural and urban areas, and (c) an index of backwardness comprising (i) illiteracy rate (ii) number of persons per bed in government hospitals and (iii) road length per sq.km. of area. For interse KSFCI identified safe drinking water supply, sanitation including garbage removal and underground sewerage, street lights and roads in that order as the most essential services which should be provided by all urban LGs at a reasonable level. For PRIs supply of safe drinking water, street lights, roads, primary education and primary health care in that order were identified. The SFC also spelt out the standards upto which these services to be raised over the next five years and unit cost for upgradation worked out and estimated the financial implications. The idea clearly is to upgrade LGs to a desirable level of providing essential public services. Those LGs which have already achieved the standards are not punished and allowed them to improve their standards further.

KSFC–II basically followed the first but made very important changes in the normative standards of water supply, road, streetlight etc. KSFC-II was more concrete in that they worked out the normatively assessed the capital investment needed. KSFC-III made some important departures. The indicators selected were population, area, SC/ST population, illiteracy, population per hospital bed and density of population. Population was given the highest weightage of 40% followed by area with 20% and the remaining 40% divided equally among the other four indicators. Without going into finer details one can say that these indicators were chosen, mutatis mutandis, for horizontal distribution as well as for ULGS.

SFCs in general in Tamil Nadu do not give importance to provision of minimum services as a dominant criterion in horizontal allocation of resources (for details see Appendix A). True, the first SFC of Tamil Nadu (TNSFC-I) considered core civic service deficiency (with 20% weightage) in horizontal distribution. All other tiers including urban local governments were left out. TNSFC-V considers some valid horizontal equity consideration like per capita consumer expenditure distance. But they have no relevance for ensuring minimum public services.

As regards Kerala SFCs (KESFC) the most prominent horizontal equity criteria of ensuring core services are considered only by the KESFC-IV. KESFC-IV elaborates in detail not only its constitutional mandates but outlines its approach as the delivery of economic development with social justices, and emphasizes the need to improve the quality of public services. An important aspect that this SFC tries to focus is the general principle that it is horizontal equity that should be the primary concern of the sub-state level transfer system. This Commission sought inter-jurisdictional equity in basic services using a devolution index, besides giving special grants to gram panchayats identified as comprising the most deprived people of the state. After identifying district-cum-social group-wise vulnerable gram panchayats (GPs), they were ranked and meticulously chose 74 most deprived GPs for special grant. KESFC-IV made a bold beginning to include the marginalized communities into the mainstream of development as part of fiscal decentralisation process and devoted one chapter exclusively to explain this devolution strategy. Using well-defined criteria fiscally weak LGs were also identified. The commission significantly changed the development fund allocation formula of the previous Commissions and brought more equity in the interse distribution. This is given in Table 1.

Table 1
Criteria for Inter-tier distribution of Development Fund

Criteria	GP	BP	DP	.ULGs
Population (Excluding SC/ST)	50	50	50	50
Deprivation Index	30	30	30	30
Tax Effort	10	-	-	-
Area	10	20	20	20

Source: SFC-IV, Kerala Report; p. 186.

The deprivation index indicates the magnitude of deprivation with respect of housing sanitation (percentage of families reported as without latrines), drinking water, electricity (percentage of families without electricity connection) and percentage of landless families. This is a great step forward.

Working Towards Institutions of Self-government

As well exemplified in Articles 243G and 243W, a cherished goal of the decentralized governance reforms in India is to create institutions of self-government at the local government level. Undoubtedly the primary task of the SFC is to work towards accomplishing this. The fundamental, principle of financial responsibility expounded in public finance literature demands that every institution should raise its own resources even in a federation. As far back as the early 1930s, B P Adarkar (1933) noted:

> The basic principle of practical public finance is that as far as practicable, the responsibility of raising revenue and the freedom of spending it ought to go hand in hand must be granted as more or less fundamental to federal as to other financial system [Adarkar (1933): 219].

Most of the SFCs have acknowledged this principle. A Government that fosters fiscal illusion or dependency syndrome can never aspire to be a self-reliant entity. India has a tradition of cultivating a grant-supported local government. The purpose of creating self-reliance is to dethrone the culture of dependency and promote autonomous actions and development. No SFC in India seems to have made such an evaluation specifically. Hazarding an impressionistic inference, I may say that the country is drifting away from the goal of creating autonomous local governments.

A government that can generate at least 50% of its own revenue to meet its expenditure could be considered self-reliant in a federation. Given the built-in mismatch in resources and responsibilities, this margin can be scaled down if the intergovernmental transfers are absolutely unconditional and seeks progressively to reduce vertical gaps in resources. We do not have reasonably reliable historical data except for Kerala and Tamil Nadu to analyse this. It is very difficult to analyse Karnataka from the data given by KSFC-III which ventured to collect time series data. So only some general observations regarding financial position are made. Table 2 and 2.1 give the OSR of Kerala and Tamil Nadu as percentage of total expenditure from 2005-06 through 2013-14 for village panchayats and for ULGs. Kerala which had very high OSR-expenditure ratios that was well above 50% in the 1990s (not reported in Table 2) comes down to 14.35% in 2004-05. Table 2 shows a steady decline and reaches 9.16% in 2013-14. The story of ULGs is somewhat different. It is within a comfortable range of 38% to 45%. With greater effort the municipalities of Kerala can hope to progress towards institutions of self-government. The CAGR of expenditure for the nine years of gram panchayat since 2005-06 rose to 20.73% per annum, as against a CAGR of 12.98% per annum for OSR. But the experience of ULGs shows that CAGR of OSR expanded in tandem with that of the increase in expenditure [see Table 2.1]. To be sure there is need for better performance.

Table 2
OSR as percentage of Total Expenditure (Kerala & Tamil Nadu)-GPs

Year	OSR Rs. Lakh	Expenditure	OSR as Percentage to TE	OSR Rs. Lakh	Expenditure	OSR as Percentage to TE
	Kerala-GPs			Tamil Nadu GPs.		
2005-06	217.33	**1514.66**	14.35	92.57	**1101.47**	8.40
2006-07	256.66	**1717.85**	14.94	109.38	**1382.13**	7.91
2007-08	295.68	**1981.88**	14.92	130.34	**2102.98**	6.20
2008-09	315.37	**2373.51**	13.29	146.21	**2979.59**	4.91
2009-10	403.10	**3334.40**	12.09	173.43	**3953.00**	4.39
2010-11	482.31	**4229.85**	11.40	186.00	**5621.45**	3.31
2011-12	493.63	**4801.69**	10.28	219.00	**6550.71**	3.34
2012-13	534.41	**5499.99**	9.72	258.69	**9480.10**	2.73
2013-2014	544.05	**5939.13**	9.16	301.85	**9578.42**	3.15
CAGR	**12.98**	**20.73**		**15.39**	**33.50**	

Source: SFC Reports 4 and 5 of Kerala and Tamil Nadu.
CAGR – Compound Annual Growth Rate

The Tamil Nadu experience of village panchayats is disquieting. OSR as a percentage of total expenditure in 2005-06 is 8.4% (which itself is very low). It declined to a very low 2.73% in 2012-13 and picked up only marginally next year. The ULGs also although start with a relatively higher proportion has steeply declined as could be seen from Table 2.1. While the expenditure of CAGR of Tamil Nadu gram panchayats increases by 33.5%, OSR expands at a pace way below at 15.39%. Tamil Nadu GPs need to scale up their mobilization efforts significantly to travel on the road to autonomous development. The performance of the ULGs of Tamil Nadu also is relatively very weak. The OSR as percentage of total expenditure of Tamil Nadu which was as high as 45.96% in 2006-07 declined to 27% in 2013-14. This certainly is not a promising trend. Also the CAGR of the OSR of ULG in Tamil Nadu increased at 14.42% per annum, the CAGR of expenditure expanded at the rate of 22.46% per annum.

Table 2.1
OSR as percentage of Total Expenditure (Kerala and Tamil Nadu)-ULGs

Year	OSR Rs. Lakh	Expenditure	OSR as Percentage to TE	OSR Rs. Lakh	Expenditure	OSR as Percentage to TE
	Kerala-ULGs			Tamil Nadu - ULGs		
2005-06	151.95	**400.47**	37.94	1264.70	**2805.39**	45.08
2006-07	185.36	**415.66**	44.59	1460.29	**3177.43**	45.96
2007-08	199.76	**451.10**	44.28	1610.04	**3770.25**	42.70
2008-09	224.46	**532.95**	42.12	1769.75	**4498.98**	39.34
2009-10	395.59	**966.53**	40.93	2093.68	**5056.71**	41.40
2010-11	478.84	**1068.48**	44.82	2303.93	**7257.00**	31.75
2011-12	575.46	**1395.52**	41.24	2713.02	**7864.00**	34.50
2012-13	635.80	**1582.19**	40.18	3325.69	**11499.00**	28.92
2013-2014	775.50	**1938.93**	40.00	3709.01	**13728.00**	27.02
CAGR	**24.38**	**24.76**		**14.42**	**22.46**	

Source: SFC Reports 4 and 5, Kerala and Tamilnadu.

As regards Karnataka, for want of data we cannot make direct inferences regarding self-reliance. Even so we piece together some data relating to deficit (defined as revenue – expenditure) for gram panchayats as well as for urban local governments. Table 1 in Appendix B shows the deficit per GP from 2002-03 through 2006-07. Table 2 in the Appendix B shows the percentage distribution of GPs with financial deficit, financial surplus and chronic deficit. There is definite acceleration in per GP deficit growth which doubles from Rs. 1.83 lakh in 2002-03 to Rs.3.69 lakh in 2005-06 and bulges much higher to R.4.49 lakh in 2006-07. That 6.6% GPs suffer from chronic deficit and their average deficit is much higher than that of the state average of Rs. 2.20

lakh for GPs tells a disturbing situation. Table II which shows the relative percentage of deficits is presumably worse in that it does not speak highly of the transfer arrangements of the period. It is evident that GPs with chronic deficit raised 16.1% by way of own revenue as against only 15.8% by those with financial surplus. Here it is also important to note that the share of own revenue ranges from 7.6% in the case of the GPs of Bidar district to 53.3% in the richer districts of Bangalore Urban and 38.4% in Bangalore Rural (see KSFC Report-III). Apparently the revenue potential of GPs is extremely uneven. Appendix C presents the situation relating to the ULGs, of Karnataka. The story of deficit shown in the Table in Appendix C for city corporations is also a cause for concern. The analysis of KSFC-III report does not go deeper into this.

The last section is in lieu of a conclusion and focuses more on policy options that lie ahead. Given the fact that the fiscal decentralisation process of India cannot be placed within the theoretical framework of Western federal literature, policy options cannot be easily borrowed or adopted from elsewhere. Evidently the fiscal decentralisation experience has been very halting and lacked vision. Several states have violated the constitutional mandates with impunity. Unless the nation is seized of the seriousness of the situation the future of decentralisation is bleak. It is very important for state governments to take corrective steps including appropriate amendments to their panchayat and municipality Acts and take efforts in streamlining activity mapping and move towards mobilization of tax and non-tax revenues. SFCs should never be made a post for retired or serving IAS officers. They seldom can make independent policy changes. No wonder the GPs and municipalities are drifting away from the avowed goal of creation of institutes of self-government. Evidently the Union government which took the bold initiative to implement the 73rd / 74th CAs has lagged way behind. We have stressed the need to drop item No. 5 of the state list and spell out a detailed local list including revenue handles. The main burden of this chapter may be seen as drawing attention to the tremendous potential for the UFC for reducing interstate vertical disparities and SFCs to reduce intra-state horizontal disparities in the provision of minimum essential services and in ushering in territorial equity in the long run. This is an important need.

Endnotes

1 World Bank stresses the governance reform aspect See World Bank [(1997); (2004) among others].

2 The term local self-government is widely used in political science to refer to those functions of domestic administration which were best managed by the personal services and contributions of local communities [See Redlich and Hirst (1903); Langrod (1952);

Whalen (1960)]. From the days of the Mayo Resolution of 1870 this term has been used in Indian official documents on local government and found its way into the Indian Constitution which uses the term 'institutions of self-government' (Article 243G &243W) as a cherished goal to be achieved in local democratic governance in India.

3 Many including 'experts' prefer the term local body to local government although Part IX and IXA of the Constitution never use it.

4 The sixth, seventh and eighth UFCs made some efforts to equalize essential public services across the states. But the amounts were very measly and certainly not critical to have any impact.

5 Local government, that is to say, the constitution and powers of municipal corporations, improvement trusts, district boards, mining settlement authorities and other local authorities for the purpose of local self-government or village administration. [Article 246, Schedule VII, Part II, Item 5].

6 The Indian Constitution has borrowed approximately 250 Articles "verbatim or with minor changes in phraseology from the 1935, Government of India Act" [M.Brecher (1961):207]

7 On this it is useful to read Chapter 10.

8 This author was a member of that Committee.

References

Adarkar B P (1933), *The Principles of Problems of Federal Finance,* P S King and Son Ltd., London .

Bahl Roy, Geeta Sethi and Sally Wallace (2008), "West Bengal: Fiscal Decentralization to Rural Governments: Analysis and Reform Options," International Center for Public Policy Working Paper Series, at AYSPS, GSU paper 0907, International Center for Public Policy, Andrew Young School of Policy Studies, Georgia State University.

Brecher M. (1961), *Nehru: A political Biography,* London: Oxford University Press.

Council of Europe (1995), *The Size of Municipalities, Efficiency and Citizen Participation,* Strasbourg, Council of Europe.

Francis Wrigley Hirst and Josef Redlich (1903), *Local government in England,* London : Macmillan and Co.

Georges Langrod (1953), 'Local Government and Democracy', *Public Administration,* Volume 31, Issue 1, March 1953, Pages 25-34

GOI (2001), Report of the Task Force on Decentralisation of Powers and functions upon Panchayati Raj Institutions, Krishi Bhavan, New Delhi.

Government of Karnataka, Report of the State Finance Commission (SFC-1, II, and III), Government of Karnataka.

Government of Kerala, Report of the State Finance Commission (SFC-1, II, III, IV and V), Government of Kerala.

Government of Tamil Nadu, Reports of the Finance Commission (SFC-II, III, IV, and V), Chennai.

Hugh Whalen (1960), Democracy and Local Government, *Canadian Public Administration,* Volume 3, Issue 1, March 1960, Pages 1-13

Musgrave A Richard (1959), *The theory of Public Finance: A study in Public Economy,* McCraw-Hill: New York.

Oates Wallace E (1972), *Fiscal Federalism,* Harcourt Brace Jovanovich Inc.

.... (1981), 'On Local Finance and the Tiebout Model', *American Economic Review,* 1981, vol. 71, issue 2, 93-98.

.... (2005), 'Toward A Second-Generation Theory of Fiscal Federalism', *International Tax and Public Finance,* Springer, 12, 349–373.

Tiebout M. Charles (1956), 'A Pure Theory of Local Expenditures', *The Journal of Political Economy*, Vol. 64, No. 5, (Oct., 1956), pp. 416-424.

Weingast R Barry (2009), "Second generation fiscal federalism: The implications of fiscal incentives", *Journal of Urban Economics*, 65 (3): 279-293

World Bank (2004), '*Fiscal Decentralization to Rural Governments in India*', Oxford University Press, World Bank, New Delhi.

World Bank (1997), The State in a Changing World, Washington, DC: World Bank

Appendix A
Criteria for Horizontal Distribution of Tamil Nadu

First SFC

Criterion	Panchayat Union	VPs	TPs	Municipality	Corporation
Total Population	50%	50%	45%	45%	40%
SC & ST Population	25%	15%	20%	10%	10%
Financial viability	25%	-	-	-	-
Per capita House Tax Collection Performance	-	15%	-	-	-
Core Civic Services Deficiency	-	20%	-	-	-
Per Capita Own Resources	-	-	15%	15%	15%
Per Capita Expenses on Core Services	-	-	20%	30%	35%
Total	**100%**	**100%**	**100%**	**100%**	**100%**

Second SFC

Criterion	Panchayat Union	VPs	TPs	Municipality	Corporation
Total Population	60%	60%	50%	50%	50%
SC & ST Population	10%	10%	10%	10%	10% (Slum population)
Agricultural Labourers	10%	10%	-	-	-
Area	10%	10%	-	-	-
Asset Maintenance	-	10%	20%	10%	10%
Resource Gap on inverse per capita land revenue	10%	-	-	-	-
Per capita own income	-	-	20%	20%	20%
Salary and pension expenses	-	-	-	10%	10%
Total	**100%**	**100%**	**100%**	**100%**	**100%**

Government did not accept the criteria recommended by 2nd SFC and determined following criteria	
Total Population	40%
Women Population	40%
SC / ST Population including Slum Population	20%
Total	**100%**

Third SFC

Criterion	Panchayat Union*	VPs	TPs	Municipality	Corporation
Total Population	32%	32%	32%	32%	32%
Women Population	32%	32%	32%	32%	32%
Financial viability	-	-	-	-	-
SC / ST Population and Slum Population	16%	16%	16%	16%	16%
Area	20%	20%	10%	10%	10%
Debt Burden	-	-	10%	10%	10%
Total	**100%**	**100%**	**100%**	**100%**	**100%**

Fourth SFC

Criterion	Panchayat Union	VPs	TPs	Munici-pality	Corporation
Total Population (2011 census)	60%	60%	80%	80%	80%
SC / ST Population	20%	20%	-	-	-
Area	20%	20%	15%	15%	15%
Debt Outstanding	-	-	5%	5%	5%
Total	**100%**	**100%**	**100%**	**100%**	**100%**

Fifth SFC

Sl.No	Criterion	Weight	
		RLB	ULB
1	Population as per 2011 census	60	65
2	Area	15	15
3	Per capita consumption expenditure distance	10	10
4	Proportion of slum population	--	10
5	SC/ST Population	15	--
	Total	100	100

Source: SFC (TN) 5th Report, pg. 247 and 251.

Source: TNSFC-V Report – Annexures, pg.290

Note: VPs: Village Panchayats, TP-Town Panchayats. *-On cross verification we found that column 2 of Third SFC is wrongly reported and add upto 119%. Hence we have corrected the column using the data on page 202 of the Third SFC Report.

Appendix B

Table I: Percentage of GPs with Financial Deficit, Chronic Financial Deficit and Average (per GP) Deficit for the period 2002-07–Karnataka

Year	Percentage of GPs	Average amount of Deficit (in Rs.)
2002-03	32.7	183225
2003-04	37.0	185483
2004-05	33.9	257465
2005-06	27.5	369345
2006-07	31.0	449832
2002-07	27.1	220359
Chronic Deficit	6.6	253104

Source: KSFC-III, P.39

Table II
Percentage Distribution of GPs with Financial Deficit, Surplus and Chronic Deficit by various sources of Revenue - Karnataka

Financial Sources	GPs with financial Deficit	GPs with Financial surplus	GPs with chronic financial deficit	Total GPs
Central Grant	36.2	36.6	39.2	35.8
State Grant	39.2	40.7	36.2	40.6
Own Revenue	16.8	15.8	16.1	16.5
Others	7.8	6.9	8.5	7.1

Source: KSFC-III, P.40

Appendix C

Percentage Distribution of Financial Condition of ULG (2002-07) in per cent–Karnataka

Type of ULG	Deficit	Surplus	Total
City Corporation	33.30	66.70	100%
City Municipal Council	3.03	96.97	100%
Town Municipal Council	9.80	90.20	100%
Town Panchayats	6.12	93.88	100%
Total	7.35	92.65	100%

Source: KSFC-III, P.189

Part II
Trends, Issues and Options

CHAPTER 6

Devolution of Resources to Rural Local Governments: A Comparative Study of the First State Finance Commission Reports of Five Major States*

Introduction

Devolution, which denotes the transfer of power and resources to subnational political entities is decentralisation par excellence. It is much broader than deconcentration, or even delegation.. Devolution which encompasses a wider horizon of decentralisation often has statutory backing accompanied by a functional, organisational and fiscal autonomy. Only then, decentralisation becomes a fact of life. As Parker (1995) aptly puts it "like a souffle' that requires an appropriate proportion of milk, eggs and heat to rise, so a successful programme of decentralisation will need to include the right combination of political, fiscal and institutional elements". Naturally, it involves a continuous process of modification, reflecting changes in social, political and economic conditions. Rightly so, UNDP (1993) considers devolution as the strongest form of decentralisation.

The 73rd and 74th Constitutional Amendment Acts, 1992 have added a new dimension to fiscal federalism and decentralised public finance in the Indian federal system. The structure of inter-governmental fiscal relations and transfers necessarily will have to undergo significant changes. The provisions relating to the creation of State Finance Commissions (SFCs) meant to rationalise state and sub-state level fiscal relations and make periodic fiscal corrections assume significance in this context. Their recommendations will have to set norms, conventions and practices relating to fiscal federalism and local governance in the country. Nearly a dozen SFCs have submitted their reports. This chapter seeks to critically review, recommendations of five SFCs: viz 'Karnataka, Kerala, Punjab, Rajasthan and West Bengal on fiscal devolution with reference to the Panchayati Raj Institutions (PRIs). The study is broadly organised under three heads: (a) Expenditure and Revenue Assignments, (b) the Design of Transfers, and (c) the Approach.

The Constitutional Tasks of SFCs

A one to one correspondence between functional requirements and 'financial resources at various level, of government is impossible in any federation. The problem is compounded when the constitution provides for a deliberate mismatch as in India. A further worry is added because the 73rd and' 74th Constitutional Amendments have left the tasks of devolving more powers,' authority, functions, finance, etc. to the, State Legislatures, of course subject to Part IX and Part IXA of the Constitution and Schedules 11 and 12, thereof.

Largely patterned on the Union Finance Commission (Article 280), the responsibilities of SFCs are laid down in Articles 243 I and 243Y. Closer interpretation of these shows that the SFCs cannot perform their tasks independent of Articles 243G, 243H, 243J, 243ZD and 243ZE. Broadly, the tasks of the SFCs may be outlined as:

(a) to review the finances of the local governments, of course, in accordance with the functional responsibilities which include the preparation of plans for economic development and social justice;

(b) to fix the size of the divisible pool taking into account the functional domain of the state on the one hand, and that of the PRIs and urban local governments (ULGS), on the other;

(c) to broadly evaluate the vertical gap at the various levels taking into account the tax assignments, on the one hand, and functional responsibilities, on the other;

(d) to suggest measures for improving the financial position of panchayats and ULGS which include revenue sharing and grants-in-aid;

(e) to design methods for the inter se distribution of the share of PRIs and ULBs on an equitable and efficient basis; and

(f) to make explicit the principles underlying the measures suggested.

Given these tasks, what have been the recommendation of the five State Finance Commissions (hereafter referred to as KSFC for Karnataka, KESFC for Kerala, PSFC for Punjab, RSFC for Rajasthan and WBSFC for West Bengal) made vis-a-vis the Panchayati Raj Institutions (PRIs)? Tables A1, A2 and A3 of Appendix A give a brief summary of the recommendations of the SFCs with reference to tax assignments, tax sharing and grants with brief comments and remarks.

Expenditure and Revenue Assignments

The local fiscal policy framework is a delicate exercise. There is a need to strike a balance between local and national needs. Fiscal balance at the subnational level is important to macroeconomic stability. In this section, the expenditure and revenue assignments are discussed to find out how far fiscal decentralisation has been promoted by the SFCs under study.

Expenditure Assignments

Fiscal federalism literature argues that expenditure assignment must precede tax assignment. This is because tax assignment would, in general, be guided by expenditure requirements at different levels and these cannot be worked out in advance of expenditure assignment. A moot question is whether SFC can discharge its constitutional mandate "to review the financial position of the panchayats" without reference to their functional domain. This calls for some review of the functional mapping done by the concerned state vis-a-vis the intentions of the 73rd Constitutional Amendment. The 'decentralisation theorem' of Wallace Oats that 'each public service should be provided by the jurisdiction having control over the minimum geographic area that would internalise benefits and costs of such provision' (Oats (1972: p. 55) and other economic logic could serve as guidelines in this exercise. In a country like India where gram panchayat size varies from 500 to over 50,000, it is difficult to practice this. Only PSCF tried this exercise and did it reasonably well. WBSFC recommended clear demarcation of "functions between State sector and District sector" in a manner somewhat similar to the division of powers between the central and state governments in the Seventh Schedule of the Indian Constitution (WSCF (1995) p. 7), they stopped there.

The prime rationale of a third tier of governance rests in increasing the basic services and improving the quality of these services so that no citizen should be discriminated for the choice of her residential location. All the SCFs except WSCF have addressed these questions in their expenditure need assessment. KSFC has identified the normative standard of public/civic services and estimated the unit cost of providing such services by PRIs. Accordingly, that much amount is earmarked as additional (upgradation) grants to the PRIs which are lagging behind the normative standard. PSFC separately makes recommendations for the devolution of obligatory and essential functions of the panchayats. The obligatory functions are the civic functions such as cleaning of streets and drains, etc. In order to perform these functions it recommended that Rs. 600/- per house per year should be available to each gram panchayat (GP) out of the resources now available through sharing of taxes on services, additional mobilisation and grants.

Neglect of maintenance of assets created has been the bane of rural development. All the SFCs (except WSCF) have provided for maintenance expenditure although with varying degrees of emphasis. KESCF provides for maintenance expenditure based on current cost of construction indexed for inflation. RSCF makes provision for the maintenance of roads and school buildings largely on the basis of ad-hoc grants. PSCF recommends that 3 per cent of capital cost be set apart for maintenance with the proviso that 85 per cent should be spent for physical maintenance and the rest for salaries. KSFC has assumed 10 per cent of current capital cost of assets as the normative level of maintenance expenditure for purpose of ensuring proper repairs and maintenance of assets of PRIs. In projecting the expenditure requirements, KSFC has used two components, namely real rate of growth of 5 per cent and a 10 per cent inflation rate. Not only that this will ensure real expenditure, it may even mean larger real expenditure if inflation is less than ten per cent. Both PSFC and RSFC break-up expenditure into establishment and staff, development and other items.

Once expenditure assignment is agreed upon, revenue assignment and design of transfers become critical elements in providing the resources to the local governments. Revenue assignment refers both to tax and non-tax revenue.

Tax Assignments

Needed tax assignments, along with rationalization of local tax structure are tasks the SFCs have to take up. Measures to promote fiscal autonomy and building cost-effective tax administration are key aspects in this respect. Bardhan (1996) and several others argue that devolving power to tax to the local level is to induce fiscal responsibility and a stake in the cost-effectiveness of expenditure. In Appendix -A, we have summed up the basic principles of local taxes as suggested by Bird and Wallich (1993) as a sort of norm for reference.

SFCs of Punjab, Rajasthan and most prominently that of Kerala besides mentioning some principles, have tried to rationalise the local tax structure. KESFC recommends a revision in the number of taxes besides adding several new taxes to be included in the local list of taxation. As regards building tax KESFC made the important suggestion that annual rental value should be replaced by tax based on the plinth area. A comprehensive reform packages for building tax, advertisement tax and land tax were recommended. Important recommendation for reforming profession tax and entertainment tax were also made a uniform rate structure for rural and urban areas besides reducing slabs as regards profession tax were a great step towards rationalization. PSFC also lays down: the principles of tax assignment following Musgrave (1983), besides recommending several new taxes and rationalisation of old ones. Although Punjab is the richest state in India with the strongest agricultural base, the proportion of tax revenue from agriculture to total income of all the PRIs in Punjab in 1993-94 was below 0.6 per cent of total revenue. The PSFC recommends that the total land revenue and land revenue cess should be assigned to the GPs and other PRIs. The distribution among different tiers recommended by PSFC is GP — 50%; PS (Panchayat Samiti) — 30% and ZP — 20%. It has analysed the resources of local governments during the pre- and post- 73rd and 74th amendment regimes. GPs are assigned house tax and a share of 40 per cent of state land revenue, while the PSs and ZPs are not assigned any tax handlers. It recommends that PRIs should be given freedom to levy taxes and fee and also to fix the rates thereof. To quote the PSFC: "The Gram Panchayats, Panchayat Samitis and the Zila Parishads should be given freedom to levy taxes and fee and also to fix the rates thereof, without the State Control as has been imposed under Section 88, 149 and 189 of the Punjab Panchayati Raj Act, 1994". This is a remarkable recommendation in view of the stress it lays on the autonomy of the PRIs. It is important to note that no Conformity Act in India gives this autonomy to PRIs. Mandatory tax handles for GPs were increased (e.g. taxes on advertisement brick kilns, rice shelters, stone crushers, petrol pumps etc., besides small scale industries). By and large, PSFC has tried to follow certain basic principles of local taxation and tax assignment. RSFC recommends the following taxes - tax on the rent on use of agricultural land up to 20% of the rent, tax on land holder, tax on assumed rental value if no rate is payable, tax on prescribed tradings, callings, professions and industries, primary education cess and tax on fairs in its jurisdictions. The recommended cess on primary education is in a way unwarranted given the low general and female literacy rate of the state. The RSFC wants the higher tiers like ZPs and PSs to impose more taxes (land tax) and share them with GPs. It takes the view that GPs would find it difficult to use their taxing powers because of "the fear of tax payers". It is doubtful whether RSCF's recommendation to tax petrol/diesel pumps, repair shops, hotels etc., on national highways passing through panchayat areas is in strict agreement with the principles of local taxation, If the PRIs have something tangible to show to the people, the rural people in all probability would be prepared to bear the burden of taxation, Burdening them without benefits is the real problem. The vicious cycle of low benefits, low taxation may have to be broken. Moreover, the dictum 'you pay I spend' should not be promoted as far as possible in the interest of sound finance and accountability: One should make a mention here that in West Bengal, the local voluntary contributions in terms of: cash, kind, technical support and labour inputs have been quite significant (see Oommen and Datta (1995 (a)).

Greater fiscal autonomy can be secured by endowing PRIs, notably GPs, with more taxes with adequate powers and freedom. It was recommended that taxes like entertainment tax imposed and collected by states should be handed over to LGs. WBSFC has recommended a new regime of tax collection in which. tax administration works in co-operation with Panchayats and giving a portion of tax collection as entitlement to these bodies. (Incidentally, the PRIs are also participating in small savings collection). By and large the taxes assigned to PRIs in the Conformity Acts and the liberal assignments recommended by PSFC and KESFC conform to some of the well-known principles of tax assignments. However it is doubtful- whether the criteria that "tax yield should be adequate to meet local needs and sufficiently buoyant over time" (Appendix A) is a distant goal, although a desirable one. Of course, this is also a matter of fixing the rate and making reasonable tax effort.

Non-Tax Revenue

Greater autonomy can be promoted by increasing the non-fax revenue raising capabilities of the PRIs. Sometimes it also helps to reduce the tax burden without compromising on fiscal autonomy: KESFC and PSFC make recommendations to improve upon the resources from non-tax revenue. KESFC recommends some important measures for rationalising income from properties owned which is the major non-tax revenue source. Instead of specifying a unique rite of licence fee, government may specify only the minimum rate and leave it to the local governments to fix rates above it. It recommends that fines and fees from unauthorized *porombokes* (backyard lands belonging to government) and revenue from porombokes need to be revised. For Punjab this source of revenue was as high as 34.8 per cent in 1993-94. PSFC suggests a number of measures to enhance the income from shamlat lands (village common lands) for GPs (see Table Al). For PSs and ZPs of Punjab, the sole source of non-tax revenue is income from property and fee and fines. Other SFCs do not suggest any measures to improve upon the sources of non-tax revenue, although there is great potential to augment the resources of PRIs. Investment of Panchayat's resources for the generation of revenue could not however be pressed too far. As the KESFC rightly remarks: "It is ironic that many local governments have constructed shopping complexes, but there is no single modern garbage treatment facility in any Local Body. The SFC is of the view that construction of shopping complexes and office complexes should not be a high priority item to Local governments" (KESFC Report: p. 79).

Borrowings

KSFC has looked into the loans and advances of PRIs. It has examined in detail the specific purpose for which loans and advances were given to the specific local governments, the amount of loan outstanding, the financial implications of repayment on the financial position of the specific local governments and also the need for ensuring the recycling of loan funds. But it has found that there are no loans outstanding from the PRIs to the state governments. PSFC recommends have the freedom to borrow from banks and other financial institutions for the development projects without state government sanction and guarantee. KESEC and RSFC recommended that one of the sources of financing the local governments is through loan from financial institutions. The borrowing potentials of PRIs, especially market borrowings are not dealt with by any of the SFCs concerned. Borrowing should be the exception for PRIs, and that too must be for productive self-financing projects.

Inter-Governmental Transfers

The way taxing and spending authorities are delineated and the manner in which inter-governmental transfers are structured in a country have come to be recognised in modern public finance as of fundamental importance in the efficient and equitable provision of public services (Shah (1991)). Following the theoretical and empirical literature on fiscal federalism and the needs of genuine decentralisation, certain principles in designing inter-governmental fiscal transfers are outlined below:

(i) Transparency - the basis on which transfers are made, (including, any equalization formula) must be clearly stated;

(ii) Predictability - intergovernmental fiscal transfer mechanisms should ensure predictability of subnational government shares from year to year to permit advanced planning; and

(iii) Autonomy – subnational governments should have complete independence and flexibility in setting their own development priorities (A.N.Parker (1995): pp. 29-30).

In addition to the above-mentioned principles, Oommen (1996) suggests the following criteria for designing the inter-governmental transfers, viz., absorptive capacity—the resource transfer should be in tune with the utilization capability, including that of the personnel; simplicity—the allocation formula should be simple and should have adequate built-in-arrangements for encouraging resource mobilisation and penalising waste and uneconomic policies.

The major instruments of transfers provided in the scheme of transfers to local governments are revenue sharing and grants. In the pre-Amendment regime, transfers to PRIs have been dominated by grants. This has promoted a dependency syndrome. (See Oommen in Oommen and Datta (1995)). There is an unquestionable need to build a strong local financial base in the country under the new regime which ought to be a major task of the SFCs.

Revenue Sharing

Revenue sharing basically is tax revenue sharing. Revenue sharing mechanisms are quite common in developing countries. Besides sharing of revenue *per sé*, they attempt to address multiple objectives such as equalisation, regional development, earmarking, etc. These mechanisms also vary a great deal across countries.

Wiseman (1981) argues that revenue sharing would have to be based on some criteria. Such criteria would have to be associated with clearly defined specifications of responsibility like the following:

i. A scrutiny of locally-provided services, with the purpose of distinguishing (a) obligatory local services, (b) discretionary services (c) activities better administered by special agencies.
ii. A review of local tax and fee sources for locating a more effective source of local revenues, and
iii. Estimating the extent: to which the revenue gap should be filled by revenue-sharing or conditional grants.

PSFC has categorically divided the functions of local governments into: obligatory, discretionary, etc. All the SFCs except WSCE have reviewed the structure of local taxes and fees and suggested measures to augment the resources as well. Some of them notably PSCF have followed most of the criteria mentioned by Wiseman. PSCF has tried to follow certain other principles of tax sharing which it has made explicit in the report.

Unlike in the case of the Union revenues, all tax revenues of a state government are shareable with local governments. The Tenth-Finance Commission has expressed itself strongly in favour of treating total tax revenue of the Union as shareable and even recommended a constitutional amendment to implement this.[1]

All SFCs except Kerala have recommended tax sharing. While KSFC, WBSFC and RSFC have brought the entire tax revenue within the divisible pool, PSFC has recommended the sharing of five taxes (stamp duty, motor vehicles tax, electricity duty, entertainment tax , and cinematograph tax), besides certain proportion of the auction money on liquor vends and state excise on Indian made foreign liquor (See Appendix A Table A2).

The revenue share for local governments recommended by the SFCs under study ranges from a low 2.18 per cent of the total net tax revenue of the state recommended by RSFC to 36 per cent of the total non-loan gross own revenue receipts of the state government by KSFC and 16 per cent of all tax revenue collected by the state in the case of WBSFC. The share of the divisible pool due to PRIs is fixed on the basis of clear criteria by KSFC and WBSFC. Although details of weightages and measures of backwardness differ, they have suggested population, area and index of backwardness as the key variables to fix rural urban shares as well as inter se distribution among the various tiers of PRIs. The devolution formulas recommended by KSFC and WBSFC seem to keep in view the principles of territorial equity, transparency and predictability. For instance, in KSFC's scheme the most developed ZPs like Bangalore Urban and Uttar Kannada get the lowest share. The revenue sharing approach especially as an entitlement (in refreshing contrast to the award approach), does not promote a dependency syndrome as transfers are automatic and according to norms. At the same time, the incentives and initiatives of the local governments are not affected. The devolution scheme envisaged by KSFC and WBSFC has the added advantage of providing predictability, which enables the local governments to plan firmly for the future.

RSFC's recommendations in this regard are in sharp contrast to those made by WBSFC and KSFC at least in two important respects. One, the tax share of a little over two per cent is too low and does indicate a poor commitment to decentralisation, RSCF recommends an additional devolution of Rs. 55.4 crore or 2.18 per cent of the State's net tax revenue for 1995-96, and works out to only 0.51 per cent of the total receipts of the State government for 1995-96. Two, the only variable recommended for inter tier and intra tier distribution is population. Population is a neutral criterion and relying entirely on it to rectify territorial imbalances is not the right approach. It cannot also be considered as a sole measure of fiscal need.

PSFC ostensibly tries to follow the principles of revenue sharing such as - financial adequacy of local governments, maintenance of essential services, creation of a fiscal surplus to plan for augmentation, upgradation and expansion of services, incentive systems to improve the fiscal and administrative practices, equity to correct horizontal and vertical imbalances and autonomy. Collection which favours the rich regions does not help the process of reducing territorial imbalances. While inter tier distribution is arbitrary, inter se distribution is based on population which, as we have already pointed out, is not a good measure of fiscal need. Besides the above mentioned principles, PSFC also attempts to adopt the following:

(i) Taxes identified for sharing should fall within the fiscal domain of the local government and to the proceeds of which the local governments have legitimate right. Accordingly, it proposes selective sharing of taxes which legitimately belong to local governments.

(ii) Taxes identified should be elastic and buoyant in nature to provide a proportionately enhanced flow of income to the local governments, and

(iii) The proportion of the share of the local governments should be fixed, preferably on percentage basis, taking in view the fiscal needs of the local governments. This would ensure transparency and predictability. PSFC has fixed the share in terms of percentages.

In sum, it is useful to examine the consolidated position of PRIs, taking into account their revenue and expenditure because bridging resource gap is one of the important tasks of fiscal devolution. The difference between the total PRI revenue and PRI expenditure (surplus/deficit) of those states for which the required data are available in the SFC Reports are given in Table 1.

Table 1
Consolidated Position (Surplus/Deficit) of PRIs (Rs. in Crore)

States	1991-92	1992-93	1993-94	1996-97*	1997-98*
Kerala	7.84	11.17	12.81	n.a.	n.a.
Punjab	(-)19.88	12.53	46.46	43.71	53.38
Rajasthan	0.78	10.76	31.21	Nil	nil

*indicates the projected figures
Source: State Finance Commission Reports

Only PSCF and RSCF make projections regarding the impact of their recommendations and the possible fiscal scenario. Kerala's PRIs have a surplus even before the devolution because statutorily they have to maintain a surplus. What the actual position will be in the coming years is not projected. Punjab PRIs had a total deficit of Rs. 19.88 crore in 1991-92. This was turned into a surplus even in 1993-94 and the trend is projected to be maintained from 1996-97 through 2000-2001. RSCF's projections are done in such a way as to balance the budget. Although such exercises are crude and are based on several assumptions it is worthwhile to make them. This is a point of reference for future evaluation and possible efforts towards making more realistic projections in the future.

Grants

Broadly speaking, there are two types of grants - general grants and specific or conditional grants. The general grants provide local authorities with untied additional resources. On the other hand, conditional grants take the form of a payment towards the cost of providing a particular local service or may have some conditionalities attached to their use. Unlike the general grants, the specific grants alter the opportunity cost of local authorities. General grants increase the level of provision of all local services, whereas specific grants affect both the mix and size of local expenditure on services.

Grants sometimes provide for matching provisions. They are called matching grants which require subnational governments to contribute funds of their own if they are to obtain access to counterpart funding from the higher government. They involve a significantly enhanced role for local governments in decision-making regarding which projects and programmes to support at the local level. Matching grants in principle have important economic and fiscal advantages in terms of both allocative efficiency (spillovers) and the efficient use of scarce (higher level government) resources to attain desired levels of certain services. They may also have the important political advantage of introducing an element of local involvement, commitment, accountability and responsibility for the aided activities. Properly, designed matching grants may contribute to equalisation (horizontal fiscal balance) and like all other transfers, they help to resolve any basic fiscal mismatch (vertical fiscal balance) problem. KSFC recommends a matching contribution by the PRIs in order to be eligible for the non-plan maintenance grants, which may be used for paying the wage bill. However, no other SFC has recommended for a matching grant.

Rationalisation of the entire scheme of sub-state level grants is an important task of SFCs especially because the prevailing grant regime is unsystematic, *ad hoc*, dependency-promoting and above all too many in number (see Oommen (1995a)). Even assuming that via tax assignments, revenue sharing and other devices, the required resources are provided to PRIs, grants as an equaliser of fiscal capacity (most prominently of gram panchayats) and also as a lever to achieve certain goals are indispensable as a mode of transfer of resources to PRIs by both Union and State governments.

Ensuring minimum standards of basic services at the local level so that backward areas also get a level of acceptable services is the hallmark of good local self-government. The Union and State level devolution should help in this process. KSFC's recommendations for earmarked grants for upgrading the delivery of safe drinking water, primary health, primary education, roads and street lighting in gram panchayat areas need special mention in this respect. KSFC has identified the panchayats which fall below certain normative standards, and made several useful suggestions which the next SFC in the state may do well to review to find out how far these are implemented on the ground.

KESFC has tried to bring in some rationality into the bewildering variety of statutory and non-statutory grants that existed in the pre-Amendment regime in Kerala. There is an effort in KESFC's recommendations to combine selective tax sharing with grants. But, the inter se distribution recommended is heavily weighted in favour of population both in regard to non-plan and plan grant allocation. The KESFC favours population because it is a neutral criterion. That exactly is its weakness when the need is promotion of territorial equity. More allocation to panchayats falling in low income (revenue) categories does not necessarily reflect financial needs. Out of the 15 per cent share allocated for financial needs in the total plan-grants, 50 per cent is recommended to panchayats in Group-IV category, which get the lowest income, 42.5 per. cent is devolved among Group-III category, whose incomes are just above those of the lowest income category and the rest 7.5 per cent is distributed among Group-II and the Group-I category panchayats. The high income panchayats with income above Rs. 20 lakh do not get any share in the allocation based on financial needs. Expenditure needs of panchayats have to be normatively arrived at and equitably distributed (reckoned in terms of relevant criteria of backwardness). KESFC has, however, recommended a good scheme of maintenance grant for schools and hospital buildings based on current construction costs with allowance made for inflation.

PSFC recommends general and specific purpose grants, besides a grant scheme for promoting incentives for better performing PRIs. It has recommended that weak gram panchayats defined as those below a per capita revenue of Rs. 100 have to be given grants to bring them up to that level with 50 per cent grant, the rest to be made good through additional tax effort and donations. PSFC and RSEC make provisions for incentive grants mainly for better tax collection and better utilisation of resources. WBSFC also makes provision to encourage collection of all revenues which is visualised as a joint effort of both the state and the local governments. RSFC recommends awards for the best three GPs and PSs in every district and similarly for the best three ZPs in the State. The first prize is as high as Rs. 2 lakh for GPs, Rs. 5 lakh for PSs and Rs. 8 lakh for ZPs.

PSFC takes the view that grants-in-aid to local governments are for reduction of horizontal revenue gap, provision of a desirable level of civic services and meeting the expenses of undertaking state assigned responsibilities and tasks. PSFC mentions a number of principles of grants-in-aid for general purpose grants such as system of grant should be transparent, predictable and based on objective measurable factors, should promote equity and justice and ensure sufficient autonomy and flexibility in planning the priorities; incentive to encourage the local governments for better resource mobilisation and management of their resources should also be granted and the grants given should be utilised for the improvement and upgradation of essential services and not for salaries and wages. Monitoring the use of the grants for the purpose for which they are meant was also mentioned as a guiding principle. When you have to grapple with a multitude of principles, their operational significance is reduced.

The specific purpose grants are basically given to stimulate specific local functions and to share local expenditure for providing essential services having national or state-wide priorities: PSFC suggests the following principles in regard to specific purpose grants. They should be conditional and matching, local governments' own commitment for the functions for which the grants have been received should be insisted upon; the local governments should be accountable to the higher levels of government for proper utilisation of the grants and there should be provisions to cover the emergency expenditure and cost of performance of the state functions entrusted to the local governments through reimbursement by the state government. The inter tier and inter se distribution of grants is not worked out by PSFC. PSFC evidently is aware of the essential principles to be followed. However its recommendations on grants do not seem to reflect these principles. For instance, it recommends a lump sum of Rs. 18 crore per annum during the period 1996-97 to 2000-2001, for financing the weak gram panchayats, which have per capita revenue less than Rs.100. This appears to be somewhat arbitrary.

RSFC makes the largest use of grants and recommends several categories of them such as start-up grant, establishment grant, maintenance grant, general purpose grant, incentive grant and so on. Almost all the grants are ad hoc and discretionary, negating the principles of transparency, predictability and autonomy. Most of them are probably small in size compared to the incentive grants. Enhanced flexibility is being achieved at the cost of transparency, objectivity and accountability. Given the fungibility of funds, it will be an extremely difficult task to ensure the realisation of the various grants in terms of specific purposes for which they are meant. A grant-based regime of this type does not promote either fiscal autonomy or proper accountability.

Fiscal Effort and Financial Autonomy

Fiscal capacity is the ability of government units to raise revenues from their own resources. The estimation of fiscal capacity is difficult both conceptually and empirically. Crude macro indicators such as income or output (personal income, personal disposable income, state domestic product, etc.) are commonly used to serve as indicators of ability to bear tax burdens by the residents of a state. However, it is a highly imperfect and partial measure of ability to impose taxes. To measure tax effort, strictly speaking it has to be related to taxable capacity. A good operational measure of tax effort would be actual tax collection, tax base and tax rate. Shah (1991) does not suggest the inclusion of tax effort in the allocation formula largely on account of the measurement problems. According to Bird and Wallich (1993) it is not good to include explicitly fiscal effort element in a transfer formula. Although putting too much weight on fiscal effort in allocating grants may penalise the poorer areas, omitting it altogether would be counterproductive in view of the known reluctance of local governments to impose taxes.

KSFC and KESFC do make some efforts to measure fiscal effort of the PRIs. KSFC has estimated the maximum potential revenue which the GPs can raise from tax on houses and buildings. It has projected the revenue of GPs based or the demand, collection and balance (DCB) of taxes on houses and buildings at the rate of 12 per cent per annum at 60 per cent collection performance. In KESFC report, financial need is one of the factors in the devolving criteria for distribution of rural and urban pool (see Table A3). Further, its suggestion that all local governments should conduct a systematic tax mapping for all taxes is an important one.

PSCF has found the tax efforts of PRIs in Punjab unsatisfactory. The only tax being used at present by the PRIs, and that too in a limited way, is the domestic property tax. The profession tax is not currently levied in Punjab either by panchayats or municipalities, PSFC suggests that to optimise the use of their own fiscal effort, some incentive grants should be given to those local governments which manage their fiscal affairs.

more efficiently, WBSFC recommends 2 per cent of the entitlement to the districts to stimulate tax effort.

Too much dependence on grants, especially those bound by restrictive conditionalities will affect fiscal autonomy. This is true in regard to PRIs which are excessively preoccupied with agency functions. Rajasthan is a typical case in point. The own sources of income of Rajasthan PRIs in 1993-94 was as low as 3.5 per cent. But RSFC has done little to alter the scenario.

To sum up, given the tasks of SFCs and the constitutional provisions especially Articles 243G, 243ZD and 243I a systematic approach means identifying the functional responsibilities, followed by estimation of the financial requirements and then determining the principles for tax assignment, revenue sharing and grant-in-aid mechanism, besides reviewing the financial position of local governments and suggesting methods for inter-se distribution which would ensure territorial equity and efficiency. Recommending measures towards proper budgeting, auditing, autonomy and transparency are also right steps to be pursued by the SFCs with regard to fiscal devolution. The first generation SFCs had a responsibility lay the foundations of viable state sub-state level fiscal relations. In regard to most SFC recommendations, the chasm between the ideal and the actual yawns wide.

Approach of the Five SFCs: A Synoptic Critique

We evaluate the approaches of the five SFCs by asking four basic questions. Have they done a meaningful review of the panchayat finances? How they taken a total view of development and finances? What is their approach in regard to the effort towards creating institutions of local self-government? and what is their approach to horizontal equity?

SFCs will have "to review the financial position of the panchayats". WSCF has not done this much needed exercise: Others have done this much exercise, some with professional rigour, a few with relative ease. A proper financial review provides the basis and backdrop for the recommendations made. Although KSCF has done a brief review of ZP and the Taluk Panchayats GPs have been left out. KESCF did a comprehensive fiscal survey covering all GPs except eight. This, can help a great deal in building a good financial data base for the panchayat system. PSCF reviews the financial structure of all the tiers, besides.

comparing the pre-devolution and projected post-devolution scenario for the period 1996-97 through 2000-2001. Indeed PSCF does provide a normative bench mark for the second SFC of Punjab to do a meaningful financial review. RSCF which also does a comprehensive review brings out the parlous state of the GPs.

A normative assessment of vertical gaps is also needed, not for any gap filling, but for informed recommendations. Most SFCs have not done this. PSCF and RSCF had done some estimation of the magnitudes involved.

The resilience and viability of local democracy rests a great deal on how the PRIs especially the gram panchayats are strengthened. In-1993-94 the average income per Gram Panchayat in Kerala was Rs. 13.85 lakhs as against Rs. 62,000 in Punjab. Along with the tasks of endowing Panchayats with greater responsibility and resources, the question of making them viable entities largely remains unaddressed.

The Union and State governments have a long established format for organising and presenting their annual financial statements. This is woefully missing in regard to local finance in the country. Also there is a need to build up a strong standardised data base. Such information is regularly needed for understanding the capabilities and viabilities of local governments in the country. The Union Finance Commission will be taking a good step if they consider this question because some uniformity in the financial statements of local governments is needed for making meaningful comparisons, and evaluations, as also for addressing the question of tax harmonization. This will be in line with Article 243J of the Constitution.

A total view of finance can be taken only with a total view of development requirements. At least in regard to local governments, the distinction between plan and non-plan is irrelevant for a variety of reasons. True, the Union Finance Commissions (UFCs) since the Third Commission have implicitly endorsed a division of labour as between UFC confining to non-plan devolution and the Planning Commission to plan devolution to states. This practice is not a constitutionally neat one. Apparently, the Ninth and Tenth Finance Commissions have tried to break from this watertight approach. The District Planning Committee (DPC) required to be constituted in every district of the country (Article 243ZD) is a statutory body entrusted with the task of planning from below, unlike the Planning Commission and the State Planning Boards (which in many states are only a wing of the State Planning Department) which do not have any statutory backing. The DPC can take up a meaningful exercise of planning for the subjects falling under the 11th and 12th Schedules only by taking a total view.

Transferring of more functions to local governments logically means transferring more resources as well. The WBSFC and KSFC take a total view of development needs and financial requirements. WBSFC's approach of treating the resources required as entitlements (entitlements on tax revenue) seems to be relevant given the constitutional mandate to promote institutions of self-government (Article 243G) and autonomous planned efforts (243ZD). The WBSFC notes that the entitlements suggested "are only a redeployment of funds which are now being spent for the districts already" (WBSFC (1995): p. 4.) This fundamental flow should be rectified by all states.

SFC's task of reviewing panchayat finance required by Article 243I implicitly means a normative review of the state finance as well as its fiscal management. The SFCs of West Bengal, Kerala and Rajasthan have reviewed the financial position of their states. However, none of them has made any normative evaluation especially with reference to the expenditure liabilities the states have to undertake along with a review of their fiscal management record. Also a meaningful review of panchayat finance cannot be undertaken without a critical evaluation of the Conformity Acts (CAs) 'in terms 'of the constitutional provisions under which they have been enacted. Equally important is the task of relating the financial powers and responsibilities of panchayats with their functional responsibilities. Parastatals that duplicate the works of local governments necessarily will have to be abolished and the funds and personnel, too, will have to be redeployed. Needless to say, this exercise of reviewing CAs has to be made in the letter and spirit of the 73rd Amendment. PSCF has made very useful recommendations for amending the Conformity Acts, including "freedom to levy taxes and fees and also to fix the rates thereof without State government control and for making autonomous borrowings". The WBSFC calls for redeployment of staff from State government departments to ZPs and others along with the transfer of functions and finances.

The dissenting note appending to the Rajasthan SFC's main Report points out how a defective CA can sabotage the efforts towards autonomy and self-government. However, it is interesting to cite the RSFC's main report, "In our view evolution of panchayats to this level of efficiency would take some time and therefore we do not want to get into an area of speculation to suggest anything with regard to the devolution of functions. We would only consider the functions that are presently being performed by the PRIs" (pre -73rd Amendments) (RSFC Report: p.31). At the same time, RSFC recommended that "the State should press for a centrally sponsored scheme for environmental improvement programmes".. (RSFC Report, p. 57). Any SFC, which tries to preserve the pre-Amendment regime or does not honestly seek to promote fiscal and functional autonomy envisaged in the Amendments could not be said to be honouring the Constitution.

As argued elsewhere [(see Oommen and Mahipal (1994); Oommen (1995 (a))], there is a dire need to maintain minimum standards of essential services like drinking water, primary health care, primary education, good roads, etc, throughout the country. No citizen should suffer because of her choice of residential location. It is a poor reflection of the planning efforts of the country during the last fifty years that both the States and the Union have failed to ensure territorial equity in the allocation of resources and ensuring desirable civic services. There is clear lack of planned improvement of local areas as well as the failure to maintain and repair assets already created. Equally important to note are the distortions in the planning and prioritization introduced by schemes like MPs Local Area Development Scheme, MLA projects and the like.

As already noted Working Groups constituted by the Resource Group formed by the Planning Commission in 1995 to help SFCs has worked out detailed minimum standards and expenditure norms, for five basic services viz., water. supply, sanitation/sewerage, solid waste collection, primary education and primary health. For different states the list of core services may vary. KESCF has carefully identified a different set of services which are relevant to the conditions of Kerala and worked out the norms based on sample studies conducted by experts. RSCF makes no normative evaluation. Where it works out it is crude. (For example the additional requirements for cleaning the villages are worked out by increasing the number of times from two times a year (Holi and Diwali) to three times a year). PSCF does not lay down any minimum standard of quality. It recommends a blanket sum of Rs. 600 per household per GP to carry on their obligatory civil duties. By virtue of the methodology it chose, WSCF absolves itself from any other responsibilities like this.

The KSFC has really made general recommendations in taking Panchayati Raj System a step forward, particularly when compared to most other SFCs. Besides recommending measures towards bottom up planning, abolition of Regional Development Boards and the scheme of allotting funds to MLAs for spending on development works in their constituency, KSCF has recommended the transfer of 36 per cent of the non-loan gross own revenue to local governments and recommending a scheme of inter se distribution of resources to PRIs giving weight to backwardness.

As far as the general principles followed by the SFCs are concerned, PSFC and KSFC apparently try to follow some of the principles of fiscal federalism. These SFCs acknowledge the basic principles of fiscal federalism like efficiency and equity. KSFC tries to keep in view the principle of financial responsibility of local governments in estimating their expenditure and financial requirements. KSFC and WBSFC suggest devolution criteria based on population, area and index of backwardness, for revenue sharing. These devolution criteria attempt to ensure territorial equity and predictability. KESFC has used population for determining the rural urban shares. It has evolved a criterion for the distribution of grants from the Rural Pool created for the purpose based primarily on population (80 per cent) with a small allowance of 5 per cent for tax effort and 15 per cent on financial need. Inter se distribution does not make allowance for backwardness. In examining the resource mobilisation of local governments, KESFC and PSFC recommend privatisation of certain specific local services, which would ensure their cost-effectiveness. PSFC and RSFC recommend that there should be financial corporations to look after the credit and technical needs of PRIs. Access to financial corporations without relation to prudent house-keeping and tax effort does not seem to be the right step.

When the issues on development, finance, governance and territorial equity are considered together, one can certainly say that KSFC and WBSFC made several useful recommendations. Still, these two SFCs too have left many things to be desired. By choosing to confine its work to the entitlements to local governments, WSCF deliberately opted out of several constitutional obligations. and desirable choices. WSCF and PSCF have ignored the resource effort aspect of local governments. PSCF's recommendation that Gram Panchayats with less than Rs. 100 per capita income-should be given grants to bring their income upto Rs. 100 per capita to enable them to perform their obligatory functions is not likely to go too far towards promoting horizontal equity. The design of grant transfers envisaged in the RSCF scheme could not also be considered as working towards territorial equity. A large variety of grants with multiple criteria governing them ranging from adhoc per GP grant to per capita grant for establishment grant for salaries/wages could not be considered as rational or equity-oriented. KESCF's design of transfers to PRIs also does not work decidedly towards horizontal equity.

An Evaluation and Summing Up

This section, besides giving a brief summing up, tries to evolve a framework for evaluating fiscal decentralisation with reference to sub-state level local governments. Only two SFCs - WBSFC and KSEC, have taken a total view of finance. Their approach unmistakably was towards creating institutions of self-government. In regard to promoting horizontal equity, too, KSFC has made some specific recommendations.

Keeping in mind the rural-urban disparity, the approach of both KSFC and WBSFC has been to reduce it. This is evident in the devolution formula suggested by them. WBSFC includes rural population of the district and a measure of banking development in the devolution criteria for PRIs in addition to illiteracy, area and the backward population, which are the components for ULGs' devolution as well. The most important aspect of the WBSFC Report is that it has taken district as a unit for devolution. KSFC in its devolution criteria, has included rural population, rural area, road length, some measure of health status and illiteracy. In the total share of 36 per cent of non-loan gross own revenue receipts, 30.60 per cent will be the share of PRIs. It is a substantial share. But how far will it lead to the reduction of rural urban disparity could be evaluated only in the future. PSFC has recommended a 20 per cent share for PRIs in five specific taxes.

The devolution of the share is largely on the basis of derivation. The derivation principle can only widen the rural-urban divide. But by and large PSCF too has tried to promote decentralisation and local self-government. As mentioned already, the functional and financial powers of the PRIs are clearly demarcated in its report which is an important step towards autonomy. RSCF's efforts on these lines have been crude and certainly not significant reckoned in terms of building institutions of local self-government.

The SFCs have a responsibility to recommend measures to build up the financial capability at the local level. Otherwise, autonomy cannot be promoted. In this regard, KESFC and PSFC have made notable efforts and suggested measures to augment the resources as well. KESFC has tried to rationalize and revise the existing tax structure, besides suggesting new taxes. If local governments are allowed unrestricted transfers without an appropriate system of checks and balances it can lead to fiscal profligacy. Simple gap-filling transfers can discourage mobilisation and give perverse signals to the subnational governments. On no account "financial irresponsibility" should develop on the part of local governments. This would also impair their financial sovereignty and expenditure responsibility. Hence, there should be a system of accountability along with fiscal autonomy at local level. Future SFCs will have to take this factor into account more explicitly.

To reiterate, the recommendations of the SFCs must lay the foundations of a decentralised, but sound public finance in Indian federal system, besides promoting regional balance especially through ensuring certain basic services of reasonable quality. The scheme of fiscal devolution flowing from the SFC recommendations will have to promote not only financial autonomy, but functional and administrative autonomy as well. It may not be out of place to record here the fact that the S. B. Sen Committee on Decentralisation constituted by the Kerala Government have made very comprehensive recommendations towards promoting institutions of local self-government. Future SFCs may do well to refer to this as a 'model' if they want to abide by the letter and spirit of the 73rd and 74th Constitutional Amendments.

The Constitution requires all SFCs to spell out the principles on which their recommendations are based. Reproduction of the text book principles is not what is expected. The purpose of making explicit the principle/principles on which the recommendations are based is to know the rationale of specific recommendations. Most of the SFC reports leave many things to be desired in this respect. Even KSF C whose recommendations go a long way towards promoting autonomy and decentralisation does not stress such principles as transparency. PSCF mentions several principles relevant to tax assignments, revenue sharing, transfer of grants etc. But it has not taken pains to explain how far it has incorporated these principles in its recommendations. Even so, it is good for all SFCs to spell out the principles that have governed their recommendations. At least they provide a point of reference and a set of norms for evaluation by others.

Following UNDP (1993), some exercises such as Expenditure Decentralisation Ratio (EDR), Revenue Decentralisation Ratio (RDR) and Financial Autonomy Ratio (FAR) have been attempted to evaluate the progress of each state towards fiscal' decentralisation. Table 2 summarises the relevant ratios for some of the states under study. They give a pre-devolution and post-devolution scenario as illustrative examples. The data required have been taken from the State Finance Commission Reports and relevant issues of the *Reserve Bank of India Bulletin*.

Table 2
Expenditure and Revenue Decentralization Ratios and Financial Autonomy Ratio of 3 States (Figures-in %)

States	1993-94			1996-97		
	EDR	RDR	FAR	EDR	RDR	FAR
Kerala	4.6	3.2	48.28			
Punjab	7.7	6.36	45.00	13.1	5.81	52.0
Rajasthan	9.9	5.47	3.98	9.4	5.17	3.06

Source: SFC Reports

The expenditure decentralization ratio (EDR) is the percentage of local government spending to total state government expenditure. Revenue Decentralisation Ratio (RDR) is the percentage of local government revenue to total state government revenue. The Financial Autonomy Ratio (FAR) is the percentage of locally raised revenue to the total local expenditure. Locally raised revenue includes both tax and non-tax revenue. While EDR and RDR are calculated with reference to both. PRIs and urban local bodies, FAR is worked out only with reference to PRIs. These ratios could be conceptually and operationally refined according to the types of measures sought. EDR, RDR and FAR are worked out for the SFCs for which relevant data are available and are given in Table 2, to compare the actual situation of 1993-94 with that of 1996-97 which shows a post-recommendation scenario.

Kerala's decentralisation ratios in 1993-94 are very low. In Kerala the "Peoples Plan Campaign" seeks to devolve 35-40 per cent of plan outlay to the local governments. This works out to over 10 per cent of the total expenditure outlay of the State. When the Sen Committee's recommendations are fully implemented the EDR and RDR of Kerala will increase substantially. FAR ratio for Kerala even in the Pre-Amendment regime is fairly high.

It is instructive to compare the existing and projected decentralisation scenario of Punjab and Rajasthan. By any reckoning Rajasthan. seems to put the clock back. Taxation decentralisation of Punjab also shows a declining trend. The actual situation in 1996-97 in the two states may even be worse.

In fact, Rajasthan has done very little decentralisation in regard to PRIs. The own income of the PRIs of Rajasthan which was below Rs. 20 crore in 1993-94 was projected to increase only to Rs. 29 crore - a 45 per cent increase as against an increase from Rs. 241 crore to Rs. 459 crore in regard to ULBs – 90.5 per cent increase. When we note that in industrial countries, local governments normally account for 20-35 per cent of total government expenditure (in Denmark it is as high as 45% and Finland 41%) (see UNDP (1993) p. 69). India's decentralisation remains a distant goal. Indeed most States have miles to go on the road of fiscal decentralisation.

In industrial countries, the local governments enjoy considerable authority in the sphere of taxation. The RDR in these countries accounts for about 25 per cent of the total government revenue. In the developing countries, the local governments could raise their revenue only around 6 per cent of the total government receipts. Unlike the developed countries, their taxation options are very minimal. Even these minimal options are not exercised, as is correctly pointed out by PSCF and RSCF. Therefore, the chances are that the revenue decentralisation ratio will fall far short of even what is projected.

Financial autonomy gives an indication of the local government's independence from central and state government funding. The Financial Autonomy Ratio (FAR) of both industrial and developing countries turn out to be the same-around 60 per cent. But the reality is that the industrial countries have 60 per cent discretion over significant share of public spending. On the contrary, in the developing countries LGs have control only over a very small proportion of public spending. The high FAR ratios for Kerala and Punjab probably may be seen in this light also. To be sure development from below is 'development from within' (i.e., with own resources).

In short, the second series of State Finance Commissions have to build on the first. They have to review and try to remedy the sins of omissions and commissions of the first Finance Commission and make recommendations towards building a truly decentralised federal polity. The Eleventh Finance Commission certainly cannot remain a passive spectator to what happens to the Constitutional mandates and federal public finance.

Appendix - A

Main characteristics of local taxation as suggested by Bird and Wallich (1993):

i. The tax base should be relatively immobile, to allow local authorities some leeway in. varying rates without losing most of their tax base.
ii. The tax yield should be adequate to meet local needs and sufficiently buoyant. over time (i.e. it should expand at least as fast as expenditures).
iii. The tax yield should be relatively stable and predictable over time.
iv. The tax base should be visible, to ensure accountability.
v. The tax should be perceived to be reasonably fair by taxpayers and
vi. The tax should be relatively easy to administer efficiently and effectively.

In practice, a local tax having all these characteristics is a rare possibility. But the local governments must ensure that at least some of the important characteristics are followed.

* ISS Occational paper series-21 1998. This paper was orginally presented at an all-India conference on panchayats; powers and finance organized by Institute of Social Sciences, New Delhi, December 2-4, 1997.

Endnote

1 The Reports and this paper was written before the 80th Amendment was passed.

References

Bardhan, P (1996), "Decentralised Development", *Indian Economic Review*, Vol. 31, No. 2.

Bird, R and C. Wallich (1993), Fiscal Decentralisation and Intergovernmental Relations in Transition Economies: Toward a Systemic Framework of Analysis, *Policy Research Working Papers*, No. 1122, World Bank, Washington, DC.

Fisher R.C (1979), "A Theoretical View of Revenue Sharing" *National Tax Journal*, Vol. 32.

Musgrave, R.A (1983), "Who Should Tax, Where and: What?" in C.Mclure (ed.), *Tax Assignment in Federal Countries*, Australian National University Press, Canberra.

Oates, Wallace, (1972), *Fiscal Federalism*, HarCourt Brace Jovanovich, New York.

Oommen, M.A. and Mahipal (1994), "MPs Local Area Development Scheme: Dangerous Portent", *Economic and Political Weekly*, January, 29.

Oommen, M.A. (1995), *Devolution of Resources from the State to the Panchayati Raj Institutions: Search for a Normative Approach*, Institute of Social Sciences: Occasional Paper Series, No. 18, New Delhi.

Oommen, M.A. and A Datta (1995a), *Panchayats and Their Finance*, Institute of Social Sciences and Concept Publishing Company, New Delhi.

Oommen, M.A. (1996), "Panchayat Raj System: Issues in Resource Mobilisation and Resource Transfers", *Kurukshetra*, Vol. XLIV, No. 7.

Parker, A. N. (1995), "Decentralisation: The Way Forward for Rural Development?", *Policy Research Working Paper*, No. 1475, World Bank, Washington. D.C.

Shah, A (1991), "Perspectives on the Design of Intergovernmental Fiscal Relations", *Policy Research and External Affairs Working Papers*, No.726, World Bank, Washington D.C.

Slavet, J.S, K.L.Bradbury and P.I. Moss (1975), *Financing State-Local Services*, Lexington, London.

UNDP (1993), *Human Development Report*, Oxford University Press, Oxford.

Wiseman, J (1981), "Revenue Sharing between Central and Local Governments in a Developing Country with a Unitary System of Government", Institute of Social and Economic Research, University of York.

CHAPTER 7

Fiscal Decentralisation to the Sub-State Level Governments in India*

Fiscal decentralization is a subset of decentralization. Given the manifold ways, decentralization is interpreted and the vast diversity of country experiences, it has to be contextually defined and understood [Bird and Vaillancourt (1998)]. For the purpose of this paper, decentralisation is defined as the empowerment of the local people through the empowerment of the local governments. Fiscal decentralization therefore is fiscal empowerment of lower tiers of government which involves the devolution of taxing and spending powers along with arrangements for rectifying mismatches in resources and responsibilities. [See Fukasaku and De Mello, (1999), V. Tanzi (1996) and Oommen (2004)]. This definition is important as it is in broad agreement with the 73rd/74th constitutional amendments which seek to establish a third stratum of government in India. The local government has relevance not only because of its instrumental significance in providing efficient delivery of public services and local goods, but also because of the failure of national and state governments in providing basic services of comparable quality to the citizens during the last half a century. On the basis of a detailed analytical study Rao and Singh (2005) conclude that neither union finance commission nor Planning Commission nor centrally sponsored schemes have made a substantial dent into regional disparities. In contemporary world, only India constitutionally empowers the local governments to prepare 'plans for economic development and social justice' along with the mandate to establish panchayats or rural local governments as institutions of self-government. [See Articles 243 G, 243W and 243ZD of the Indian Constitution]. Fiscal decentralization is the key variable in this new dispensation of governance. This paper tries to analyse the trend in fiscal decentralization in India focusing on the fifteen major non-special category states based on the data set relating to panchayati raj institution (PRIs) and urban local governments (ULGs) given as Annexure to chapter 8 of the Twelfth Finance Commission (FC-12) report. We are aware of the serious limitations of such a set of aggregate data reported by the various state governments. However, it is a matter of comfort that these data are canvassed through a common format prepared and collated by the FC-12. This analysis is supplemented by a study of the second state finance commission (SFC) reports of five states.[1] The state finance commission (SFC) is a constitutional counterpart of the union finance commission (UFC) at the state level to mediate between the state and the local governments. [See Article 243 I and 243 Y].

Trend in Fiscal Decentralization

The extent of fiscal decentralization depends on the expenditure responsibilities and revenue assignments devolved to the lower tiers. The total expenditure of local governments (PRIs and ULGs), as a proportion of the combined expenditure of union, state and local governments works out to about 6.4 per cent in 1998-99 and 5.1 per cent in 2002-03[2]. The decline in the expenditure of PRIs (from 3.9 per cent in 1998-99 to 3.3 per cent in 2002-03) which cover nearly 73 per cent of the people, needs special mention because decentralized governance is envisaged primarily to improve the quality of life in the rural areas. The PRIs expenditure in 2002-03 as a proportion of GDP works out only to 1.07 per cent. The own source revenue (tax + non-tax revenue) of local governments as a proportion of the combined tax and non-tax revenue of the union, states and local governments for 1998-99 which was around 2.7 per cent, declined to 1.9 per cent in 2002-03. Reckoned in terms of GDP, in 2002-03, the own source revenue of local governments is only 0.39 per cent, more than 82 per cent of which is accounted for by ULGs. The extent of fiscal decentralisation which being already very low has shown a pronounced declining trend. When we know that in most advanced countries local governments, normally account for about 20-35 per cent of total government expenditure (in some countries like Denmark it goes as high as 45 per cent), India with two major constitutional amendments ostensibly to transfer power, authority and resources to local governments has very little to write home about.

The trend in the overall scenario of decentralization in India raises several questions. We may address some of them for the purpose of this paper: What has been the state-wise scenario? What interstate differences are in the structure and pattern of transfers by states to local governments? What role has the SFC constitutionally created to rationalise state sub-state level fiscal relations and transfers in the context of decentralization played?

Third Strata of Government and Fiscal Decentralization:

Table 1 shows the state-wise progress in regard to expenditure and tax decentralization as well as the changes in the relative magnitudes of these variables by comparing two years, 1998-99 and 2002-03. The proportion of local governments' expenditure of all states to the expenditure of all states and local governments combined declined from 11.24 per cent in 1998-99 to 9.47 per cent. Among the 15 major states shown in Table 1, only Bihar, Haryana, Tamil Nadu and Uttar Pradesh seem to have made some progress. In all the other eleven states the percentage has declined. The progress of Bihar and in the other three states are due to their very low base in 1998-99. In 1998-99 the percentage of local government expenditure to total expenditure comprising state and local governments ranged from 0.92per cent in Bihar to 21.73 per cent in Karnataka, followed by 20.90 per cent in Kerala[3] (18.76 per cent if RBI figures are used) and 20.36 per cent in Gujarat. In 2002-03, the corresponding range was from 0.93 per cent in Assam to 18.22 per cent in Karnataka and 14 per cent in Kerala (13.32 per cent with RBI figures) and Gujarat. Karnataka occupies the top position in expenditure decentralizatin in both the years. It could be firmly confirmed from the Table in Appendix A which gives the rate of growth of the total expenditure of each of the 15 states and that for all states for the period, 1998-99 – 2002-03 that the decline in the ratio is due to the lower growth rate of the expenditure of the local governments. While the all-states average rate of growth of expenditure increased at 11.6 per cent during the period, the rate of growth in the total expenditure of PRIs was only 6.87 per cent and of ULGs 4.07 per cent. Actually the trend in Gujarat, Kerala and Orissa for PRIs and in Gujarat, Haryana, Karnataka, Madhya Pradesh and Maharashtra for ULGs is negative. [See Appendix A].

Table 1
Expenditure and Tax decentralisation at the State-sub-state levels (Major States) (1998-99 and 2002-03)

No.	States	Local Government Expenditure as per cent of State Expenditure + Local Government Expenditure		Local Government Own Tax as Per cent of State Own Tax Revenue + Local Government Own Tax Revenue	
		1998-99	2002-03	1998-99	2002-03
1	Andhra Pradesh	18.12	18.05	3.07	3.90
2	Assam	1.08	0.93	2.07	1.45
3	Bihar	0.92	2.65	1.53	2.40

No.	States	Local Government Expenditure as per cent of State Expenditure + Local Government Expenditure		Local Government Own Tax as Per cent of State Own Tax Revenue + Local Government Own Tax Revenue	
		1998-99	2002-03	1998-99	2002-03
4	Gujarat	20.36	14.06	12.30	8.04
5	Haryana	3.63	4.64	2.95	0.73
6	Karnataka	21.73	18.22	6.14	3.68
7	Kerala*	18.76	13.32	3.87	3.99
8	Madhya Pradesh	9.90	9.30	8.20	8.98
9	Maharashtra	16.30	13.60	9.97	5.17
10	Orissa	3.33	3.13	3.54	0.55
11	Punjab	5.62	4.71	9.67	7.55
12	Rajasthan	12.34	11.47	2.71	0.48
13	Tamil Nadu	9.19	9.42	3.63	4.22
14	Uttar Pradesh	3.98	4.64	1.27	1.36
15	West Bengal	5.93	4.69	3.27	4.87
16	**All States**	**11.24**	**9.47**	**5.71**	**3.97**

Basic Data Source: Twelfth Finance Commission and RBI, State Finances: A study of Budgets for the relevant years.

* State Expenditure figures are obtained from RBI's State Finances: A study of Budgets. From the state total expenditure, figures given in the RBI document item IV of Appendix II i.e. Compensation and Assignments to local governments and Panchayat Raj is deducted. We have checked with RBI sources and learn that all the payments to local governments (ULGs + PRIs) are not included under this item. The real figures have to be obtained from the Ministry of Finance as audited by the C &AG. For Kerala we have used the figures from C&A.G Reports. As per the Report of C&A.G, the figures for 1998-99 and 2002-03 are Rs.1309.78 crore and Rs.989.98 crore respectively for Kerala. Hence the percentage when reworked will be 20.9 for 1998-99 and 14.1 for 2002-03. Similar figures for other states are not readily available and the given figures are possibly underestimates.

Turning to tax decentralisation, Table 1 shows that at the all-states level the percentage of own tax revenue of local government as a percentage of state's own tax revenue plus local tax revenue declined by 1.74 percentage points in 2002-03 compared with 1998-99. Only in seven states we see marginal increase during this period. The decline ranges from 0.62 percentage points in Assam to 4.80 percentage points in Maharashtra with Gujarat closely following. The magnitude and the pathology of the own revenue situation may be captured better in the three tables given under Appendix B. Table (i) shows the per capita own tax (OT) and per capita own source revenue (OSR) of PRIs along with the average growth rate from 1998-99 through 2002-03. Table (ii) shows the corresponding growth rate for ULGs. Table (iii) shows the ratio of own source revenue to total expenditure for PRIs and ULGs in the states under study for 1998-99 and 2002-03.

The per capita tax and per capita OSR of urban local governments are several times higher than that of the PRIs in all the states [See Table (i) and Table (ii) of Appendix B]. Appendix B Table (i) shows that in 2002-03, the per capita OT of PRIs is below one rupee (zero in Bihar) or around it in five states. The highest per capita OSR among PRIs in all the five years consistently is reported in Kerala (as high as Rs. 101.96 in 1999-2000). The per capita OSR of PRIs is below the all state average in the nine states in 2002-03. The rate of growth for all-states in regard to PRIs during the quinquennium 1998-99 to 2002-03, is over 7.7 per cent for tax and 5.7 per cent for own source revenue. The rate of growth in tax revenue of PRIs, however, is negative in Gujarat, Orissa and Punjab. Although the level of OSR of ULGs is very high compared to PRIs and in 2002-03, the per capita OSR ranges from Rs. 75.34 in Orissa to Rs. 743 in Punjab, the overall rate of growth of OSR of ULGs for all states has been negative (-3.14 per annum) during the period from 1998-99 to 2002-03. The growth rate of per capita taxes of ULGs is negative in Gujarat, Haryana, Karnataka, Maharashtra, Orissa and Rajasthan. Indeed, the own source revenue situation at the third tier of government especially that of PRIs does not seem to support a healthy decentralisation process in the country. The ratio of OSR to total expenditure which could be considered as a measure of the fiscal autonomy of the states [Appendix B Table (iii)] presents a some what misleading picture. The picture of ULGs is encouraging and definitely better than that of the PRIs. If we assume that a local government raises 50 per cent of its expenditure through OSR, it could be considered as fairly autonomous. By this standard except in a few states the ULG scenario is in fairly good shape. The share of OSR to total expenditure for ULG is over 52 per cent in 2002-03 as against 6.7 per cent for PRIs for the same year. In the case of Assam and Punjab the high OSR ratio of PRIs is presumably because of poor expenditure assignments.

Trends in Revenue Transfers to Local Governments

The effectiveness of fiscal decentralisation to the sub-state level governments depends on: (i) appropriate expenditure assignments (illustrative guidelines follow from Schedule XI and XII of the Constitution) broken up into activities and sub-activities accompanied by transfer of funds from the concerned state department head of accounts in the State Budget to the local governments; (ii)

Appropriate revenue/tax assignments and (iii) efficient design of the transfer system and its proper implementation. The latter, of course, is the primary responsibility of the State Finance Commission and the concerned state governments.

Table 2 presents the state-wise trend in the ratios of transfers (tax devolution plus grants-in-aid)[4] to net state domestic product (NSDP), to state's total revenue, as well as to state's total expenditure excluding loans and interest payments. Besides that, Table 2 contains a column [No. 3] which shows the ratio of tax devolution to local governments as a percentage of state's own tax revenue. All these are different ways to measure the magnitude of transfers.

Table 2
Select Indicators of Revenue Transfers to LGs by Major States (1998 - 99 and 2002-03)

No	State	Transfers as per cent of NSDP		Transfers as Per cent of State Revenue		Tax Devolution as per cent of State's Own Tax Revenue		Transfers as per cent of State Expenditure	
		(1)		*(2)*		*(3)*		*(4)*	
		98-99	02-03	98-99	02-03	98-99	02-03	98-99	02-03
1	Andhra Pradesh	2.68	3.39	19.54	21.20	4.44	4.54	15.33	16.48
2	Assam	0.03	0.04	0.17	0.18	0.27	0.29	0.16	0.16
3	Bihar	0.03	0.54	0.13	2.39	0.00	0.00	0.10	1.77
4	Gujarat	3.49	2.61	24.57	16.72	2.08	1.24	17.54	12.62
5	Haryana	0.27	0.58	1.88	3.87	0.88	2.59	1.28	3.43
6	Karnataka	4.81	4.43	33.74	27.52	52.63	42.62	27.34	21.01
7	Kerala	1.67	1.17	11.88	7.82	3.86	2.71	8.70	5.40
8	Madhya Pradesh	1.31	1.19	7.07	6.35	15.54	10.44	5.41	5.12
9	Maharashtra	1.71	1.99	15.05	16.87	0.36	0.31	11.41	12.07
10	Orissa	0.59	0.80	4.03	3.69	5.09	6.51	2.38	2.84
11	Punjab	0.13	0.17	1.12	1.03	1.28	1.24	0.68	0.76
12	Rajasthan	1.73	1.76	13.21	10.13	1.95	1.97	8.49	6.96
13	Tamil Nadu	1.09	1.27	8.12	8.26	12.03	12.00	6.50	6.68

No	State	Transfers as per cent of NSDP		Transfers as Per cent of State Revenue		Tax Devolution as per cent of State's Own Tax Revenue		Transfers as per cent of State Expenditure	
		(1)		(2)		(3)		(4)	
		98-99	02-03	98-99	02-03	98-99	02-03	98-99	02-03
14	Uttar Pradesh	0.58	0.25	4.45	1.59	9.58	2.99	2.83	1.25
15	West Bengal	0.44	0.45	4.97	4.76	0.09	0.66	3.16	2.92
16	**All States**	**1.19**	**1.12**	**10.76**	**8.96**	**8.35**	**6.25**	**7.92**	**6.86**

Source: Twelfth Finance Commission RBI State Finances A study of Budgets and Government of India Economic Survey 2004 - 05.

NSDP – Net Domestic Product

Table 2 which focuses on the magnitude of transfers made by the major state governments to local governments has to be seen along with the poor revenue and expenditure decentralization noted in Table 1 and Appendix B. Transfers to local governments as a percentage of SDP, has declined in the country as a whole. However it improved in ten states in 2002-03 albeit marginally compared to 1998-99. SDP is not a good fiscal variable to measure the magnitude of transfers. The best way is to reckon transfers with reference to state's expenditure and state's revenue. We have also examined the tax component of the transfers vis-à-vis the own tax revenue of the state. In nine states total transfers have registered a decline as a proportion of the total state expenditure. This includes such prominent states upholding decentralisation like Karnataka, Kerala, Madhya Pradesh, Rajasthan and West Bengal. An important measure of fiscal decentralisation is the percentage of tax revenue devolved (e.g. tax assigned, plus state taxes shared) to total state tax revenue. In 1998-99 it ranges from zero in Bihar to 52.63 per cent in Karnataka and in 2002-03, the same pattern continues except that Karnataka's share has fallen to 42.62 per cent. Karnataka is followed by Tamil Nadu and Madhya Pradesh in 2002-03. Transfers as a percentage of state revenue declined in nine states as well as for all states. Table 2 clearly shows that only Karnataka has above all-state average in regard to all the four measures in all the years. Maharashtra and Rajasthan fall in the second best category as they qualify for all measures except tax devolution as percentage of state's own tax revenue. In brief, the record of fiscal decentralization, to the sub-state level governments through transfers has been very poor. As regards Karnataka it is important to note that the transfers are linked to the schemes transferred by the state government. The system that prevailed in 1993 continues. The local governments do not have any autonomy to determine priorities, discontinue schemes or change the composition of expenditures. Moreover, the gram panchayats in the state account for only 5 per cent of the total allocation of state funds to PRIs in 2002-03 and in 2000-01 as low as 3.5 per cent. [See Karnataka second SFC Report (2002), p. 27]. In all other states the share of village panchayats is high. Indeed, the efficiency of resources use and the quality and effectiveness of the delivery of basic services depend on the quantum of expenditure at the cutting edge level.

Table 3
Per Capita State Revenue and Per Capita Transfers to PRIs and ULGs (2002-2003)

No	State	Per Capita Revenue of State (in Rs.)	Per Capita Transfer (Combined) (in Rs.)	Per Capita Transfers to PRIs (in Rs.)	Per Capita Transfers to ULGs (in Rs.)
1.	Andhra Pradesh	2941.78	623.78	775.43	219.87
2.	Assam	2464.25	4.54	0.00	35.53
3.	Bihar	1318.96	31.57	34.21	8.97
4.	Gujarat	3382.16	565.45	835.44	112.60
5.	Haryana	3882.39	150.18	188.00	57.18
6.	Karnataka	2955.19	813.14	1175.61	110.33
7.	Kerala	3274.34	256.02	293.29	149.16
8.	Madhya Pradesh	2114.19	134.29	65.23	325.92

No	State	Per Capita Revenue of State (in Rs.)	Per Capita Transfer (Combined) (in Rs.)	Per Capita Transfers to PRIs (in Rs.)	Per Capita Transfers to ULGs (in Rs.)
9.	Maharashtra	3073.10	518.57	816.05	114.69
10.	Orissa	2225.93	82.08	56.54	227.43
11.	Punjab	4369.67	44.84	47.72	39.25
12.	Rajasthan	2190.99	221.84	250.56	127.62
13.	Tamil Nadu	3266.99	269.74	231.31	318.52
14.	Uttar Pradesh	1593.29	25.39	32.04	0.00
15.	West Bengal	1729.35	82.36	24.12	232.37
16.	**All States**	**2656.85**	**238.04**	**269.55**	**152.10**

Before we conclude this discussion, we may try to discern the pattern in the structure of transfers to local governments. Table 3 juxtaposes the state-wise distribution of per capita state revenue and per capita transfers in 2002-03 to PRIs and ULGs for the 15 states. One important aspect to be noted from the table is the higher per capita transfers to the rural areas (PRIs) than the urban areas for the country as a whole. By and large this is true in the case of most of the states. This is a healthy trend. But there are significant exceptions. Assam makes no transfers to PRIs[5]. It is very significant that Madhya Pradesh and Orissa which are admittedly backward states with a very high tribal population, the per capita transfers to PRIs is way below that to ULGs. In West Bengal the per capita transfers to PRIs is only Rs. 24.12[6] as against Rs. 232.37 for ULGs. Although Tamil Nadu's case is not that glaring as West Bengal, Madhya Pradesh or Orissa, the hiatus is very conspicuous.

Figure.1 seeks to illustrate the association between per capita state revenue and the transfers made to the local governments. The per capita state revenue is shown in the x-axis and per capita transfers in the y-axis with the median lines relevant to these two variables being drawn making the whole figure into a box with four quadrangles identified as A,B,C and D [See Fig.1].

Figure 1
Per Capita Revenue of States and Per Capita Transfers Received by Local Governments, 2002-2003

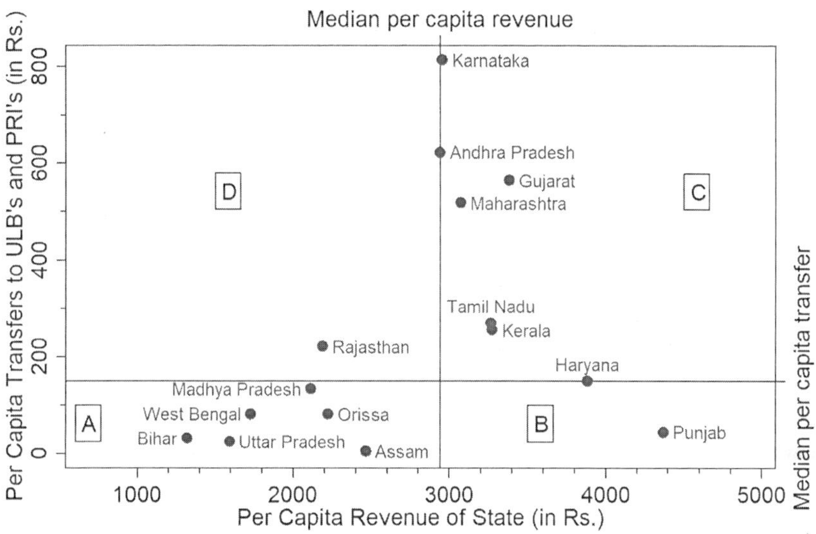

In Figure 1 Quadrangle A represents the case of states with low per capita revenue (less than the median level of per capita revenue, or states with per capita revenue less than the middle 50 per cent, when the states are arranged in order of increasing per capita revenue), and low per capita transfers to the LGs (less than the median level of per capita transfers). Quadrangle B represents the case of states with high per capita revenue (greater than median level of per capita revenue) and low per capita transfers to LGs (less than median level of per capita transfer). Quadrangle C represents the case of states with high per capita revenue and high per capita transfers to LGs. Quadrangle D represents those cases with low per capita revenue but high per capita transfers.

What Fig. 1 shows is that though higher transfers are mostly seen to be made by the richer revenue states, it is not true in all cases. Punjab with the highest per capita revenue has the lowest per capita transfer. More or less the same story is narrated in the case of Haryana. The highest per capita transfer is made by Karnataka which is a state with per capita revenue in the middle fifty per cent of states when they are ranked by their per capita revenue.

It may also be seen that most of the states with low per capita revenue devolves less or even nil to LGs with Rajasthan standing out as an exception. Though a low per capita revenue state, Rajasthan devolves funds to LGs in much larger magnitude in per capita terms than that of Punjab, Haryana or West Bengal. This is shown by it being the sole state in Quadrangle D

The Role of SFCs: Study of Five Second SFCs

Interalia poor progress of fiscal decentralization may be considered as reflecting the ineffectiveness of the institution of SFC. It is as well be due to the failure of the states in implementing SFC recommendations. The primary task of the union finance commission (UFC) is to mediate in the sharing of revenues between the centre and the states by rectifying the mismatches between responsibilities and resources as well as to reduce the horizontal fiscal imbalances between states in an equitable manner. The SFC which is a counter part of the UFC at the state level is mandated to perform these tasks at the state sub-state level. The task is probably more complex and onerous for the SFCs because of the lack of clarity in regard to expenditure responsibilities in many states. Except in a few states like Kerala where the responsibilities of the panchayats and urban local governments are broken down into activities and sub-activities, every function of the LG is state-concurrent and therefore administratively complex. Because the local governments are constitutionally required to create institutions of local self government and prepare plans for economic development and social justice under the new decentralization regime, the responsibilities of a state finance commission in ensuring vertical and horizontal equity and balance are very high. Economically poor gram panchayats and municipalities will have to be helped in providing comparable services through equalizing allocations (grants) which will compensate for genuine revenue raising problems and cost disadvantages such as distance, mountainous or marshy regions and the like. In what follows we examine very briefly how five second generation SFCs (Karnataka, Kerala, Punjab, Rajasthan and Tamil Nadu) have tried to improve vertical and horizontal imbalances in their respective states.

The size of vertical transfers logically depends on the goals to be achieved and the needs of local governments which certainly will have to take into account the magnitude of the mismatches in resources available and the expenditure responsibilities. All the SFCs under study except Kerala have made estimates of vertical gaps. But none has made this exercise with reference to functional assignments and needs following from that. Actually a clear demarcation of functional domain is not available in most cases. All the five SFCs agree in regard to the need for providing basic public services of comparable quality at the level of rural and urban local governments. Tamil Nadu, Punjab and Rajasthan SFCs estimate the fiscal gap including capital requirements mostly taking civic functions into account. Rajasthan SSFC takes the view that investment requirements for providing civic services are "large and ought to be met from plan funds including cess and externally funded projects" (Rajasthan SSFC Report: p.82).

In Appendix C we present a broad outline of the scheme of vertical transfers of the five SSFCs which shows the magnitude of transfer, the instrument of transfers and the basis of vertical distribution between PRIs and ULGs. The size of transfers ranges from 2.25 per cent (this includes 0.05 per cent as incentive grant for raising additional revenue) of state's own net tax revenue in Rajasthan to 40 per cent of non-loan gross own revenue receipts (NLGORR) in Karnataka. All SFCs except Karnataka consider net tax revenue as the instrument and source of transfer. Kerala SSFC which endorses the prevailing practice of giving one third of plan outlay to the LGs, as plan grants-in-aid, additionally recommends the devolution of a maintenance grant (5.5 per cent of net own tax revenue of state) based on a current cost of replacement and a general purpose grant to the tune of 3.5 per cent of the net own tax revenue.

We also see from Appendix C that the basis of vertical distribution between PRIs and ULGs is population in most cases. Besides population, Karnataka takes illiteracy rate and population per hospital bed into consideration and the ratio works out to 80 per cent for PRIs and 20 per cent for ULGs. Tamil Nadu takes besides population (50% weight) needs (operation and maintenance, capital and debt) and resource potential, and the rural-urban proportion works out to 58:42. It is clear that the choice of criteria and the weightage given to them which in turn depends on the objectives and priorities underlying the design of transfer of the concerned SFC assume significance in determining the vertical share of PRIs and ULGs.

Turning to horizontal distribution, we may make some general observations based on the five SSFC reports. We have noted in Table 3 that in 2002-03, [See also Fig. 1] that Karnataka has the highest per capita transfer. This is obviously due to the high vertical transfers through the transfer of schemes of the state government as we have already mentioned. The real question is whether it also results in higher horizontal equity or not. The answer is in the negative. For one the allocation to gram panchayats[7] in Karnataka as we have already noted is only around 5 per cent of the total allocation to PRIs in 2002-03. The criteria for *interse* distribution such as population, area, illiteracy rate, the ratio of population per bed and so on are applicable only in the case of Zilla Panchayats and Taluka panchayats. Gram Panchayats get only a fixed amount (Rs.3.5 lakh per GP). In the case of the other states, the tax shares recommended to gram panchayats ranges from 60 per cent of the share of PRIs in Tamil Nadu to 100 per cent in Punjab. Kerala SSFC besides giving nearly 70 per cent plan grant share to GPs, 78.5 per cent of general purpose grant is also earmarked for them.[8] While in Kerala the *interse* distribution among the municipalities and corporations should be entirely on the basis of population, as regards GPs, a corpus of Rs.100 million is recommended to be set apart as a horizontal gap filling to fill the gap between obligatory expenses and own revenue plus general purpose grant of GPs. A 100 per cent gap filling in the case of Second and Third grade GPs, 50 per cent in the case of First grade GPs and 25 per cent in the case of special grade GPs are recommended. The balance is to be distributed on the basis of population.

The most rational horizontal distribution is to give adequate weightage to equity and efficiency. For *interse* allocation among GPs, all SFCs other than Karnataka use population as the dominant criterion followed by area, tax efforts and some indicators of backwardness. The choice of a relevant backwardness criteria with appropriate weightage, incentivising revenue efforts and ensuring delivery of quality of services assume significance. On this score most of the SSFCs require improvements and need to incorporate better efficiency and equity elements. Besides the horizontal gap filling recommendations of Kerala SSFC, two recommendations of the Tamil Nadu SSFC need special mention: one relates to the introduction of the Report Card system for the *interse* distribution of Incentive Funds. Five per cent of the total devolution is set apart for providing incentives to local governments for efficient resource mobilization as well as for delivery of quality public services. The Report Card system is a way of assessing the quality of public services from the perspective of citizens or users of civic services. Users can provide feed back on the quality, efficiency and adequacy of the services through the various entries in the card. The other is the Equalisation Fund to compensate for fiscal disabilities. Any GP with less than Rs. 17 per capita tax (which is the state average for all GPs) is considered a weak village panchayat deserving this fund. The shortfall from Rs. 17 is made good from the Equalisation Fund. It may be noted here that one may do well to compare fiscal capacity at a given average tax rate rather than the actual per capita tax, which may be low due to lower tax effort. This type of compensation may even disincentivise tax effort. Even so the promotion of equalization is a relevant effort towards horizontal equity. A great weakness of the Tamil Nadu SSFC is that it left 20 per cent of devolution to be discretionary and only 80 per cent as formula-based. A rational devolution mechanism should be fully formula-based which of course should be operationally simple.

By and large, the SSFC reports are better than their first generation counterparts in terms of analytical content and quality of recommendations. Despite the innumerable shortcomings of the first series of SFC reports pointed out by the Eleventh Finance Commission (FC-11) and those raised by the FC-12 about SFC reports they examined, that SSFCs raised the magnitude of vertical devolution compared to the previous regime cannot be gainsaid. However, the pertinent question is the cavalier fashion in which most state governments have treated the recommendations of the SFCs. All the five SSFCs under study have reviewed the progress the respective states have made in implementing the first SFC, devolution packages and recommendations. All of them report very serious lapses on the part of the state governments. The constitutional provisions contained in Article 243 (4) that "The Governor shall cause every recommendation made by the commission under this article together with an explanatory memorandum as to the action taken thereon to be laid before the Legislature of the State" have been violated by almost all the states. By dishonouring and soft-peddling on the recommendations of successive SFCs most state governments have put the fiscal decentralization process in reverse gear.

Presumably, the most striking mistake in regard to the transfer system emerging at the state sub-state level following decentralization reforms is treating the transfers to LGs as an additional financial allocation. Yes, there is need for extra resources. But the basic principle that as part of decentralization of funds[9], budgetary provision of an item of expenditure responsibility that has been transferred to the LGs should be followed with corresponding reduction in the concerned departmental budget of the state has not been followed in most states. So long as the necessary adjustments are not made the entire state transfers to the LGs become an additional burden on the state. It is a grave mistake on the part of the SFCs that they have not taken into account this in arriving at the vertical gaps. Economic efficiency and efficiency in governance are enhanced by the division of governmental functions among different levels depending on their comparative advantage or what is called the principle of subsidiarity. Although Kerala State has made functional demarcations between the state and LGs and LGs, *interse*, and Kerala Government introduced a separate budget document for panchayats and ULGs as Appendix IV to the budget papers, there was no *pro tanto* reduction at the state departmental level except in the case of a very few departments. So decentralization resulted in additional burden on the state exchequer even in Kerala. There is also need to insure local government from the impact of the fiscal imprudence of the state governments.

To conclude, even after more than a decade of decentralized governance under the new dispensation, the emerging fiscal decentralization scenario is disquieting. The percentage of local government expenditure in relation to total government expenditure has declined significantly during the period 1998-99

– 2002-03. The progress of expenditure decentralization in eleven out of the 15 states appears to be on the decline. The revenue decentralization trend is also no better. That the average rate of growth in the tax revenue of PRIs and ULGs in most of the states in the country had been negative or declining provides a wrong signal. It renders efforts towards building autonomous local governments impossible. As regards transfers to the local governments, reckoned in terms of SDP, state revenue and state expenditure, the overall trend has been very discouraging, although there are significant exceptions. Again while by and large per capita transfers to rural governments are higher than that of ULGs, the per capita transfers to ULGs is very high in states like Madhya Pradesh, Orissa, Tamil Nadu and West Bengal. The performance of SFCs which have the responsibility to mediate in the revenue sharing between the state and the LGs leaves many things to be desired. Functional mapping with reference to state and LGs on the one hand and that among the three tiers of PRIs has not made much progress in most states. Sometimes functions are transferred without making any change in the budgetary head by way devolution to local governments. This makes transfers an additional burden on the state exchequer. Needless to say, economic efficiency and political efficiency is best ensured when the functions among the different levels are organized on the basis of comparative advantage followed by corresponding transfers. The design of the transfer system at the state sub-state level needs drastic reform. SFC recommendation is one thing, but implementation is the responsibility of the state. It is the state governments who should bear the major responsibility about the poor progress of fiscal decentralization in the country.

Appendix A

Average Rate of Growth in the Total Expenditure of State, PRI and ULGs (1998-99 – 2002-03)

No.	States	Growth Rate of State Expenditure (1998-99 – 2002-03)	Growth Rate of Expenditure of PRIs (1998-99 – 2002-03)	Growth Rate of Expenditure of ULGs (1998-99 – 2002-03)
1	Andhra Pradesh	12.83	11.92	15.44
2	Assam	13.53	2.25	10.07
3	Bihar	4.93	96.20	12.57
4	Gujarat	8.95	-1.65	-5.68
5	Haryana	6.92	26.72	-9.41
6	Karnataka	12.41	5.86	-3.81
7	Kerala	10.04	-2.09	3.46
8	Madhya Pradesh	2.94	2.04	-1.50
9	Maharashtra	10.42	11.09	-0.25
10	Orissa	10.88	-3.37	19.45
11	Punjab	12.60	9.70	5.47
12	Rajasthan	10.22	5.67	9.48
13	Tamil Nadu	9.70	7.73	8.30
14	Uttar Pradesh	7.01	5.14	11.32
15	West Bengal	12.45	5.52	4.00
16	**All States**	**11.59**	**6.87**	**4.07**

Appendix B
State-wise Distribution of Per Capita Own Tax and Per Capita Own Revenue with average Growth Rate
Table (i)

State	Panchayati Raj Institutions											
	1998-1999		1999-2000		2000-2001		2001-2002		2002-2003		Growth Rate	
	Per Capita Own Tax	Per Capita Own Revenue	Per Cap-ita Own Tax	Per Capita Own Revenue	Per Cap-ita Own Tax	Per Capita Own Revenue	Per Capita Own Tax	Per Capita Own Revenue	Per Capita Own Tax	Per Capita Own Revenue	Own Tax	Own Revenue (OSR)
Andhra Pradesh	12.03	23.83	12.11	24.92	13.46	27.37	13.56	28.66	13.65	30.05	3.72	6.23
Assam	3.12	3.14	3.12	3.15	3.13	3.16	3.13	3.16	3.14	3.17	0.16	0.18
Bihar	0.00	0.84	0.00	0.42	0.00	1.04	0.00	0.47	0.00	0.85	0.00	1.33
Gujarat	22.52	25.48	22.34	25.80	20.99	23.95	19.50	22.14	18.48	21.10	-5.18	-5.17
Haryana	5.07	40.67	3.71	39.70	4.91	46.76	4.88	49.44	5.43	49.43	4.17	6.29
Karnataka	15.30	15.30	16.69	16.69	19.15	19.15	14.75	14.75	16.47	16.47	0.25	0.25
Kerala	38.08	72.68	42.84	101.96	49.16	93.08	48.08	81.36	51.27	94.07	7.36	2.94
Madhya Pradesh	28.24	29.26	28.01	29.61	28.38	32.00	27.46	31.33	33.34	37.55	3.17	5.71
Maharashtra	29.46	44.54	32.31	52.15	36.64	58.78	48.08	67.39	59.48	80.65	19.75	15.53
Orissa	0.16	2.05	0.15	2.81	0.15	2.89	0.15	2.77	0.07	1.71	-15.95	-3.70
Punjab	0.77	42.61	0.58	52.94	0.72	50.11	0.70	39.64	0.52	59.08	-5.64	3.71
Rajasthan	0.74	7.76	1.12	8.69	1.10	8.52	1.08	8.34	1.06	8.23	6.96	0.77
Tamil Nadu	10.09	15.26	11.26	17.24	13.10	16.39	14.51	17.68	13.64	18.34	8.95	4.01
Uttar Pradesh	0.75	3.70	0.90	4.15	0.89	4.47	0.81	4.39	0.80	4.57	0.07	4.89
West Bengal	1.24	5.28	1.22	5.26	1.56	5.64	1.62	5.69	1.63	5.17	8.71	0.37
All India	**8.86**	**16.34**	**9.34**	**18.40**	**10.18**	**19.15**	**10.72**	**18.95**	**12.03**	**21.29**	**7.77**	**5.74**

OSR – Own Source Revenue (Own Revenue)

Appendix B
Table (ii)

State	Urban Local governments											
	1998-1999		1999-2000		2000-2001		2001-2002		2002-2003		Growth Rate	
	Per Capita Own Tax	Per Capita Own Revenue	Per Capita Own Tax	Per Capita Own Revenue	Per Capita Own Tax	Per Capita Own Revenue	Per Capita Own Tax	Per Capita Own Revenue	Per Capita Own Tax	Per Capita Own Revenue	Own Tax	Own Revenue
Andhra Pradesh	92.32	238.22	105.20	249.17	125.53	302.48	153.36	340.70	203.78	401.53	21.66	14.53
Assam	42.18	95.92	45.06	89.55	52.15	104.85	54.81	105.34	59.49	122.41	9.23	6.72
Bihar	50.51	54.38	54.35	59.68	57.75	64.37	54.88	63.10	73.84	82.29	8.00	9.24
Gujarat	552.34	657.72	623.06	739.95	632.15	745.69	605.95	719.49	390.85	494.48	-6.94	-5.81
Haryana	151.92	237.66	116.82	255.57	95.20	205.84	104.31	207.39	50.37	144.50	-20.71	-11.34
Karnataka	231.29	304.34	223.15	263.54	215.85	241.43	225.49	254.80	182.57	188.49	-4.52	-9.44
Kerala	121.31	187.07	149.09	223.39	172.58	252.14	153.28	269.85	213.04	350.17	12.23	15.52
Madhya Pradesh	220.66	300.23	251.78	350.20	288.23	364.68	242.49	327.51	270.38	361.76	3.76	3.11
Maharashtra	359.65	475.89	346.02	470.11	391.62	542.61	412.15	577.41	209.14	247.00	-8.69	-10.47
Orissa	101.45	136.01	22.94	60.38	27.24	67.80	28.71	72.67	27.69	75.34	-21.12	-9.48
Punjab	435.54	584.61	556.58	732.49	590.99	818.83	559.81	807.82	540.27	743.80	4.46	5.97
Rajasthan	85.29	150.27	11.49	64.44	15.66	82.23	17.80	126.45	18.17	123.42	-23.32	2.84
Tamil Nadu	122.13	221.31	180.36	277.91	172.28	309.81	187.59	328.02	207.50	356.40	11.62	11.84
Uttar Pradesh	28.18	55.97	31.85	60.00	35.81	67.15	40.30	80.89	45.40	90.88	12.63	13.52
West Bengal	72.25	140.23	79.42	150.11	85.08	158.37	121.54	198.87	149.28	253.76	20.64	15.81
All States	**182.59**	**263.91**	**193.71**	**277.53**	**206.91**	**304.25**	**212.33**	**207.80**	**174.59**	**260.06**	**0.02**	**-3.14**

Appendix B
Table (iii)
Percentage of OSR to Total Expenditure

States	Percentage of PRIs		Percentage of ULGs	
	1998-1999	**2002-03**	**1998-1999**	**2002-03**
Andhra Pradesh	3.93	3.34	64.09	60.81
Assam	99.86	98.83	69.55	67.67
Bihar	20.15	2.27	59.65	56.84
Gujarat	2.65	2.72	72.57	74.62
Haryana	45.35	20.82	77.94	94.00
Karnataka	1.67	1.45	70.00	56.48
Kerala	9.44	12.67	31.47	50.87
Madhya Pradesh	26.50	36.68	39.50	49.50
Maharashtra	7.88	9.98	73.01	49.68
Orissa	5.40	3.02	76.68	24.88
Punjab	66.33	55.32	100.78	113.85
Rajasthan	2.38	2.17	34.90	23.60
Tamil Nadu	14.68	12.39	41.11	46.61
Uttar Pradesh	11.60	10.62	25.11	28.96
West Bengal	16.89	17.64	39.53	60.21
All States	**6.34**	**6.77**	**57.11**	**52.58**

Appendix C
Scheme of Vertical Transfers of Five SSFCs

Name of State	Instrument of Transfer and % to be transferred	Basis of arriving at the divisible Pool	Basis and proportion of vertical Distribution Between PRIs & ULGs	Remarks
Karnataka	**40%** of Non loan gross own Revenue Receipts (NLGORR).	Normative estimate to provide minimum public /civic services of comparable quality in rural and urban areas	Population, SC/ST, Illiteracy rate and population per hospital bed. **PRIs - 80% ULGs - 20%**	Raised NLGORR ratio from 36% recommended by first SFC to **40%** by the SSFC.
Kerala	**Plan** Grant-in-aid – **33 1/3%** of the state plan. **Non Plan** (i) **5.5%** of Own Tax revenue for main-tenance of assets (ii) **3.5%** of Own Tax revenue as general purpose grant (uncondi-tional) **10%** of plan grants (excluding special component plan and Tribal sub plan) to be distributed as Incentive Fund (in proportion of additional revenue collected by GPs and ULGs).	Maintenance grant based on current cost of replacement. (Details spelt out). General purpose grant based on normative assessment of establishment cost and office expense requirements for District Panchayat and Block Panchayat. The balance is distributed as **Gram Panchayat – 78.5%** **Municipalities – 8.5%** **Corporations – 13%**	Population of Urban and Rural areas.	It may be noted that the general purpose grant is in lieu of assigned taxes, shared taxes and various statutory and non statutory grants-in-aid.
Punjab	**4%** of net collection of Own Taxes.	Normative projection of income and expenditure and estimating vertical gaps of PRIs and ULGs.	**PRIs – 67.5%** **ULGs – 32.5%** *Interse* distribution among ULGs: Population (70%), SCs (15% (and shortfall of per capita tax as compared to average per capita tax of all ULGs. Enter share of taxes to GPs *Interse* distribution: Population (65%), shortfall of per capita own income as compared to per capita own income of GPs in the state. (15%) Population of SCs (15%) population in mountainous areas (5%).	Income includes additional resource mobilization also and expenditure includes capital needs and quality of services.

Name of State	Instrument of Transfer and % to be transferred	Basis of arriving at the divisible Pool	Basis and proportion of vertical Distribution Between PRIs & ULGs	Remarks
Rajasthan	**2.20%** of own tax revenue plus **0.05%** as incentive for resource mobilization (Total **2.25%**) • 15% of net proceeds from entertainment tax. • 1% of net receipts from royalty or mineral in gram panchayat of the districts where these activities are carried on.	• Assessment of minimum requirements based on additional responsibilities • Gap to be filled by additional revenue efforts • Sharing of royalty on the basis of collection.	Population the basis **PRIs – 76. 6%** **ULGs – 23.4%**	Incentive scheme of a matching allotment by state for tapping taxes and non tax sources. District wise distribution of PRIs: Population (80%) Area (10%), BPL families (5%) Illiteracy (5%) ULGs 85% population. 15% for less developed municipalities.
Tamil Nadu	Net own tax revenue. 8% in the first two years (2002-03 and 2003-04) 9% in the next two years (2004-06) and 10% in the last year (2006-07). 5% of central devolution for vertical and horizontal devolution. Horizontal distribution for village panchayats: Population (60%) SC/ST Population (10%) Agricultural labourers (10%), Area (10%) and asset maintenance (10%). Out of 100% global sharing, 13% set apart for Reserve, Equalisation and Incentive Funds.	Resource gap on the basis of normative assessment of needs for providing minimum basic services.	**Population: 50%** **Needs: 25%** (Operative & Maintenance, Capital Debt) **Resource Potential: 25%**	Quantitative and qualitative aspects of civic needs considered in Resource gap estimates. Capital needs also considered. Zero base budgeting recommended. Several measures to ensure fiscal responsibility recommended. **80% Formula - based 20% left to discretionary decisions.**

* **Publised in Economic and Political Weekly, March 11, 2006. I wish to acknowledge the helpful comments of Prof. D.K.Srivastava on the first draft of this paper.*

Endnotes

1 They are Karnataka, Kerala, Punjab, Rajasthan and Tamil Nadu.

2 The expenditure data for local governments are from FC-12 report and that for union and state governments are from Economic Survey, Government of India for the relevant years.

3 For details, see foot note to Table 1.

4 Transfers consist of tax assignment plus tax devolved plus grant-in-aid transferred to local governments (PRIs and ULGs). The TFC data contain an item 'Others', other than own source revenue and tax devolution and grants-in-aid. As it is a mixed category we have not included it in the transfers.

5 This cannot be a case of non-reporting because it is zero in all the five years.

6 In West Bengal in the year 2001-02, the per capita transfers to PRIs was above Rs. 70.

7 Moving the 73rd Amendment on December 1, 1992 in the Lok Sabha the then Minister for Rural Development said: "The Constitution (73rd) Amendment Bill casts a duty on

the centre as well as the states to establish and nourish the village panchayats so as to make them effective self governing institutions". This basic objective must be a governing consideration in the state sub-state level transfer system.

8 The GPs share is determined after allotting a one-time share for District and Block panchayats in the general purpose grant based on their establishment cost and office expense requirements.

9 For the whole process to be complete, logically the functionaries also should be transferred to the lower tiers. This is a serious deficit in the democratic decentralisation underway in the country.

References

Bird Richard Mand Francios Villancourt (1998), *Fiscal Decentralisation in Developing Countries.* Cambridge, Cambridge University Press.

Fuka Saku Kichiro and L.R.De Mello Jr. (1999), *Fiscal Decentralisation in Emerging Economies*, Paris, Development Centre OECD.

Oommen, M.A., (2004), "Fiscal decentralization in Kerala" in Geeta Sethi, ed. (2004), *Fiscal Decentralisation to Rural Governments in India*, Oxford University Press.

Rao M.G and Nirvikar Singh (2005), *Political Economy of Federalism in India*, Oxford University Press.

Report of the Second State Finance Commissions of Karnataka, Kerala, Punjab, Rajasthan and Tamil Nadu.

Reserve Bank of India, ***State Finances: A Study of Budgets*** for different years.

Tanzi, Vito (1996) "Fiscal Federalism and decentralization: A Review of Some efficiency and Macro-economic Aspects" in Michael Bruno and Boris Plesrovic, eds, *Annual World Bank Conference on Development Economics 1995*, Washington, World Bank

Twelfth Finance Commission Report, 2005.

CHAPTER 8

The Thirteenth Finance Commission and the Third Tier*

Following the 73rd/74th Constitutional Amendments, local governments notably the panchayat raj institutions (PRIs), once a neglected appendage of the rural development department, have acquired 'a habitation and a name' in Indian federal polity. It is significant that Article 280 of the Constitution establishing the union finance commission (UFC) was amended as part of the two Amendments. The addition of sub-clauses 280 (3) (bb) and (c) mandating UFC to recommend measures needed to augment the consolidated fund of a state to supplement the resources of the panchayats and municipalities in the state "on the basis of the recommendations made by the finance commission of the State" affirms the organic link in Indian fiscal federalism. All the UFCs since the two amendments have been required through their terms of reference (ToR) to make recommendations on these clauses. The tenth UFC (FC-10), although appointed before these amendments became a *fait accompli, suo moto* recommended some adhoc grants to the local governments (LGs). This paper seeks to evaluate the recommendations of the thirteenth finance commission (FC-13) with reference to the third tier. Despite several shortcomings, I try to argue that this Commission has made some significant departures from the past and made recommendations which if fully implemented could help to strengthen the process of democratic decentralisation in the country.

Some Magnitudes and Trends

The fiscal data relating to local governments are admittedly very weak. Even after 15 years under the new dispensation of decentralised regime, reliable and comparable data across states and over time are found wanting. FC-11, FC-12 and FC-13 have gathered data regarding income and expenditure of rural and urban local governments through state governments. While the first two presented the data in the text of their reports, FC-13 has placed them in its website. But none of the Commissions ventured to analyse them although FC-XI and FC-XII used the data for estimating revenue efforts of local governments. FC-XIII data covering a period of six years from 2002-03 through 2007-08 are probably more reliable because the accounting format prepared by the C&AG for LGs, following the EC-XI recommendations, has been accepted by a large number of states. This does not ensure that the fiscal data provided is beyond reproach and strictly comparable. Actually FC-XIII did not seem to have precisely defined the terms/concepts used in canvassing the scheduled data from the state governments who in turn did it through a chain of local government functionaries. Even so, in this paper I have used the data on the website to throw some light regarding the magnitude and trend in the expenditure and own source revenue of the third tier (the panchayati raj institutions and urban local governments) from 2002-03 to 2007-08 fully aware of the limitations of the data. The all-India statistics as well as those of the major 15 states in regard to selected variables are used. These states cover over 96% of the country's population. Though not as precise statistic, but as broad aggregates to provide some useful magnitudes and insights, the data are helpful.

The economic significance of LGs in a federal system may be measured by four parameters: (1) the share of local government expenditure to total public sector expenditure (the centre, states and local governments), (2) the share of LG expenditure to gross domestic product (GDP), (3) the share of local governments' own source revenue (OSR) to total public sector OSR and (4) the LG share of OSR to GDP. Table 1 attempts to capture the share of LGs with reference to public sector expenditure and OSR for six years from 2002-03 through 2007-08.

Table 1
Trend in the Percentage Share of LGs in the Public Sector Expenditure, Public Sector OSR (2002-03 – 2007-08)

Items	2002-03	2003-04	2004-05	2005-06	2006-07	2007-08
PRIs						
Share of Public Sector Expenditure	2.5	2.9	3.1	3.7	3.9	3.7
Share of Public Sector OSR	0.4	0.4	0.4	0.4	0.3	0.3
ULBs						
Share of Public Sector Expenditure	3.0	2.2	2.5	2.7	2.8	3.0
Share of Public Sector OSR	3.2	3.1	2.9	2.9	2.7	2.5

Items	2002-03	2003-04	2004-05	2005-06	2006-07	2007-08
LGs						
Share of Public Sector Expenditure	5.5	5.1	5.6	6.4	6.7	6.7
Share of Public Sector OSR	3.6	3.5	3.3	3.3	3.0	2.8

Note: Calculations based on FC-13 website data; Government of India, Economic Survey for relevant years and Reserve Bank of India, State Finances: A study of Budgets for relevant years.

It is significant that the share of local governments' expenditure in the total public sector expenditure has increased almost steadily from 5.5% in 2002-03 to 6.7% in 2007-08. Equally important is the visible stepping up of PRIs share which increased from 2.5% to 3.7% during this period. Actually, the share of urban local governments (ULGs) stagnated around 3% and even declined in some years. However, the LG share in public sector expenditure is small compared to the OECD countries where it broadly ranges from 20– 35%. Although as a share of GDP also, the LG share of expenditure demonstrates an increasing trend from 2.13% in 2002-03 to 2.42% in 2007-08, it falls way below the corresponding share of nearly 14% of GDP for OECD countries and 10.8% for China. This increasing trend has to be understood subject to two important qualifications: one is that this increase presumably is due to the step up in agency functions such as the centrally-sponsored schemes and several state sponsored programmes routed through PRIs and ULGs in recent years. Indeed this goes counter to the avowed mandate of the Constitution to create 'institutions of self-government'. We provide in Appendix A the percentage of central transfers to PRIs including Union Finance Commission transfers (as reported in the FC-13 local data set) to total receipts and total expenditures of PRIs. It may be noted that the all-states' average of central transfers including that of eleventh and twelfth finance commissions to total revenue and total expenditure have increased during the six year period from 2002-03 through 2007-08 and the percentage of transfers in regard to expenditure goes as high as 31.1% in 2007-08 while it was only 19.5% in 2002-03 (See Appendix A). The magnitude and trend of the percentage of central transfers to expenditure shows a disturbing picture in 2007-08 for Andhra Pradesh (51.8%), Assam (87%), Bihar (90.7%), Madhya Pradesh (65%), Orissa (71.6%), Tamil Nadu (39.4%), West Bengal (47.8%) and so on (See Appendix A). What autonomous space can you expect of a state like Bihar where nearly 91% of the expenditure of rural local governments is met by transfers from central government[1]. The second is the poor level of the own revenue and its declining trend and in some cases even zero revenue collection. This indicates the fragile autonomous space of the LGs notably the PRIs. The share of local governments in the total public sector OSR has declined from

3.6% in 2002-03 to 2.8% in 2007-08 (See Table 1). Nearly 90% of the OSR share is accounted for by the ULGs. The most striking aspect is the extremely poor own revenue share of the PRIs in the total own revenue base of the public sector. More over it declined from 0.4% in 2002-03 to 0.3% in 2007-08. That this works out only to a negligible percentage of 0.08% of GDP in 2002-03 and a still lower number of 0.06% in 2007-08 is surely not a promising picture. The declining own revenue and growing expenditure trend indicates a clear dependency syndrome. Fig.1 graphically illustrates this yawning gap, the y-axis represents both the expenditure and own source revenue (OSR) of LGs as percentage of public sector and the x-axis the six year period from 2002-03. While the expenditure share of local governments in the total public sector has improved, the share of own revenue has posted a decline signalling the narrowing of the autonomous space of these institutions. However, it is to be noted that the relative decline in the revenue share of the local governments may also be due to the very buoyant and faster growth of both central and state revenues in recent years vis-à-vis local revenues. The unfortunate part of the fiscal reform processes of the last two decades has been that they are concentrated only at central and state level.

Figure 1
Trend in Local Governments' Share of Public Sector Expenditure and Public Sector OSR

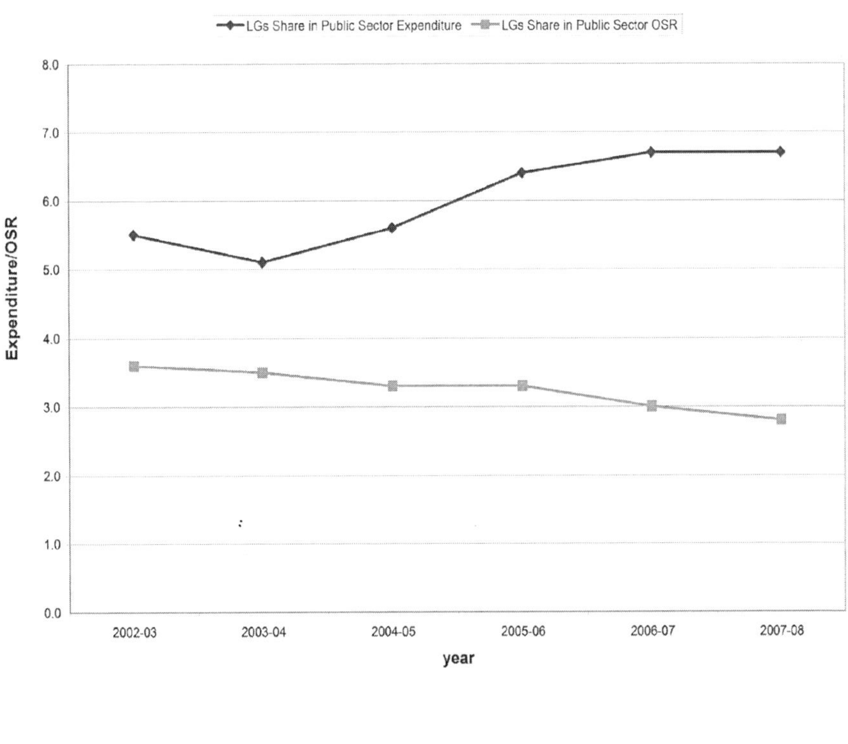

Table 2
Per capita Own Tax, Per capita OSR and Per capita Expenditure of PRIs (in Rs.)

States	2002-03			2003-04			2004-05			2005-06			2006-07			2007-08		
	PCOT	PCOSR	PCEX	PCOT	PCOSR	PCEX	PCOT	PCOSR	PCEX	PCOT	PCOSR	PCEX	PCOT	PCOSR	PCEX	PCOT	PCOSR	PCEX
Andhra Pradesh	20	51	187	22	52	192	25	60	216	28	66	263	31	70	281	33	89	371
Assam	0	4	272	0	4	489	0	4	555	0	4	863	0	6	1257	0	7	866
Bihar	0	0	18	0	0	18	0	0	1	0	0	44	0	1	45	0	1	48
Gujarat	7	22	1342	7	22	1387	14	39	1507	7	27	1718	12	34	2013	26	45	2080
Haryana	3	74	177	1	73	201	5	134	234	4	173	451	4	187	469	4	180	637
Karnataka	19	19	1199	33	33	1335	24	24	1409	36	36	2057	46	46	2391	88	88	2967
Kerala	49	86	351	48	94	600	52	107	674	66	127	760	66	133	820	63	112	874
Madhya Pradesh	5	11	77	6	12	69	7	13	341	7	15	468	3	11	868	3	13	1153
Maharashtra	64	85	1364	106	127	1531	85	109	1687	70	96	1872	73	103	2067	80	114	2268
Orissa	0	3	268	0	3	295	0	3	291	0	3	326	0	3	568	0	3	576
Punjab	2	77	175	2	70	193	11	95	235	11	95	267	12	111	520	8	29	136
Rajasthan	0	3	50	0	3	51	0	4	81	1	3	90	1	4	84	0	3	75
Tamil Nadu	14	65	686	22	55	715	24	65	828	27	70	838	29	78	979	34	74	1229
Uttar Pradesh	1	5	93	1	5	129	1	6	146	1	7	169	1	6	196	1	7	186
West Bengal	2	7	181	3	9	209	2	12	254	3	13	267	4	17	433	0	0	581
All States	**11**	**24**	**356**	**15**	**28**	**406**	**14**	**31**	**466**	**15**	**33**	**564**	**15**	**36**	**692**	**18**	**37**	**779**

PCOT: Per capita Own Tax, PCOSR: Per capita Own source Revenue PCEX: Per capita Expenditure. Source: 13th Finance Commission website
Note: State-wise rural populations as per 2001 census is used for per capita computation. No Projection is made.

Table 2 presents the state-wise distribution of per capita tax, per capita OSR and per capita expenditure of PRIs. I have left out ULGs because in their case the emerging scenario although could be disturbing has a better revenue base and a different story to tell. I think despite the many lapses and possible omissions in the basic data the major findings from table 2 are broadly relevant and reportable. One, all the three variables present an extremely uneven and disturbing scenario. In 2002-03, four states report no PRI tax revenue (See Table 2). For the others per capita tax ranges from Re. 1, in Uttar Pradesh to Rs. 64 in Maharashtra with an all-states' average of Rs. 11. Assam, Bihar, Orissa and Rajasthan continue to report zero taxing and in 2007-08, the per capita tax for the other states ranges from Re. 1 in Uttar Pradesh to Rs. 88 in Karnataka. Two, the per capita OSR which includes non-tax revenue shows a slightly altered picture with the exception of Bihar. In 2002-03 the per capita OSR of PRIs ranges from Rs. 3 in Orissa and Rajasthan to Rs.86 in Kerala with an all-states average of Rs. 24. In 2007-08 it ranges from Re.1 in Bihar to Rs. 180 in Haryana with an all-states average of Rs. 37. Three, the per capita expenditure trend is certainly encouraging with all-states PRI expenditure increasing at 16.9% per annum. In 2002-03, it ranges from Rs. 18 in Bihar to Rs. 1364 in Maharashtra with an all-states average of Rs. 356 and the minimum- maximum ratio works out to 75.7. There is a steady increase in expenditure in all the states. In 2007-08, the per capita expenditure ranges from Rs. 48 in Bihar to Rs. 2967 in Karnataka with an all-states average of Rs. 779 and a minimum-maximum ratio of 61.8. It appears 73rd Amendment has had no notable impact in Bihar and the situation in Rajasthan, Punjab and Uttar Pradesh no better compared to several other states. This means over 32 crore people or 30% of the population of the country comprising these states report no visible impact as a result of decentralised governance.

Figure 2
Per capita Own Tax, Per capita OSR and Per capita Expenditure of PRIs (All States)

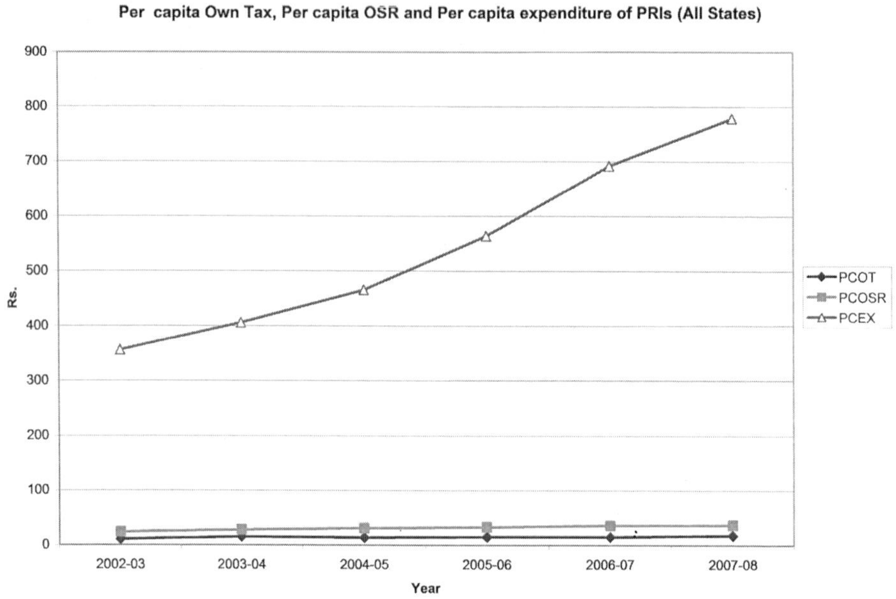

Note: PCOT: Per capita Own Tax, PCOSR: Per capita Own source Revenue PCEX: Per capita Expenditure

Fig. 2 which shows the widening trend in the per capita expenditure of all-states on the one-hand and per capita OSR and per capita tax on the other tells a depressing story. The magnitude of PRIs expenditure in absolute terms has increased and as a percentage of GDP from 1.17% to 1.36% in 2006-07 although slightly declined to 1.33% in 2007-08. At the state level in 2007-08, as may be noted from Appendix B, the percentage of PRI expenditure to GSDP ranges from 0.15% in Punjab to 4.34% in Karnataka, with Madhya Pradesh, Assam, Maharashtra and Gujarat falling in the 2.14% to 3.59% range. It is only reasonable to infer that the growing expenditure might have generated a multiplier income effect in those states which have a critical level of per capita expenditure. So long as local public goods and services are almost fully financed by grants from higher governments, it surely creates a fiscal illusion among the local people about the cost of such services and this has to be addressed as a problem. FC-13 failed to examine this problem of fiscal illusion and the possible implications thereof. The union government may do well to appoint a Local Government Taxation Enquiry Commission to examine this phenomenon and make suitable recommendations.

FC - XIII Recommendations and the LGs: A Critique

Unlike its predecessors, FC – 13 upheld the view that local governments should be supported through "a predictable and buoyant source of revenue" substantially higher than in the past (Report, p.174). The strategic recognition "that larger fiscal transfers to the local governments to encourage speedier implementation of the 73rd and 74th Constitutional Amendments regarding the transfer of functions and functionaries in consonance with the subsidiarity principle" to improve the productivity of public expenditure (Report p.26) is a great step forward towards meaningful decentralised governance. Indeed, the most important recommendation of FC-13 is its decision to relate grants to local governments to a share in the divisible pool of the union tax revenue. In the words of the Commission: "Taking into account the demand of local governments that they be allowed to benefit from the buoyancy of central taxes and the Constitutional design of supplementing the resources of panchayats and municipalities through grants-in-aid, we recommend that local governments be transferred a percentage of the divisible pool of taxes (over and above the share of the states), as stipulated by us, after converting this share to grant-in-aid under Article 275". (Report. P.174). In this way the Commission has made LGs an integral part of the public finance of the country. They are now recognized as an entity which is linked to the union tax revenue pool almost like the state governments. Not only that, in absolute amount as well as in relative terms the local government grant recommended by FC-13 could be considered as substantial as is well exemplified in table 3. However, the local governments will be a beneficiary of this recommendations only if this is done based on actual revenues of the central government instead of what has been projected in the FC-13 report. The prospect of central revenues growing at a faster rate appears bright with the introduction of GST and further reforms in direct and indirect taxes and part of that benefit will go to local governments only if the percentage of grants to them is worked out based on the actual revenues. Then the actual devolution as a percentage of GDP may be much higher than what is projected in table 3.

The increase from the twelfth commission's Rs.25,000 crore to Rs.87,519 crore is over 3.5 times. Because the projection of union tax revenue by FC-13 is clearly conservative the estimate may easily go up to Rs.1,00,000 crore. The total demands made by the Ministry of Panchayati Raj, Ministry of Urban Development and the Department of drinking water supply alone add up to a huge sum of Rs.296998 crore[2]. Reckoned in terms of the projected need the grant may be a small amount, but relatively speaking it is substantial. I think the real danger lies elsewhere. In the words of the Commission "We have not imposed any stipulation that state governments maintain their present level of transfers such that FC transfers become an additionality" (Report, p.183). This goes counter to the letter and spirit of Article 280 (3) (bb) and (c) that requires FC transfers 'to augment' the consolidated fund of a state to 'supplement' the resources of panchayats and municipalities. The laggard states can now piggy-back on the FC grants which can have adverse impact on genuine fiscal decentralisation and good local governance.

Table 3
Local Grant Allocation of Different Commissions to LGs

Commission	Total Grant (Rs. In crore)	% to Divisible pool
FC-X (1995-2000)	5,380.93	1.38
FC-XI (2000-2005)	10,000	0.78
FC-XII (2005-2010)	25,000	1.24
FC-XIII (2010-2015)	87,519	2.28*

Source: FC-13 Report, P.151 and 174. *De facto only 1.93%

It is important that FC-13 goes beyond the usual official pontifications to carry the decentralisation process forward. The local grant recommended by FC-13 has two components, a basic component and a performance-based component. The basic grant is equivalent to 1.5% of the previous year's (t_{-1}) divisible tax revenue to be further adjusted when the final accounts are available. All states will have access to this grant for all the five years (2010-15). A small portion of this grant is earmarked to special areas such as those covered by Schedule V and Schedule VI. Sixteen states stand to benefit out of this and the estimated total for the award period works out only to Rs.1357 crore or just 2.3% of the total basic grant. The performance grant, effective from 2011-12, will be 0.5% for 2011-12 and 1% thereafter, upto 2014-15. The availing of the performance grant allocated to each state is subject to fulfilling a 9-point conditionality package. This helps to promote results-based accountability. All of them are important and desirable measures to incentivise the states to carry forward and make decentralised governance durable. For example, making the devolution to the various tiers as part of the state budget in separate major and minor heads can prevent needless interference by various departments and ensures greater autonomy and predictability and if the allocations are done for each LG by name as has been the practice followed in Kerala State Budgets (Annexure IV), a major step towards building a stable and autonomous third tier system is taken. Similarly the requirements for a standardized audit system, creation of Ombudsman for local governments, (which *inter-alia* helps LGs to preserve autonomy and prevent needless state intervention and to enforce the rules of decentralisation governance), electronic transfer of central grants to local governments (which indirectly means putting in place a net-working system) in five days of receipts, (not very practicable given the present day red-tapism), legally prescribing the qualifications of SFC members, compulsory levy of property tax (creation of a Property Tax Board at the state level which will assist all ULGs to put in place an independent procedure for assessing property tax which will reduce endemic corruption), ensuring a minimum standard of public services and putting in place a fire hazard prevention mechanism in all municipal corporations are definitely welcome conditionalities. I think a large chunk of the performance grant estimated to be of the order of Rs.29826 crore remaining unutilized by 2015 is a great possibility despite the provisions for redistribution of unused funds among the general and performing local governments. If state governments do not take necessary legal, administrative action everything will remain in cold-storage. This is because you can only lead the horse to the water, however much you try you cannot make it drink unless it chooses to do so. Probably from a minimum of four or five items in the second year (2011-12) to a graduated progression to the final year would have been a more feasible proposition.

Inter se Distribution Criteria : A Critique

Once the size of vertical transfers is fixed, an equally important task of a finance commission is to determine the horizontal share on the basis of relevant criteria. Here the choice of criteria is very crucial. On apriori grounds, I think at least three criteria are basic along with some of the conventional ones. Being a grant for local governments, and that too in an environment where you have to travel miles and miles on the road to functional, financial and administrative autonomy to local governments the first priority is to arrive at a relevant decentralisation index (a wrong choice of the variables of this measure can be misleading as had happened in the case of FC-11). Second comes tax effort. Tax compliance may be treated as a form of citizen's participation. Citizen resistance is much less when it comes to the payment of non-tax revenues such as fees, charges, licenses etc. where some *quid pro quo* is involved. There are states in India where PRIs do not impose any tax (see Table 2). Some states with high local non-tax revenue (eg. Haryana, Punjab, and Himachal Pradesh) have even abolished such major sources of local taxes like property tax and profession tax. Studies have shown that individuals trusting a government particularly a local government have higher tax morale than those who do not trust them. In this background the case for tax effort as a criterion becomes more important. Third, the states and the LGs have a bounden responsibility to utilize fully the grants received. So a grant utilisation index becomes relevant. The procedural formalities and preconditions required for spending the amount by the local governments must be well laid down by the state governments concerned. Hence the accountability of both the state and local governments is at stake. Among the conventional criteria population and area are relevant candidates. Population (could include vulnerable categories like SC/ST separately) and area could be included as surrogates for need, but surely with a relatively lower weightage. Table 4 gives the criteria and weights assigned to LG grants by FC-13.

Table 4
Criteria and Weights Allotted for Grants to LGs

Criterion	Weights allotted %	
	PRIs	ULBs
Population	50	50
Area	10	10
Distance from highest per capita sectoral income	10	20
Index of devolution	15	15
SC/ST proportion in population	10	--
FC LG grants utilization Index	5	5
Total	**100**	**100**

Source: FC-XIII Report, p.177

It is clear from table 4 that population is accorded the highest weightage (50%) by FC-13. If we include SC/ST population, the aggregate weight to population in the case of PRIs rises to 60%. FC-13 gives only a smaller weightage of 15% to the index of devolution and a still smaller weightage of 5% to the FC grant utilisation index. As I have already noted given the context of an extremely poor and uneven progress in implementing the 73rd/74th Constitutional Amendments, a larger weightage to the devolution /decentralisation index is definitely justifiable. It is important to recall that in the criteria and weights used in the sharing of union tax revenue, FC-13 has given only a low weightage of 25% to population as against a weightage of 47.5% to fiscal capacity distance and another 17.5% to fiscal discipline making a total weight of 65% for fiscally relevant criteria (See Report, Table 8.1 p.122). The logic of these criteria and the weights assigned are legitimate in India's fiscal federalism that avowedly seeks to reduce fiscal disparities and promote fiscal efficiency. However this type of needed emphasis is not seen when it comes to the local grants and the weights allotted to the devolution index (ideally it should have been a decentralisation index) to LGs. Not only that FC-13 gave a lower weight to the devolution index, the components chosen by them to build the index also leave many things to be desired. In the devolution index relating to PRIs, Karnataka tops the list of allocations with a 20.93% share followed by Maharashtra, Andhra Pradesh and Uttar Pradesh. Karnataka however has made only schematic transfers (which is the enemy of genuine decentralisation) and that too only to district panchayats while only a fixed amount of Rs. 5 lakhs being allotted to each gram panchayat. On the other hand, Kerala which has devolved untied grants (this admittedly is a strong indicator of decentralisation) to LGs on the basis of a transparent formula with 70% of PRI grants allotted to gram panchayats which are at the cutting edge level, and has already implemented most of the recommended performance-based grant conditionalities and so on gets only a low rank and therefore a lower share.

FC-13 has dispensed with tax/revenue effort criterion in regard to local grants, on the plea that credible data are not available. FC-11 and FC-12 used revenue effort as a criterion based on the local fiscal data they have collected. This Commission had six years data and they could have obtained better outcomes by using tax/revenue effort. FC-13 criteria are really unfair. For example the horizontal formula with 50% weight for population and 10% weight for area shifts the scale in favour of Uttar Pradesh, Bihar and so on as against states like Kerala which has imposed five taxes and has a very high per capita tax revenue (See Table 2). The population weight including SC/ST population (here using 2001 Census) and area for Uttar Pradesh works out to 39.83% and Bihar 19.07% as against 5.67% for Kerala. These are not strictly relevant for gauging devolution or decentralisation. A wrong choice of criteria can lead to very unfair.

What then are some of the best candidates one would propose for a rational and equitable horizontal distribution of local grants to states? Besides some of the criteria which we have already discussed the following also seem to be relevant as they are important measures of decentralised governance. They could be considered among the possible parameters of any valid decentralisation index:

1. untied investible funds devolved as a percentage of state expenditure
2. OSR of LGs as a percentage of the state's own revenue
3. The number of employees under LGs as a percentage of state employees
4. percentage of PRI expenditure as proportion of SDP and
5. Progress in building online data base.

All Union Finance Commissions in recent times including FC-10, FC-11, FC-12 and FC-13 have a common mandate given in their Terms of Reference (ToR) namely that "they shall adopt the population figures of 1971 in *all* cases where population is regarded as a factor for determination of devolution of taxes and duties and grants-in-aid". The failure to follow the 1971 population affects states that have implemented the population policy of the Government of India. For example, Kerala's decadal growth rate was 0.91% per annum during 1991-2001. The current total fertility rate is 1.6 way below the replacement rate. Kerala's population share in India's total population in 1971 was 3.93%, whereas in 2001, it is only 3.18%. Use of 2001 Census can also affect adversely states like Tamil Nadu as well which have followed a family planning policy.

Some General Observations

FC-13 report says: "the quality of SFC reports continues to be patchy"; but the Commission is silent on where and how they continue to be so. Actually the Commission is only reiterating the sweeping and general comments against SFCs made by the two earlier Commissions. Presumably FC-13 could have contributed substantially had they critically studied the state sub-state level transfer arrangements recommended by the SFCs of the past or at least the third generation set and pointed out where exactly each SFC has failed in honouring its constitutional and historical responsibilities. That way it could have contributed more substantially in drawing up a better road map towards what the commission calls "accelerated decentralised governance".

However two significant recommendations of FC-13 require special mention. One is the template prepared by the Commission with the help of an expert committee to help future SFCs in preparing their reports. Although no SFC with a mind of its own will mechanically follow the template, this indeed is a great step towards streamlining SFC reports in the future. The other refers to the recommendation to amend Article 280 (3) (bb) and (c) of the Constitution such that the words 'on the basis of the recommendation of the Finance commission of the State' are changed to 'after taking into consideration the recommendations of the Finance Commission of the State.' This recommendation already approved by several expert bodies is far better than the recommendation made by FC-XI to drop the clause "on the basis of the recommendations of the Finance Commission of the State" altogether. That indeed was a retrograde recommendation because it fails to appreciate the spirit of the clause that envisages an organic link in Indian fiscal federalism.

FC-13 rightly points out that parallel agencies and bodies are "emasculating them (local governments) both financially and operationally". Having constitutionally assigned certain functional domain to the LGs, which include "Planning for economic development and social justice" and preparing a draft district development plan, it is for the union and state governments to help this process of decentralised planning and governance with funds, functionaries and technical support. Instead of that what we have witnessed during the last 15 years is a manifold growth of parallel agencies that transgress the functional domains entrusted to LGs and distorting their role in the federal structure of India. A classic case is the Member of Parliament Local Area Development Scheme (MPLADS) and the Member of Legislative Assembly Local Area Development Scheme. No one including the Supreme Court of India which endorsed these activities in a recent judgment seems to have comprehended the distortions that can happen if all the three million LG representatives ask for their 'local area development' shares (which is more legitimate than the MP, MLA cases). This dangerous temptation to follow the higher level counterparts is already underway in several ULGs of the country. Effective coordination and service delivery in areas such as drinking water, sanitation, solid waste management, slum development, housing and the like is rendered difficult because of multiple agencies. Ultimately local democracy suffers grievously.

To conclude, FC-XIII vis-à-vis the third tier despite several sins of commissions and omissions seems to have walked somewhat differently from its predecessors. The website data leads to some interesting inferences. The share of local government expenditure in the total public expenditure and in GDP has increased, while their share in total own source public sector revenue and GDP has disturbingly declined. This story is more revealing when we examine state-wise PRI per capita expenditure and per capita tax.. Future finance commissions may have to address the issue of fiscal illusion in financing local services. That local governments are recognized as an entity entitled to a share in the union tax pool is something to write home about. However it is somewhat untenable that the Commission has not chosen to treat the FC grants to local governments as an additionality "to augment" the consolidated fund of a state "to supplement" the resources of panchayats and municipalities. The criteria chosen for *inter se* distribution of local grant also leave many things to be desired. The third tier has to be made an integral component of India's federal public finance and FCs of the future cannot afford to shirk that responsibility any more.

Appendix A

State-wise Percentage Shares of Central Transfers (Transfers from Central Govt.+Transfers from FC-11/FC-12) to Revenue and Expenditure of PRIs

Sl. No.	State Item	2002-2003	2003-2004	2004-2005	2005-2006	2006-2007	2007-2008
1.	**Andhra Pradesh**						
	% to Total Revenue	25.5	32.2	30.9	34.9	35.3	41.7
	% to Total Expenditure	30.5	43.9	41.8	46.8	42.7	51.8
2.	**Assam**						
	% to Total Revenue	84.2	86.6	88.8	90.5	90.9	89.4
	% to Total Expenditure	81.3	84.6	87.2	88.5	89.4	87.0
3.	**Bihar**						
	% to Total Revenue	77.6	78.3	40.7	98.5	97.0	90.7
	% to Total Expenditure	77.6	78.3	40.7	98.5	97.0	90.7
4.	**Gujarat**						
	% to Total Revenue	4.5	4.4	4.2	6.0	5.7	5.9
	% to Total Expenditure	4.5	4.4	4.4	6.4	6.1	6.3
5.	**Haryana**						
	% to Total Revenue	45.2	43.6	33.4	30.1	31.6	22.6
	% to Total Expenditure	36.7	32.9	32.0	27.2	30.3	21.9
6.	**Karnataka**						
	% to Total Revenue	14.7	14.0	11.4	12.6	16.2	13.9
	% to Total Expenditure	15.6	14.8	12.1	13.3	17.2	14.7
7.	**Kerala**						
	% to Total Revenue	15.9	14.0	14.6	17.5	16.0	16.9
	% to Total Expenditure	28.6	18.5	19.7	24.4	22.8	24.7

Sl. No.	State Item	2002-2003	2003-2004	2004-2005	2005-2006	2006-2007	2007-2008
8.	**Madhya Pradesh**						
	% to Total Revenue	35.3	41.6	68.2	75.8	89.2	89.0
	% to Total Expenditure	29.7	33.4	35.9	46.7	67.4	65.0
9.	**Maharashtra**						
	% to Total Revenue	3.1	3.2	6.7	6.7	9.2	13.1
	% to Total Expenditure	3.3	3.4	6.9	7.1	9.5	13.5
10.	**Orissa**						
	% to Total Revenue	53.3	49.8	57.3	67.4	73.3	71.6
	% to Total Expenditure	53.3	49.8	57.3	67.4	73.3	71.6
11.	**Punjab**						
	% to Total Revenue	4.0	1.8	30.1	0.0	5.6	14.0
	% to Total Expenditure	5.6	1.9	35.6	0.0	7.7	14.8
12.	**Rajasthan**						
	% to Total Revenue	45.2	44.2	63.9	63.1	61.2	44.7
	% to Total Expenditure	45.2	44.2	63.9	63.1	61.2	44.7
13.	**Tamil Nadu**						
	% to Total Revenue	23.0	31.7	37.6	34.9	40.6	39.4
	% to Total Expenditure	23.0	31.7	37.6	34.9	40.6	39.4
14.	**Uttar Pradesh**						
	% to Total Revenue	59.5	61.4	56.6	60.9	36.4	30.9
	% to Total Expenditure	69.0	68.6	62.7	82.1	30.5	32.5
15.	**West Bengal**						
	% to Total Revenue	52.5	49.9	50.7	53.8	50.2	50.8
	% to Total Expenditure	41.3	37.4	40.2	69.8	41.8	47.8
	All States						
	% to Total Revenue	18.5	20.4	23.6	26.7	29.7	30.0
	% to Total Expenditure	19.5	21.2	24.1	28.8	30.7	31.1

Note: For Bihar, Orissa, Rajasthan and Tamil Nadu given data on revenue and expenditure are same. EFC-Eleventh Finance Commission, TFC-Twelfth Finance Commission

Appendix B
State-wise Distribution of PRIs (all tiers) Expenditure as Percentage of GSDP

State	2002-03	2003-04	2004-05	2005-06	2006-07	2007-08
Andhra Pradesh	0.62	0.56	0.57	0.61	0.56	0.63
Assam	1.45	2.40	2.45	3.46	4.53	2.81
Bihar	0.21	0.21	0.01	0.42	0.34	0.31
Gujarat	3.01	2.62	2.53	2.40	2.43	2.15
Haryana	0.37	0.36	0.37	0.64	0.54	0.62
Karnataka	3.46	3.56	3.15	3.90	4.05	4.34
Kerala	0.95	1.47	1.44	1.43	1.33	1.24
Madhya Pradesh	0.39	0.30	1.42	1.78	2.95	3.59
Maharashtra	2.54	2.51	2.44	2.38	2.27	2.14
Orissa	1.69	1.51	1.27	1.30	1.87	1.51
Punjab	0.34	0.34	0.39	0.40	0.69	0.15
Rajasthan	0.25	0.20	0.30	0.30	0.24	0.19
Tamil Nadu	1.151	1.42	1.43	1.25	1.23	1.41
Uttar Pradesh	0.60	0.75	0.77	0.80	0.83	0.71
West Bengal	0.62	0.64	0.70	0.67	0.94	1.09

Note: GSDP data taken from CSO 1999-00 series at current prices.

* *'I wish to acknowledge the computational assistance of D. Shyjan in the preparation of this paper. I also wish to thank Sri. S.M.Vijayanand IAS, for offering some useful comments on an earlier draft of this paper. Published in Economic and Political Weekly, November 2010.*

Endnotes

1 Because the term 'central transfers' is not defined, there can be serious omissions. This definitely includes all direct transfers to local governments by central government and may not include all centrally sponsored schemes by different ministries. Even so, the data are good enough to highlight the poor autonomous space.

2 This is based on the figures reported in chapter 10 of the Report.

CHAPTER 9

Towards Streamlining Panchayat Finance in India: A Study Based on Gram Panchayats in Kerala*

The progress of a well-functioning local democracy in a federal setup depends on sound fiscal decentralization and viable local finance. Of late we witness a distinct swing of the pendulum towards decentralized governance (Crook and Manor, 1998, Heller, 2001; Bardhan, 2002, Shah, 2004 and 2006, World Bank, 2008 and Raghunandan, 2012, among others). This is obviously because of the general failure of all forms of governance from above to respond to the needs of citizens at the local level. It is also widely recognized that participatory governance is not only an intrinsic democratic value but more importantly an instrumental process for ensuring better delivery of services and quality life at the local level [See Putnam (1993, 2000); Cohen and Rogers (1995); Fedozzi (1997); Elster John (ed) (1998); Bardhan (1999); Isaac and Franke (2000); Fung and Wright (ed) (2003); Baiochi et al. (2011); and Oommen (2014); (2015); among others]. For this to happen, a critical variable is to augment own source revenue besides promoting sustainable fiscal decentralization [Ter-Minassian (1997), Bird and Vaillancourt (1999), deMello (2000), Sethi (2004), Devas *et al.* (2008), Oommen (2008), and Bahl *et al.* (2010) among others].

India made history in December 1992 by legislating the 73rd/74th Constitutional Amendments which established local governments as an integral component of the Indian federal polity. Of particular significance is that rural local governments (called panchayats), once an appendage to the rural development department, have been made 'institutions of self-government' mandated to plan "for economic development and social justice" (see Article 243G of the Constitution). Before April 30, 1994 all states in India confirmed the amendments and instituted necessary statutory measures to facilitate a viable devolution process.

In many countries and conspicuously in India, the lack of comparable, consistent and reliable data continues to create serious bottlenecks not only in pursuing analytical studies and policy choices, but equally well in the progress of accountable local democracy. There continues to be a dearth of empirical analysis on the functioning of local governments in developing countries. In large part, this is due to the poor quality and availability of data, without which evaluation of decentralization becomes very difficult. No wonder, there is a woeful lack of literature on panchayat finance in India[1]. The Kerala story analysed in this study can provide powerful insights for similar studies in other states and work towards improved decentralisation and reforms in India[2]. In this paper, we take a hard look at local government finance data in the state of Kerala, with a focus on gram panchayats.[3]

The purpose of the research is to assess the efficiency of public finance in a state that has received considerable domestic and international support for decentralization over the last two decades. In terms of devolution of functions, funds and functionaries, Kerala has outdistanced other states [See (GoI (2006); TISS (2015)]. The most striking salience of decentralized governance in Kerala is the significant transformation in the size and structure of the income and expenditure of local governments (LGs) since the inauguration of the third level of government during 1993-94. The total receipts of local governments which were Rs. 247 crore in 1993-94 or 0.9 per cent of GSDP rose to Rs. 10980 crore or 2.4% of GSDP in 2013-14. The expenditure responsibilities of LGs, notably that of gram panchayats (GPs) have expanded but with very slow corresponding growth in revenue assignments. As such, a system of vertical fiscal imbalance was built into the decentralized governance A system. Through transfers, the local governments accustomed to a few lakhs of rupees in receipts and expenditure before the mid-1990s have now come to transact their finances in crore. It is incumbent on policy-makers to understand the ability of the local governments to carry out effective public sector management as the role of local governments has changed. Unfortunately, useful, comparable fiscal data are hard to come by to perform such an evaluation.

As part of the World Bank supported Kerala Local Government service delivery project (KLGSDP), the Gulati Institute of Finance and Taxation (GIFT) on behalf of the Kerala Government commissioned a study on local finance in 2014. This paper utilizes data from a field analysis conducted in Kerala during 2014-15. The chief objectives of the research are (a) to critically examine the sources and uses of the finances of the gram panchayats of Kerala,

(b) provide an analysis of the fiscal impact of the growth in transfers that has accompanied expanded decentralization in Kerala; in particular, we estimate whether or not the growth in transfers has crowded out "true" local own source revenue, and (c) to bring home the need for evolving a reliable and stable financial reporting system at the local government level with focus on gram panchayats.

The paper proceeds as follows. The next section discusses the methodology, the state of local government data and section two provides detail on the composition of local government revenue in Kerala, while the third section provides the empirical analysis of impacts of expanded transfers on revenue mobilization and effort. The fourth section adds the context of expenditure composition and the final section concludes.

Methodology, Sources and Quality of Data

To date, there is no consistent longitudinal data base of local government finances in Kerala not to speak of other states in India. It is not possible to obtain accurate data for all GPs at this time, so for purposes of this research, we have chosen a sample of 62 gram panchayats (GPs). To select the sample GPs, a multi-stage random sampling method was used. The panchayats were classified into three natural regions, which are basic to Kerala's geography and identified on the basis of the mean sea level height, viz., low-land (below 8 m), mid-land (8 m to 75 m), and high-land (above 75 m). The distribution of GPs in the low-land, mid-land and high-land gram panchayats in the state consists of 264, 487, and 227 respectively. Hence, in order to reflect the true representative character, 17 gram panchayats from low-land, 30 gram panchayats from mid-land and, 15 gram panchayats from high-land were selected applying Circular Systematic Random Sampling Method (See Table 1).

Table 1
Distribution of Gram Panchayats by Land classification

Land classification	Total GPs (as on 2013) (2)	Nos. of Sample GPs (3)	Sample Proportion (3/2)	State Proportion
Low land	264	17	6	2
Mid land	487	30	6	3
High land	227	15	6	1
Total	978	62	6	6

It is difficult to draw any meaningful inference from a single year of data. Data were therefore gathered for ten years from 2004-05 through 2013-14. A team visited some of the sample GPs and it became clear that record keeping and accounting practices were in deep disarray. Before 2011-12, GPs throughout India followed the single entry accounting system. The annual budgets proved to be unreliable and non-comparable data. Cash book, payment register, and receipts register are the basic books of accounting under the system. In the end, to track revenues and expenditures, the Annual Financial Statements (AFS) were used. The AFS is a consolidated receipts and payments statement, which every LG has to submit to the local fund audit. From 2011-12 onwards, Kerala switched to the accrual based double entry system of accounting which was evolved following the recommendations of the eleventh union finance commission. The switch over to the new system before rectifying the mistakes of the old order has led to considerable misclassification and confusion.

In 2009 Kerala established the Information Kerala Mission (IKM) for facilitating e-governance in the state. IKM developed *Saankhya*, an accrual based double entry application for budgeting. Nearly all GPs in the state now use the application for financial management. Due to the changes in systems of accounting without adequate preparation and generally poor record keeping, there are some reservations about the quality of the resulting longitudinal data from the sample GPs; however, it is considered a reasonably accurate data base of local government finance in Kerala. In this paper, we present only percentages and per panchayat and per capita data as they are better indicators of the trend rather than the actual numbers. We turn now to an analysis of receipts for the 62 sample GPs.

Structure and Composition of Receipts

The major sources of receipts of gram panchayats in Kerala are tax and non-tax revenues, general purpose fund, maintenance fund, development fund, state-sponsored scheme funds, centrally-sponsored scheme funds, other grants and contributions, capital receipts and loans and borrowings. Of these, the tax and non-tax revenues are the only own source revenues (OSR) of GPs and may be considered discretionary revenues. The general purpose fund, maintenance fund and development fund are transfers from state government. The general purpose fund is an item of transfers created by the second state finance commission (SFC)[4] in lieu of specific assigned and shared taxes and sundry grants traditionally given to LGs. The Commission estimated it to be around 3.5 per cent of state's own tax revenue to arrive at the amount of transfers. Similarly there is a maintenance fund; fixed at 5.5 per cent of the state's own tax revenue. This has to be distributed for the maintenance of road and non-road assets of LGs. Although the third SFC discontinued the general purpose and maintenance fund, the fourth commission reestablished both.

Development funds are fixed as a share of state plan outlay and a specific share is generally recommended by state finance commissions. The horizontal distribution among LGs is formula based. The fourth SFC has given a new formula with 50 per cent weight to population, 10 per cent to area, 10 per cent to tax effort and 30 per cent to an index of deprivation. The state sponsored scheme (SSS) funds are funds handed over to local governments by the state government to carry out state initiated programmes. These are tied funds and are scheme-specific and could not be counted as devolution[5] or untied transfers. However we know that several state governments treat these fund transfers as devolution which is incorrect. Centrally-sponsored schemes (CSSs) are funds entrusted with local governments for implementing specific schemes which are important ostensibly from a national or all-India perspective. SSSs and CSSs are part of the agency functions of panchayats and could not be treated strictly as part of genuine decentralized or autonomous funds. Amounts coming under *other grants* are a mixed category including joint venture projects of different tiers, beneficiary contribution, voluntary contribution, funds for flood and drought relief, solid waste management, and so on. Capital receipts by way of sale of assets, loans and borrowing are the sources for capital expenditure. All others are treated as revenue receipts and form the source for funding revenue expenditure.

Table 2 presents the per GP trend in the composition of receipts of panchayats from 2004-05 through 2013-14 with corresponding percentages (shown in italics). The average receipt of a gram panchayat which was only Rs.20.37 million in 2004-05 rose to Rs. 66.87 million with a compound growth rate of over 14 per cent. For the state as a whole comprising 978 GPs, a rough estimate of receipts works out to Rs. 19920 million or over 1.8 per cent of gross state domestic product (GSDP) for 2004-05 and Rs. 65400 million for 2013-14 which is 1.4 per cent of the GSDP. To be sure, the expenditure responsibilities of panchayats have tremendously increased although as a share of GSDP there is a fall. While the state expenditure as a percentage of GSDP declined from 16.72 per cent in 2004-05 to 14.31 per cent in 2013-14 registering a decline of 2.41 percentage points the corresponding GP expenditure/GSDP ratio fell only by 0.4 percentage points. The GPs have received substantial devolution.

Table 2
Trend in Per GP Composition of Receipts of Sample Panchayats (2004-05 - 2013-14)

	Particulars	2004-05	2005-06	2006-07	2007-08	2008-09	2009-10	2010-11	2011-12	2012-13	2013-2014	CAGR
Revenue Receipt	Total Tax Revenue	1,298,899	1,294,152	1,509,986	1,683,441	1,647,008	1,996,654	2,399,506	2,764,027	3,169,246	3,433,148	11.40%
		6.38	*5.70*	*6.58*	*6.23*	*5.85*	*6.05*	*5.31*	*5.54*	*4.81*	*5.13*	
	Total Non Tax Revenue	714,884	826,787	824,170	1,205,564	1,196,646	1,447,804	1,925,269	1,476,751	1,616,940	1,537,351	8.88%
		3.51	*3.64*	*3.59*	*4.46*	*4.25*	*4.39*	*4.26*	*2.96*	*2.45*	*2.30*	
	Total Own Source Revenue	2,013,783	2,120,939	2,334,156	2,889,005	2,843,654	3,444,458	4,324,775	4,240,778	4,786,186	4,970,500	10.56%
		9.89	*9.34*	*10.18*	*10.70*	*10.11*	*10.44*	*9.58*	*8.50*	*7.26*	*7.43*	
	General Purpose Fund	1,462,180	1,685,387	2,251,935	2,394,274	2,612,613	2,872,185	3,248,057	4,284,537	5,730,538	6,632,441	18.29%
		7:18	*7.42*	*9.82*	*8.86*	*9.29*	*8.71*	*7.19*	*8.59*	*8.69*	*9.92*	
	Maintenance Fund	2,222,444	2,573,496	2,239,737	2,440,404	2,544,823	1,653,255	1,777,129	3,127,728	6,101,239	8,324,491	15.80%
		10.91	*11.33*	*9.77*	*9.04*	*9.05*	*5.01*	*3.93*	*6.27*	*9.25*	*12.45*	
	Total Development Fund	7,934,769	7,984,455	8,021,701	8,821,145	9,659,532	10,610,390	11,557,926	13,117,373	16,911,533	21,803,134	11.89%
		38.96	*35.15*	*34.98*	*32.66*	*34.34*	*32.16*	*25.59*	*26.28*	*25.65*	*32.60*	
	State Sponsored Scheme Funds	2,390,210	2,872,691	3,244,885	4,314,522	4,591,488	5,622,216	7,079,429	8,693,709	11,851,137	12,651,324	20.34%
		11.74	*12.65*	*14.15*	*15.97*	*16.32*	*17.04*	*15.67*	*17.42*	*17.97*	*18.92*	
	Centrally Sponsored Scheme Funds	1,334,113	1,257,657	1,479,057	2,525,993	3,475,511	4,807,669	7,463,818	10,662,500	15,897,584	6,243,240	18.70%
		6.55	*5.54*	*6.45*	*9.35*	*12.35*	*14.57*	*16.53*	*21.36*	*24.11*	*9.34*	
	Other Grants, Funds and Contributions	1,336,676	2,965,822	1,879,607	1,684,122	913,307	1,605,873	2,170,599	3,357,620	2,586,508	4,518,605	14.49%
		6.56	*13.06*	*8.20*	*6.24*	*3.25*	*4.87*	*4.81*	*6.73*	*3.92*	*6.76*	
Capital Receipt	Capital Receipts (by way of sale of Assets	11,375	48,179	24,546	30,415	20,370	25,353	3,392	4,801	2,262	1,558	-19.82%
		0.06	*0.21*	*0.11*	*0.11*	*0.07*	*0.08*	*0.01*	*0.01*	*0.00*	*0.00*	
	Receipts from Loans and other liabilities	1,661,792	1,206,440	1,459,609	1,909,701	1,471,408	2,349,527	7,541,203	2,417,647	1,902,893	1,725,256	0.42%
		8.16	*5.31*	*6.36*	*7.07*	*5.23*	*7.12*	*16.70*	*4.84*	*2.89*	*2.58*	
	Total Receipts	**20,367,342**	**22,715,066**	**22,935,235**	**27,009,582**	**28,132,706**	**32,990,926**	**45,166,327**	**49,906,694**	**65,931,422**	**66,870,548**	**14.12%**

Note: Figures in italics show the corresponding percentages of each item.

The most striking feature of Table 2 is the increase in the contribution of own source revenue (OSR) in the early period and steady decline since 2010-11. The highest share reported in 2009-10 was 10.44 per cent which when compared to an earlier study in 1993-94 in the pre-Amendment Regime. [Oommen (2004): 125]. Given the exponential expansion in expenditure responsibilities of GPs, a fall in OSR share does not necessarily indicate inefficiency in revenue mobilization. The CAGR (compound annual growth rate) in the relative contribution of OSR declined at a rate of 3.12 per cent largely because of the increase in several other items. The statutory transfers showed a steady decline because of the restrictive recommendations of the third SFC which were implemented from 2005-06 through 2009-10. Since then it picked up following the recommendations of the fourth SFC. It is evident from the table that SSSs registered a spectacular growth of over 20 per cent per annum followed by CSSs with 18 per cent per annum. These are agency functions and the increase in their share from 18 per cent in 2004-05 to over 42 per cent in 2012-13 does not augur well for the future of local democracy and the constitutional goal of creating 'institutions of self-government' at the local level.

Borrowing is only a negligible item and capital receipts by way of sale of assets were insignificant. For financing capital expenditure the village panchayats of Kerala have a great potential for taking loans from institutional sources. In 2010-11, the GPs in general borrowed for housing projects in which the state took the policy initiative, to guarantee the loans besides agreeing to underwrite the interests.

Own Source Revenue

Own Source Revenue (OSR) is the real strength of any sub-national government in a federal polity because it is the basis of its autonomy. OSR comprises both tax and non-tax revenue. Although there are 11 taxes, the major taxes of the GPs are property tax, profession tax, entertainment tax, and advertisement tax. The enabling legislations to impose taxes are passed by the state legislative assembly. The LGs are offered different rate options. Although there are 33 sources of non-tax revenue, fees (such as market fee, license fee, registration fee and building permit fee), rent on land and buildings, receipts from quarry, sand mining and receipts from transferred institutions constitute the major sources of non-tax income. Despite the plethora of non-tax revenue handles, their contribution to OSR does not go beyond 42 per cent as is evident from the data given in Table 2. In 2004-05, the tax – non-tax ratio is 65:35 whereas in 2013-14, it works out to 69:31 which shows the relative increase in the share of taxes in OSR, compared to the non-tax revenue.

Table 3 provides data on the per GP distribution of major taxes. Property and profession taxes are the major taxes. The share of these taxes which in 2004-05 was 95.3 per cent rose to 98.5 per cent in 2010-11 and only marginally declined to 97.9 per cent in 2013-14. Evidently property tax is the major tax and its contribution to total tax revenue ranges from 49.9 per cent in 2008-09 to 59.8 per cent in 2006-07. However while the profession tax expanded at the rate of nearly 14 per cent, property tax increased only at 10.6 per cent per annum.

Given the unprecedented growth in the construction sector[6] in the total value added of income originating in this state, a higher increase in the property tax is to be expected. With the help of IKM, we have collected the plinth area-wise distribution of the households in the 62 GPs (not reported here) for 2013-14. Using the data and the rate of property tax collected by each panchayat we have estimated the tax potential to be Rs. 192.1 million. This estimate is based on the assumption that all the exempted households were correctly identified and all of them fall below the exempted plinth area of 30 sq.m^2. The exempted categories work out to nearly 12 per cent of the total households. As per our study the total property tax collected is only Rs. 116.4 million or 60.5 per cent of the potential. Nearly 40 per cent of the potential is not collected. This could be an underestimate due to the generous assumption made about exemptions. According to the GoI Census 2011, in Kerala, houses with over three rooms comprise 66.5 per cent of the total houses the corresponding all-India percentage is only a little over 27 per cent. Moreover, as per the census data, Kerala with 2.76 per cent of India's population accounts for over 3.4 per cent of households in India. Property tax potential of Kerala is certainly very high. We must also note that no serious rate revision or reform of property tax is done in Kerala since 1993. The elected representatives are reluctant to raise tax rates for fear of offending the electorate. In fact, state actions and public opinion generally militate against hikes in tax rates and user charges while clamouring for central grants.

Table 3
Per GP Distribution of Major Taxes (in Rs.) and Percentages to Total Tax Revenue

Item	2004-05	2005-06	2006-07	2007-08	2008-09	2009-10	2010-11	2011-12	2012-13	2013-2014	CAGR
Property Tax	759136	760207	903223	985705	821982	1122648	1276242	1524204	1742850	1878002	10.59%
	59.40	58.74	59.82	58.55	49.91	56.23	53.19	55.14	54.99	54.70	
Profession Tax	458246	481830	533987	617013	716198	839252	1087547	1165673	1328046	1482379	13.93%
	35.86	37.23	35.36	36.65	43.48	42.03	45.32	42.17	41.90	43.18	
Entertainment Tax	34890	23792	22898	21178	19128	25646	24655	21239	43330	44504	2.74%
	2.73	1.84	1.52	1.26	1.16	1.28	1.03	0.77	1.37	1.30	
Advertisement Tax	1145	651	1998	2192	1361	1995	3820	5924	5591	6639	21.56%
	0.09	0.05	0.13	0.13	0.08	0.10	0.16	0.21	0.18	0.19	
Other Taxes	24532	27673	47880	57352	88340	7112	7241	46987	49429	21624	-1.39%
	1.92	2.14	3.17	3.41	5.36	0.36	0.30	1.70	1.56	0.63	
Total Tax Revenue	1277949	1294152	1509986	1683441	1647008	1996654	2399506	2764027	3169246	3433148	11.61%

Note: Percentages are shown in Italics.

In Kerala, local governments collect the entertainment tax[7], whose contribution to tax revenue ranges from 0.8 per cent in 2010-11 to 2.7 per cent in 2004-05. It is not an important source of revenue and its CAGR (compound annual growth rate) is only 2.74 per cent. The revenue from all other taxes including advertisement tax is negligible although it records a very high growth rate due to the low base. On the basis of the data given in Table 4, we adduce more evidence to show that the tax effort needs significant improvement. The minimum to average tax ratio has increased in the mid-land where the majority of GPs are functioning. A target to increase tax effort of panchayats below average to step up collection up to mean level could be considered in order to augment tax revenue.

Table 4
Mini-max Ratio and Average Per Capita Tax and Minimum to Average Tax Ratio of Sample Gram Panchayats

GP Land Type	Per capita Tax Revenue				Average		Minimum to Average Ratio	
	Min of 2004-05	Max of 2004-05	Min of 2013-14	Max of 2013-14	2004-05	2013-14	2004-05	2013-14
Low land	20.80	71.22	70.67	267.17	40.07	121.38	1.9	1.7
Mid land	32.41	146.33	73.02	265.43	44.15	110.40	1.4	1.5
High land	22.12	94.67	57.41	304.04	55.81	142.79	2.5	2.4

Quite understandably the average per capita tax of the low-land region comprising fisher folk community in 2004-05 was lower than the other regions. But they remarkably improved their position where as the mid-land region (Admittedly a richer region of the state) saw the per capita revenue decline. The high-land region which is the home of plantation crops and tea factories has a higher per capita yield obviously because of profession and property tax. Table 5 shows the per capita distribution of property tax, profession tax and all taxes from 2004-05 through 2013-14. The level of property tax increases from Rs. 27/- per capita in 2004-05 to Rs. 68/- in 2013-14, profession tax from Rs. 16/- to Rs. 54/- and all tax revenue from about Rs. 46/- to Rs. 124/- during the same period. In terms of per capita revenue, the high-land panchayats invariably show a larger level, (see Table 5). What comes out most prominently is that the GPs in the mid-land regions have by and large performed poorly.

Table 5
Region-wise Distribution of Per Capita Tax Revenue (2004-05 -2013-14)

Particulars	Item	2004-05	2005-06	2006-07	2007-08	2008-09	2009-10	2010-11	2011-12	2012-13	2013-2014	CAGR
ALL GPs	Property Tax	27.09	27.18	32.34	35.35	29.53	40.39	45.99	55.02	63.01	68.01	10.77%
	Profession Tax	16.36	17.22	19.12	22.13	25.73	30.20	39.19	42.08	48.01	53.68	14.12%
	Entertainment Tax	1.25	0.85	0.82	0.76	0.69	0.92	0.89	0.77	1.57	1.61	2.91%
	Advertisement Tax	0.04	0.02	0.07	0.08	0.05	0.07	0.14	0.21	0.20	0.24	21.76%
	Other Tax	0.88	0.99	1.71	2.06	3.17	0.26	0.26	1.70	1.79	0.78	-1.23%
	Total Tax Revenue	45.61	46.26	54.07	60.37	59.16	71.84	86.47	99.77	114.58	124.32	11.79%
Low Land GPs	Property Tax	25.05	26.87	31.23	34.82	30.36	40.14	50.40	57.78	63.95	72.17	12.48%
	Profession Tax	13.18	13.91	17.06	19.18	21.33	26.76	31.10	37.39	42.45	46.72	15.10%
	Entertainment Tax	0.39	0.23	0.20	0.13	0.07	0.71	0.74	0.00	1.32	0.66	6.04%
	Advertisement Tax	0.01	0.01	0.03	0.08	0.04	0.04	0.05	0.09	0.27	0.18	44.43%
	Other Tax	0.07	0.09	0.34	0.40	0.40	0.12	0.08	3.99	3.11	0.73	29.48%
	Total Tax Revenue	38.69	41.11	48.86	54.61	52.19	67.77	82.38	99.25	111.10	120.46	13.45%
Mid Land GPs	Property Tax	25.58	26.84	30.61	32.73	26.99	41.70	44.36	53.01	60.00	61.37	10.21%
	Profession Tax	15.14	16.27	18.75	21.32	24.98	28.66	33.67	39.65	44.07	48.84	13.90%
	Entertainment Tax	1.32	0.81	0.89	0.90	1.00	1.17	1.20	1.36	2.30	2.76	8.52%
	Advertisement Tax	0.06	0.01	0.11	0.07	0.03	0.05	0.03	0.15	0.10	0.27	19.22%
	Other Tax	0.50	0.44	0.44	0.72	0.49	0.09	0.10	0.55	1.15	0.62	2.30%
	Total Tax Revenue	42.60	44.37	50.79	55.74	53.49	71.67	79.36	94.72	107.61	113.86	11.54%
High Land GPs	Property Tax	31.83	28.14	36.66	40.78	33.46	38.25	44.52	56.01	67.94	76.71	10.27%
	Profession Tax	21.67	22.28	21.93	26.67	31.71	36.73	58.36	51.83	61.79	70.90	14.08%
	Entertainment Tax	1.96	1.55	1.33	1.14	0.75	0.69	0.45	0.43	0.39	0.34	-17.62%
	Advertisement Tax	0.05	0.06	0.03	0.10	0.09	0.14	0.44	0.46	0.34	0.24	19.37%
	Other Tax	2.33	2.87	5.42	6.21	11.04	0.72	0.77	1.49	1.62	1.18	-7.31%
	Total Tax Revenue	57.84	54.90	65.38	74.91	77.05	76.54	104.54	110.21	132.08	149.37	11.12%

Non-Tax Revenue

Prima facie, in an expanding economy like Kerala, largely driven by the service sector, non-tax revenues should increase substantially with the economy. Table 6 shows that non-tax revenue per GP increased from Rs.0.703 million in 2004-05 to Rs.1.925 million in 2010-11 and declined to Rs.1.537 million in 2013-14 with a compound growth rate of a little over 9 per cent per annum. The CAGR of non-tax revenue is lower than the corresponding increase in taxes.

This is particularly striking when it comes to property tax. While the CAGR of property tax of Low-land region, clearly a poor region, is as high a 12.48 per cent that of mid-land is only 10.21 per cent. The relatively rich mid-land region performs poorly when compared to the low-land panchayats comprising mostly fisher folk. Comparatively speaking the high-land panchayats have a relatively good record of tax effort because "it is worth it"—their yield provides enough revenue to be effective in public sector goods provision. But the mini-max ratio of high-land is high because it is the abode of both poor labourers and rich plantation owners. Asking mid-land panchayats to raise their per capita tax to that of the low land panchayat is a desirable target the local administration can demand to augment the total tax revenue.

It is evident from Table 6 that non-tax revenues constitute a diverse and uneven source with considerable year-on-year fluctuations in revenue collection. Receipts from quarrying and sand-mining which has earned a dubious reputation for corruption in its administration has been the single largest source of revenue in 2004-05 accounting for a share of 18.17 per cent.[8] In 2005-06 it rose to 19.17 per cent. Since then it was a steady decline and the overall CAGR works out to a fall of 4.0 per cent per annum. This is largely because of leakage due to corruption[9].

One item which shows a steep fall in collection is the receipts from transferred institutions, which register a large negative CAGR of 37.8 per cent. Several departments such as public health centres, veterinary hospitals and the like which were transferred from the state to gram panchayats did not contribute much by way of user charges. Rent from land and buildings could have been much higher. Several GPs do have land and buildings of their own. The potential of this source has not been fully tapped because the administration often colludes with the rent payers and assign low rent instead of collecting the market price. Such practices lead to fall in revenue.

By and large a tendency to soft pedal on non-tax revenue collection is visible. The high average increases in building permit fee (CAGR 23.45 per cent) and registration fee (19.78 per cent per annum) is indicative of the increasing growth and buoyancy of the economy (see Table 6.). Other things being equal this should lead to increase in non-tax revenue. There is nothing amiss in inferring that non-tax revenue potential is poorly tapped and corruption and leakage is endemic. In the next section, we turn to an empirical analysis of OSR in Kerala as we attempt to identify whether OSR is developing in a way to support decentralized local government in the state.

Explaining OSR in the Gram Panchayats

As has been demonstrated by the data for the sample GPs, there is diversity in the mix of OSR and revenue growth across types of GPs and over time. However, based on the aggregate trends, we cannot determine whether GPs' OSR is related to underlying economics (capacity) or whether it is more idiosyncratic and thus not responding to market and economic forces. It is important to understand the reason for variation in OSR so that, where appropriate, policies may be developed to move the needle forward on OSR generation—an important component of true decentralization. We therefore turn to a simple empirical question: What might explain the variation in OSR per capita?

We estimate an ordinary least squares (OLS) regression of OSR per capita as a function of the following independent variables for GPs. We expect that population size will be positively related to per capita own source revenues because agglomerations of population suggest greater taxable capacity. However, there may be decreasing returns to size. With a larger population, there should be greater levels of economic activity, regional markets that would draw non-resident buyers and sellers to the GP, more commercial dwelling units to tax, and more services financed by user charges up to a point.

There are a handful of additional variables available to address economic activity: per cent of scheduled caste/scheduled tribe (SC/ST)[10] population, per cent of agricultural workers, and the literacy rate. The first two are hypothesized to be negatively related to OSR as they demonstrate a less robust economy and in the case of agricultural workers, less of a tax handle. A high literacy rate suggests a greater taxable capacity and a positive relationship with the level of own source revenue. For 2013, we also obtained information regarding property by five classifications of size of property. Very small plots and houses are exempt from property tax, so we include a variable measuring the per cent of taxable property as a share of total property as another measure of capacity. The results are reported in Table 7 as a panel (2004-2013) and for 2013.

Table 6
Per GP Distribution of Non-tax Revenue by Sources

Particulars	2004-05	2005-06	2006-07	2007-08	2008-09	2009-10	2010-11	2011-12	2012-13	2013-2014	CAGR
Market Fee	30225	29587	42300	26044	28015	34857	68675	58039	48045	66531	9.16%
Market Fee as % to Total NTR	4.30	3.58	5.13	2.16	2.34	2.41	3.57	3.93	3.00	4.33	
Licence Fee	39176	42701	51054	93964	75246	81851	101455	110879	88218	101719	11.18%
Licence Fee as % to TotalNTR	5.57	5.16	6.19	7.79	6.29	5.65	5.27	7.51	5.51	6.62	
Registration Fee	6029	9549	6241	9222	12723	17396	40909	43012	42862	30607	19.78%
Registration Fee as % to Total NTR	0.86	1.15	0.76	0.76	1.06	1.20	2.12	2.91	2.68	1.99	
Permit Fee	19507	33478	40955	126221	173607	192019	354548	106916	106095	129908	23.45%
Permit Fee as % to Total NTR	2.77	4.05	4.97	10.47	14.51	13.26	18.42	7.24	6.63	8.45	
Rent on Land and Buildings	90328	129874	112520	134752	138293	149917	172063	205029	293423	320906	15.13%
Rent on Land and Buildings as % to Total NTR	12.84	15.71	13.65	11.18	11.56	10.35	8.94	13.88	18.34	20.87	
Interest receipts	57916	50649	44778	104876	57865	77766	164573	133120	121376	119726	8.40%
Interest receiptsas % to Total NTR	8.23	6.13	5.43	8.70	4.84	5.37	8.55	9.01	7.59	7.79	
Penalties and Fines	71177	58170	45574	65174	55991	60956	88809	101466	109210	147139	8.40%
Penalties and Finesas % to Total NTR	10.12	7.04	5.53	5.41	4.68	4.21	4.61	6.87	6.83	9.57	
* Receipts from Transferred Insti-tutions	78268	140997	136164	202658	200074	365263	384825	209238	36733	1093	-37.79%
Receipts from Transferred Institutions as % to Total NTR	11.13	17.05	16.52	16.81	16.72	25.23	19.99	14.17	2.30	0.07	
Receipts from Quarry, Sand etc	127819	144171	160489	152222	208120	191900	149349	162507	149586	88540	-4.00%
Receipts from Quarry, Sand etc as % to Total NTR	18.17	17.44	19.47	12.63	17.39	13.25	7.76	11.00	9.35	5.76	
Other Non Tax Receipts	182908	187611	184097	290431	246711	275879	400064	346546	604182	531182	12.58%
Other Non Tax Receipts as % to Total NTR	26.01	22.69	22.34	24.09	20.62	19.06	20.78	23.47	37.77	34.55	
Total Non Tax Revenue	703354	826787	824170	1205564	1196646	1447804	1925269	1476751	1599730	1537351	9.08%

Table 7
Determinants of Own Source Revenue Per Capita

Variable	2004-2013	2013
Population	0.0009 (0.0008)	0.001 (.001)
Proportion SC/ST population	1.14 (0.97)	2.46* (1.43)
Proportion Agricultural workers	-0.83 (1.54)	-0.13 (3.18)
Proportion literate population	0.51 (2.80)	-1.10 (4.19)
Year	12.88** (0.52)	
Per cent of property taxable		509.50** (201.26)
Constant	-25836** (1085)	-221.23 (448.25)
N	620	62
R-sq	0.52 (overall)	0.17

Standard errors in parenthesis, * significant at the 90% level, ** at 95%

In the case of the time-series for GPs, we find no convincing explanation for variation in OSR other than the time trend for the 2004-13 series but we do find that the per cent of taxable property is correlated strongly with OSR per capita in our one-year cross-section, as might be expected.[11] This result suggests that a portion of the GPs tax capacity is being realized in terms of actual revenue. The lack of significance of other "capacity" measures is somewhat disheartening and different from findings in West Bengal—one of the few empirical studies of GPs (Bahl et al 2008). We also analyzed the regression using log forms with no substantial difference in results.

The focus in Kerala on decentralization has been accompanied by various grant programmes. One hypothesis regarding the variation in OSR is that it is directly affected by the level of per capita grants. If grants were incentivizing, we might see higher OSR in places where grants have been larger. Whether or not grants stimulate revenue mobilization or serve to crowd out local motivation is an important question that we investigate by way of regression. Table 8 reports the raw data on the set of taxes, OSR (which includes non-tax revenue) and all grants received for ten years from 2004-05 for GPs included in the sample.

Table 8
Grants Vs Revenue effort: The Raw Data (GPs)

Year	**Tax Revenue**			OSR			Total Transfers		
	All GPs	Per GP	Per Capita	All GPs	per GP	per capita	All GPs	Per GP	Per Capita
2004-05	79232843	1277949	46	122840761	1981303	71	1017503912	16411353	586
2005-06	80237416	1294152	46	131498188	2120939	76	1199049507	19339508	691
2006-07	93619121	1509986	54	144717675	2334156	84	1185249270	19116924	684
2007-08	104373335	1683441	60	179118320	2889005	104	1375188522	22180460	795
2008-09	102114507	1647008	59	176306566	2843654	102	1475430939	23797273	855
2009-10	123792545	1996654	72	213556380	3444458	124	1684638503	27171589	978
2010-11	148769343	2399506	86	268136041	4324775	156	2064411316	33296957	1200
2011-12	171369658	2764027	100	262928215	4240778	153	2681095025	43243468	1561
2012-13	196493223	3169246	115	296743512	4786186	173	3662869440	59078539	2136
2013-14	212855204	3433148	124	308170972	4970500	180	3730740589	60173235	2179

*Total Transfers include General Purpose Fund, Maintenance Fund - (Road and Non Road Assets), Total Development Fund, State Sponsored Scheme Funds, Centrally Sponsored Scheme Funds, and Other Grants.

The relationship between own source revenue per capita and grants per capita is estimated using OLS. In addition to grants per capita, a time trend (year) was used to control for general growth in revenue, SC/ST population, the per cent of agricultural workers, and the per cent of property that is taxable are included as proxies of income (capacity), and total population is included as a control for economies of scale in revenue and expenditure.

The results of this estimation are presented in Table 9. It is interesting to note that across GPs over the entire period, grants do not appear to crowd out local revenue mobilization as the sign of the coefficient on log per capita grants is positive and significant. This is evidence that grants are stimulating to revenue mobilization in GPs. The only other robust result is the log of the proportion of property that is taxable, which is positively correlated with own revenues per capita. This is consistent with the hypothesis that more advantaged such as those more urbanized or richer GPs would generate more own revenue per capita among GPs. These results suggest that the grants are not squelching the revenue mobilization of the GPs—a result that is good for the GPs in terms of developing some level of autonomy.

Table 9
Determinants of Own Source Revenues including Per capita Grants (all variables in log except year)

Variable	2004-2013	2013
Population	0.17 (0.18)	0.22 (0.18)
Log Proportion SC/ST population	0.092 (0.94)	0.18 (0.10)
Log Proportion Agricultural workers	-0.102 (0.08)	-0.083 (0.082)
Log Proportion literate population	0.130 (1.49)	-0.92 (1.49)
Log per capita grants	0.22** (0.04)	0.574** (0.25)
Per cent of property taxable		2.63** (0.82)
Year	0.76** (0.01)	
Constant	-156.7** (15.92)	2.77 (8.07)
N	619	62
R-sq	0.13 (overall)	0.27

Standard errors in parenthesis, * significant at the 90% level, ** at 95%

A Brief Expenditure Analysis

A picture of GP finances in Kerala would not be complete without a review of expenditures. The expenditure classification into seven broad categories given in Table 10 is functional. Establishment and administrative expenses, funds for development activities, core function (27 functions defined as obligatory by the Kerala Panchayat Act, 1994) and welfare activities constitute the major items of expenditure. The closing balance figures are available only from 2011-12.

Table 10 gives the percentage distribution by major expenditure categories. Figure 1 presents a region-wise graphical presentation of per GP expenditure. Table 10 helps to show how much money is spent on establishment and administration, on core or mandatory functions, on welfare activities, on development and so on. Expenditures on welfare activities include education, sports, youth affairs, culture, housing, welfare of SC/ST and other backward communities, social security and welfare, Kudumbashree and the like. This may include some of the items that fall under core functions and may sometimes exaggerate the expenditure numbers.

It is clear from Table 10 that welfare activities account for the lion's share of the total expenditure. The funds spent on this item increases from 36.1 per cent of the total in 2004-05 to 51.35 per cent in 2009-2010 although it falls to 46.95 per cent in 2012-13 and to 35.1 per cent in 2013-14. In the low-land areas the share of welfare activities is well above 50 per cent in several years and in 2012-13 crosses over 56.8 per cent. The 27 core functions which are mandatory as per the Panchayati Raj Act 1994 do not occupy a conspicuous place in the scheme of expenditure priorities. It is a matter to be investigated especially in the context of the growing problem of solid waste management in the state. Table 10 shows that development activities occupy only a second position in the application of funds received. Expenditure on development activities includes public works, crop cultivation, animal husbandry and animal health services, fisheries, forestry and wildlife, cooperation, special programmes for rural development, irrigation, small scale industries, non-conventional energy etc. It is a matter for consideration whether development activities should receive greater priority in the planning and project formulation in the decentralized governance and planning process in Kerala in the future or not? Each GP has to reexamine its development strategies.

Table 10
Per GP Distribution of Major Expenditure Categories

Payment Category	2004-05	2005-06	2006-07	2007-08	2008-09	2009-10	2010-11	2011-12	2012-13	2013-14
Establishment Expenses	1377914	1428029	1702739	2039327	2265408	2631271	2887189	4470731	5133133	5935104
	7.79	*7.75*	*8.66*	*8.51*	*8.26*	*8.36*	*6.07*	*8.40*	*6.88*	*7.16*
Administrative Expenses	531725	662216	631053	945623	894780	855299	976824	1086337	941195	1184034
	3.00	*3.60*	*3.21*	*3.95*	*3.26*	*2.72*	*2.05*	*2.04*	*1.26*	*1.43*
Development Activities	5577620	6159263	5571785	6739719	7276883	7097722	9424952	11252584	11271156	20764188
	31.52	*33.45*	*28.35*	*28.14*	*26.54*	*22.55*	*19.80*	*21.15*	*15.11*	*25.07*
Core Function	1328654	1988606	2213267	2059986	2201813	2455293	2849362	3548373	4070322	6273719
	7.51	*10.80*	*11.26*	*8.60*	*8.03*	*7.80*	*5.99*	*6.67*	*5.46*	*7.57*
Welfare Activities	6389283	6344842	7929282	9930019	12365585	16164970	23958300	26190699	35029782	29075792
	36.10	*34.45*	*40.34*	*41.46*	*45.11*	*51.35*	*50.33*	*49.23*	*46.95*	*35.10*
Loans, advances and repayment of loans	714876	170375	62486	346522	362755	108124	4036031	1461603	1408304	2134780
	4.04	*0.93*	*0.32*	*1.45*	*1.32*	*0.34*	*8.48*	*2.75*	*1.89*	*2.58*
Expenditure by way of discharge of liabilities other than loans	1616715	1491417	1415413	1763955	1847096	2006666	3235042	2360635	3628584	2780460
	9.14	*8.10*	*7.20*	*7.36*	*6.74*	*6.37*	*6.80*	*4.44*	*4.86*	*3.36*
Others	159633	170776	128594	126276	200583	162733	232106	301923	485804	948099
	0.90	*0.93*	*0.65*	*0.53*	*0.73*	*0.52*	*0.49*	*0.57*	*0.65*	*1.14*
Closing Balance	0	0	0	0	0	0	0	2531140	12636843	13744153
	-	-	-	-	-	-	-	*4.76*	*16.94*	*16.59*
Total	17696420	18415524	19654618	23951427	27414903	31482079	47599807	53204026	74605122	82840329

Note: Because Kummili Gram Panchayat was established only at the close of the year 2004-05, no data available for the panchayat, so we omit the panchayat in per GP calculation for the year 2004-05. Figures in italics show the percentage of the corresponding payment category.

Figure 1
Per GP Total Expenditure by Region

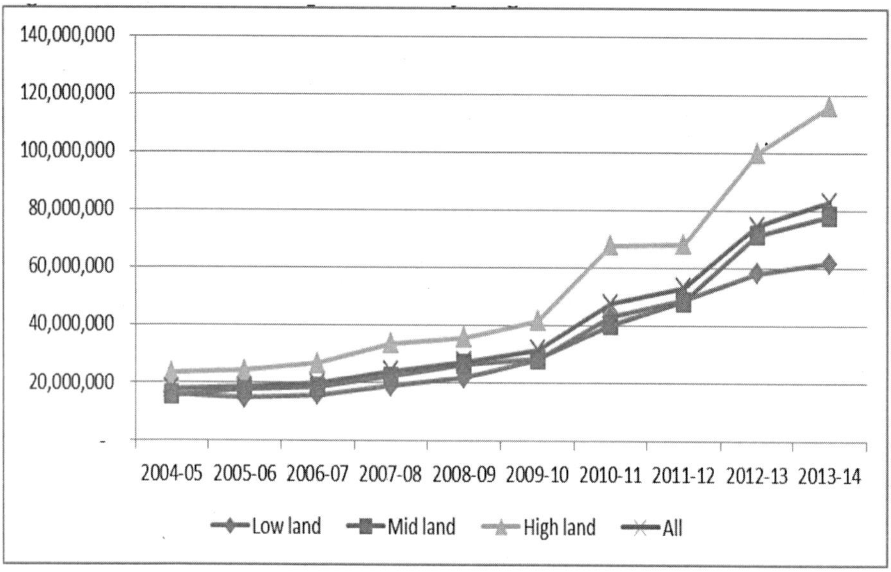

Table 10 shows that establishment and administrative expenses generally do not occupy a very large share in the total expenditure. It ranges from 8.12 per cent in 2010-11 to 12.46 per cent in 2007-08. The establishment expenditure of high-land region is lower than the all-state average in all the years. One major reason for the low establishment cost is because the salaries of all officials of the transferred institutions are paid by the state government directly. The table also shows that loans, advances and discharge of liabilities generally are not important except in certain years.

We can see from Table 10 that the total expenditure per GP increased from Rs.17 million in 2004-05 to Rs.81.99 million with a CAGR of 19.1 per cent per annum. The per GP expenditure is generally higher among the GPs in the high ranges and lower in the mid-land regions. By and large as Figure 1 shows the per GP expenditure of the high-lands is higher than in other regions and has the highest CAGR of 20.9 per cent. The per capita total expenditure in 2004-05 ranges from Rs. 562.8 in the mid-land region to Rs. 755.7 in the high-land areas. In 2013-14 the corresponding range is from Rs. 2305.9 in the low-land region to Rs. 4158.5 in the high-lands. Given the standing rule that LG should maintain a 5 per cent surplus budget and the high underutilization of funds by many GPs, per GP expenditure should be less than per GP receipts. But we find that expenditure exceeds receipts from 2010-11 onwards. This shows that the accounting system and public management should be revisited, scrutinized, and corrected. The lack of a full-fledged financial reporting system is conspicuously visible.

An increasing share of OSR in total expenditure could be taken as an index of the viability of panchayats. Table 11 presents the proportion of per GP OSR to per GP expenditure. For all panchayats the proportion ranges from 6 per cent in 2013-14 to 12 per cent in 2007-08. That the ratio declines in all regions is a disquieting trend. This is an important message of the analysis and while the analysis of OSR provides some evidence of small growth in OSR, overall, the results are weak. It appears that the GPs in Kerala are not making substantial strides in terms of autonomy and therefore we suggest, not making progress in terms of meaningful decentralization.

Summing Up and Conclusion

The progress of a well-functioning local democracy depends on a sound fiscal decentralization framework coupled with a viable financial reporting system. Regular evaluation of decentralization is also important for informing policy adjustments and choices that might need to be made, understanding the impact of incentives including intergovernmental grants, and discovering the experience of decentralization across GPs. This paper provides a detailed analysis of the trends in the village panchayat finance of Kerala and analyzes the growth in OSR and impact of intergovernmental grants on revenue mobilization.

We demonstrate that the GPs have shown a marked increase in expenditure responsibility without commensurate increase in revenue authority and without a demonstrated growth in OSR out of their own capacity. The study shows that reckoned in terms of per GP receipts and expenditure Kerala has demonstrated remarkable progress. If we use the per capita number of a GP to make an estimate for the entire state it works out to Rs.19920 million or 1.8 per cent of GSDP in 2014-15. But in 2013-14 while the absolute number has tremendously increased, as a share of GSDP, the proportion declines to 1.4 per cent of GSDP. It appears gram panchayats do not partake in the general prosperity as years move on due to poor revenue mobilization and resource allocation.

While the level of revenue has grown during the study period (2004-2014) own source revenue as a share of total revenue has declined from 10.7 per cent in 2007-08 to 7.43 per cent in 2013-14. The share of tax revenue in total revenue was also not substantial. This shows a reduction in the autonomous space of GPs. State grants and central government grants have played an expanded role. Presumably agency functions have crowded out the focus on the core functions. Being conditional they affect the autonomy of panchayats and certainly the quality of local democracy. And while we find evidence that grants do not directly crowd out revenue mobilization, mobilization is still at relatively low levels. Property is an important source of OSR variation and, as is the case in many countries, may provide a critical link to the success of decentralization vis-à-vis the property tax.

Property and profession taxes are the major sources of own revenue for GPs. The shares of these taxes in the total tax revenue have remained relatively steady over the past decade with current shares of 54.7 (property tax) and 43.2 (profession tax) respectively. However, an analysis of property tax potential shows a tax effort of only 60.5 per cent (tax collected/potential revenue). Tax revenue mobilization *potential* is certainly high. The non-tax revenue potential is also inadequately tapped. There is certainly great fiscal space for GPs to expand own revenue and thereby improve the quality of services.

Grants to the local governments may enhance or dampen the growth of own revenues. An empirical analysis included in the paper regresses own revenues per capita as a function of grants per capita, year, and income-proxy variables. The results show that grants appear to enhance (and not crowd out) own revenues. It may be hypothesized that this could be due to local governments effectively using grants to stimulate economic activity and/or collection.

Expenditures in GPs are largely concentrated on welfare activities, with development activities being the second largest user of funds. These patterns are similar for all GPs in all the regions in the survey. There are several short-comings associated with the financial data at the local government level in Kerala. A number of activities are underway to increase the reliability and availability of data. In particular, efforts should be expended to create a recent time series of comparable revenue and expenditure data by major heading. These data are needed for analysis and also for general checks and balances as warranted in a democracy.

That opening balance plus receipts must equal payment plus closing balance is a basic tenet of accounting. This should be true for all accounts such as the OSR, maintenance, GPF, SSSs, CSSs and so on. Then only one can ensure a consolidated accounting heralding a reliable financial reporting system. Presumably it is important to introduce a data check and control mechanism to review the data provided by each LG. All financial transactions are consolidated through Annual Financial Statements. But Budgets, although passed by all LGs dutifully before March 31st are not made instruments of financial control and fiscal management among the LGs of Kerala. This is a major deficiency.

Unless and until this is rectified once and for all through systemic reforms, the situation is not going to improve not only for this state but for the country as a whole. It is important to restructure receipts and payments under revenue and capital heads as is followed by the union and state governments in India. Why is it that the Budget and Annual Financial Statement (AFS) stand apart and do not form mutually supportive documents? An effective answer to this can help to solve the major hurdles in local finance and lay the foundations of a sound and corruption free financial reporting system.

* This paper is written jointly with Sally Wallace and Abdu Muwonge, and published in *Economic and Political Weekly*, September 23,2017

- This paper is in part based on data gathered as part of work commissioned under the Kerala Local Government and Service Delivery project by the World Bank. The findings are those of the authors and do not represent the views of the World Bank. We wish to thank Pinaki Chakraborty for helpful comments on an earlier draft.

End Notes

1 Geeta Sethi (ed.) (2004) is an important exception.

2 In Kerala, gram panchayats constitute 85 % of all local governments.

3 In Kerala the gram panchayats constitute 85 per cent of the total local governments.

4 Following the 73rd/74th constitutional amendments, the constitution provides for (Articles 243I and 243Y) the creation of State Finance Commission every five years to rationalize state sub-state fiscal relations.

5 Devolution is an important concept in federal finance and needs to be clearly understood. We use it here as defined by the Task Force on Decentralisation of the Government of India:

"Devolution in the context of the Panchayats, means that when the authority in respect of a specific activity is transferred from the state to the local governments, the latter should have the prerogative of taking decisions in respect of planning and implementation of such activity. In fact functions, funds and functionaries are complementary to one another in the process of devolution of responsibilities and powers upon the Panchayats". GOI (2001): 5.

6 From mid 1970s, Kerala witnessed a regular outmigration to Gulf countries leading to an unprecedented inflow of foreign remittances a sizeable proportion of this inflow having gone to investment in buildings (see Zachariah, K.C. (2002); Zachariah, K.C. and Irudaya, Rajan S (2012); among others).

7 As per the 122nd Constitutional Amendment entertainment tax is subsumed under the goods and services tax (GST) and can turn out to be a potential loss for LGs in India.

8 The local newspapers in the districts where sand mining occurs generally carry stories of the corruption and collusion between revenue collectors and police. The endemic corruption and leakages in revenue collection at the local government level is well documented (Isaac and Franke, 2000, Pillai AVR et al, 2000).

9 Given the growing expansion of construction activities, the demand for materials like sands and stones are high which given the restrictive rules for conservation, the scope for corruption is very high.

10 Scheduled castes refer to the so called low castes popularly called dalits and scheduled tribes refer to adivasis or tribal communities, both listed in separate schedules of the Indian Constitution.

11 Unfortunately, we do not have data for property values over the entire time frame.

References

Baiocchi, Gianpaolo, Patrick Heller, and Marcello K Silva (2011), *Bootstrapping Democracy Transforming Local Governance and Civil Society in Brazil*, Stanford University Press, Stanford, California.

Bahl, Roy, Geeta Sethi and Sally Wallace (2008), The Structure of PRI Finances in West Bengal" (Kolkata: Department of Rural Development, State of West Bengal).

Bahl Roy, Geeta Sethi and Sally Wallace (2010), "Fiscal Decentralization to Rural Local Governments in India: A Case Study of West Bengal State", *Publius,* Vol. 40, No. 2, Non-Metropolitan Policy and Governance (Spring 2010): 312-331.

Bardhan, Pranab (1999), "The State against Society: The great Divide in Indian Social Science Discourse" in Sugara Bose and Ayesha Jalal, (eds) *Nationalisms, Democracy and Development,* Oxford University Press, New York: 184-95.

Bardhan, Pranab (2002), "Decentralization of Governance and Development," *Journal of Economic Perspectives,* Volume 16, Number 4, Fall 2002: 185–205.

Bird, Richard M. and Francois Vaillancourt (eds.) (1999), *Fiscal Decentralisation in Developing Countries,* Cambridge University Press, Cambridge.

Cohen, Joshua and Joel Rogers (1995), *Association and Democracy*; Verso, London, New York.

Crook, C Richard and James Manor (1998), *Democracy and Decentralisation in South Asia and West Africa: Participation, Accountability and Performance,* Cambridge University Press.

De Mello, L R (2000), 'Issues in Fiscal Decentralisation: Ensuring Resources Reach (the Poor at) the Point of Service Delivery', Paper presented at the DFID workshop on Improving Service Delivery in Developing Countries, Eynsham Hall, 24-30, November 2002. Downloaded from http://www.gsdrc.org/docs/open/ds19.pdf.

Devas, Nick, Munawwar Alam, Simon Delay, Roger Oppong Koranteng, Pritha Venkatachalam (2008), *Financing Local Government*, Commonwealth Secretariat Local Government Reform Series, Commonwealth Secretariat, UK.

Elster John (ed) (1998), *Deliberative Democracy,* Cambridge University Press, New York.

Fedozzi Luciano (1997), *Orcamento Participativo: reflexes sobre a experience de Porto Alegre,* Tomo Editorial, Porto Alegre.

Fung, Archon and Erik Olin Wright (2003), *Deepening democracy: Institutional innovations in empowered participatory governance,* Verso, London.

GOI (2001): *Report of the Task Force on Decentralisation of Powers and functions upon Panchayati Raj Institutions*, Krishi Bhavan, New Delhi.

GOI (2006), The State of the Panchayats: A Mid Term Review and Appraisal, Volume 1, Ministry of Panchayati Raj, New Delhi.

Heller, Patrick (2001), 'Moving the State: The Politics of Democratic Decentralization in Kerala, South Africa, and Porto Alegre', *Politics & Society*, Sage Publications, Vol. 29, No. 1: 131-163.

Isaac, Thomas and Richard W Franke (2000), *Local democracy and development,* Left Work Books, New Delhi.

Oommen, M.A. (2004), 'Fiscal Decentralisation in Kerala', in Geeta Sethi (ed); *Fiscal Decentralisation to Rural Local Bodies*, Oxford University Press, New Delhi.

Oommen, M.A. (ed.) (2008), *Fiscal Decentralisation to Local Government in India*, Cambridge Scholars Publishing, New Castle, UK.

Oommen, M.A. (2014), "Deepening Democracy and Local Governance" *Economic and Political Weekly,* Vol. 49, Issue No. 25, 21 June, 2014.

Oommen, M.A. (2015), 'Local government in the Fiscal Space of Indian Federalism: Towards More Rational Arrangements', RULSG Occasional Papers 2015: 2, Research Union on Local Self Governments, Centre for Development Studies, Thiruvananthapuram.

Pillai, A.R.V, N Jayaprakash and Ajith Bhashkaran (2000), *Beneficiary committees: An experiment under people's planning,* Paper presented at the International Seminar on Democratic Decentralisation, Thiruvananthapuram, May 23-27, 2000.

Putnam, Robert D. (1993), *Making Democracy Work, Civic Traditions in Modern Italy,* Princeton University Press, Princeton

Putnam, Robert D. (2000), *Bowling Alone: The Collapse and Revival of American Community,* Simon and Schuster, New York.

Raghunandan, T. R. (2012), *Decentralisation and Local Governments The Indian Experience,* Reading on the Economy, Polity and Society, Orient Blackswan, New Delhi.

Sethi, Geeta (ed.) (2004), *Fiscal Decentralisation to Rural Local Bodies,* Oxford University Press, New Delhi.

Shah, Anwar (2004), 'Fiscal Decentralization in Developing and Transition Economies Progress, Problems, and the Promise', World Bank Policy Research Working Paper 3282

Shah, Anwar (ed.) (2006), *Local Governance In Developing Countries* Public Sector Governance and Accountability Series, The International Bank for Reconstruction and Development / The World Bank, Washington, DC.

Ter-Minassian, Teresa (ed.) (1997), *Fiscal Federalism in Theory and Practice,* International Monetary Fund, Geneva.

Tata Institute of Social Sciences (2015), Devolution Report 2015-16 Where Local Democracy and Devolution in India is heading towards?, Ministry of Panchayat Raj, Government of India.

World Bank (2008), Decentralisation and Local Democracy in the World, A co-publication of the World Bank and United Cities and Local Governments.

Zachariah K C, Kannan K P and Irudaya Rajan S (ed.) (2002), *Kerala's Gulf Connection,* CDS studies on International Labour Migration from Kerala State in India, Centre for Development Studies, Thiruvananthapuram.

Zachariah, K.C. and Irudaya, Rajan S. (2012), *Kerala Migration Survey (2011),* Centre for Development Studies, Thiruvananthapuram.

CHAPTER 10

Local Government Budgets and Local Governance: Towards a Systematic and Rational Financial Reporting System*

"Well! I've often seen a cat without a grin,' thought Alice 'but a grin without a cat! It's the most curious thing i ever saw in my life!"
– Lewis Carroll, *Alice in Wonderland*

The 73rd/74th Constitutional Amendments (CAs) gave constitutional status to local governments (LGs) which were once part of the rural or urban development departments besides providing for quinquennial elections, uniform institutional structures, and regular flow of funds. Within the parameters set by the CAs, the states have been given adequate flexibility to build and promote local governments as a viable component in delivering local development and social justice in the Indian federal polity. While the fiscal federalism literature of the West treats citizens as customers or consumers, the CAs envisage citizens as political entities engaged in the transformation of their area and consider LGs as autonomous institutions responsible, responsive and accountable to the people. The CAs mandate the LGs (as per 243G, 243W and 243ZD) to plan and implement schemes and policies for 'economic development and social justice' besides preparing a draft development plan for each district. Kerala is one state that took the CAs seriously and comprehensively amended the Kerala Panchayat Act, 1994 and Kerala Municipal Act 1994 to devolve funds, functions and functionaries in order to create 'institutions of self-government' on the basis of the recommendations of an expert committee popularly called Sen Committee (1996-98). The state legislature also amended all the important allied legislations to empower and facilitate the LGs to act on their own. To be sure, CAs and the significant reforms taken by Kerala could be considered as important steps towards ushering in a strong local democracy.

Even so, the CAs at best are only necessary conditions, several sufficient conditions are also needed to see local governance at work on a stable and sound footing. An important pre-requisite for any government to function efficiently and transparently is to have a regular financial reporting system. Financial reporting is the process of producing reliable and consistent fiscal data and statements that disclose an organization's financial status to the concerned stakeholders which for local governments consists of elected representatives, administration, civil servants, and the wider local community. No meaningful decision-making or inference can be made be it by the gram sabha/ward sabha, the local government, policy-makers, researchers or by any rational entity without a credible financial data. In this study we proceed on the hypothesis that the budgets of LGs in Kerala do not provide a consistent and reliable fiscal data and economic information that reflect the needs and priorities of the people and do not serve as a source of a reliable and regular financial reporting system. A well-orchestrated, rule-based and fully comparable budget system remains a distant goal. In Kerala the PRIs (Panchayat Raj Institutions) [941 Gram Panchayats, 152 Block Panchayats and 14 District Panchayats] and the ULGs (Urban local Governments comprising 87 municipalities and 6 corporations) function independently of-course subject to guidelines by the Local Self-Government Department. This study is important as it can initiate debates that can contribute to the theory, practice and policies relevant to local budget and budget-making which is virtually an unexplored field.

A Historical Backdrop

Before the two CAs, Kerala's local bodies were governed by the Kerala Panchayat Act, 1960 and the Kerala Municipalities Act, 1960 and the Kerala Municipal Corporation Act 1961. Accounting rules based on cash-based single entry system were framed for the local bodies comprising village panchayats and municipalities based on these Acts. Budget making was a routine affair with no consequence and was not an integral part of finance management. That the receipts of local governments (LGs) in 1993-1994 which was Rs. 237 crore or about 0.9% of the GSDP, rose to Rs. 14925 crore in 2015-16 or 2.61% of GSDP around 63 times increase signals a sea change in public finance and policy. A fiscal management system based on simple account books such as cash book, receipts register and payments register was far too inadequate for the proper and efficient functioning of the new generation LGs. The devolution of functions, funds and functionaries, along with the decision to devolve 35-40% of the state plan outlay to LGs, the introduction of Appendix IV to the state budget from 1997-98 onwards to ensure annual legislative sanction to the transfers to LGs and so on necessitated reforms in accounting and accountability standards and arrangements. The reform initiatives taken up by the Comptroller and Auditor General (CAG) following the recommendations of the Eleventh Finance Commission (FC-11) (2000-2005) was a much-needed and timely reform for Kerala. The FC-11 required the CAG to introduce reforms to facilitate a comparable, computerized accounting and audit system. The CAG prescribed the accrual-based double entry system of accounting for municipalities. It was introduced in selected municipalities using a software and handholding by M/s. A Ferguson Co. in 2007-08 based on an ADB grant support. After the support to the company was withdrawn, the Information Kerala Mission (IKM) stepped in to carry forward the reform process. The Mission designed and implemented what has come to be called Saankya application of accrual-based double entry system of accounting. From 2011-12 onwards it was introduced in all panchayats, municipalities and corporations. We are in the sixth year of the new regime of accounting. The moot question is whether the new accounting system and budget practices have succeeded in delivering a sound financial reporting system based on a viable and running budget system.

Local Budget: Its Functions and Role

In public finance Budget is a financial plan of governance and development besides a major instrument of financial management and financial reporting. Although the term budget as such does not appear in the Indian Constitution, the Central Government (as per Article 112) and the State governments (as per Article 202) are mandated to prepare and submit before parliament and state legislatures an annual financial statement containing estimated receipts and expenditures. Besides setting limits, a budget is the system of expenditure control, resource management and accounting in which all the operations are forecasted and planned in advance to the extent possible and the actual results compared with them. It is the best way to exercise control, find deviations and slippages and facilitate effective utilization of resources, besides revising plans and programmes. It is also a standard practice to present the original budget, revised budget of the current year and the actual account of the previous year as part of the Annual Budget. The fiscal data are made available to all stakeholders which include the general public. The conformity legislations following the CAs generally mandate the Panchayati Raj Institutions (PRIs) and Municipalities/ Corporations in every state including Kerala to prepare a budget (the term is explicitly used) and get it approved before 31st March of every fiscal year. While this exercise is dutifully done not much happens in practice, beyond this. However, it is important to note that all the 1209 Local Governments (LGs) have switched over to an accrual based double entry system of accounting from 1st April, 2011 onwards along with the introduction of a computerized accounting system. The question this study seeks to address is: Are the LG budgets in Kerala credible and operational financial statements on the basis of which financial decisions and actions are done in each local government?

The general accounting practice and fiscal accounting arrangements currently followed in Kerala's local governments consist of (a) preparation of a Budget and (b) preparation of an Annual Financial Statement (AFS). I am not certain why the two practices are religiously worked out and pursued separately. The actuals in a budget must be based on the AFS. The numbers in a state or central budget reflect the real accounts.

Preparation of Budget by the LGs

Budget is a statutory document for the LGs. There are provisions in the Kerala Municipality Act 1994 and the Kerala Panchayat Raj Act 1994 on the preparation of Budget. As per section 286 of the Kerala Municipality Act, the Standing Committee for finance shall prepare a budget estimate of the receipts and expenditure of the Municipality for the next financial year. The budget estimates shall provide for the payment of all instalments of principal and interest for which the Municipality may be liable on account of loans. As per Section 293 of the Kerala Municipality Act, the Budget shall be prepared in the prescribed form and manner, and got approved with modifications as it deems fit. The working balance shown in the budget should not be less than 5% of the current year's estimated receipts excluding the receipts from endowments, Government grants, contributions and debt heads. In particular it is specified that the estimated receipts should be detailed and real and apparent differences, if any, from the actual receipts of the last year should be accompanied by detailed notes and explanations. While incurring expenditure, no amount other than those included in the current budget estimates shall be expended except under unavoidable emergent circumstances. No expenditure, out of the amount granted by the Government for the implementation of any scheme, project or plan entrusted and delegated to the Municipality under this Act shall be incurred for any other purpose including the implementation of any other scheme, project or plan. Section 214 of the Panchayat Raj Act provides for almost similar procedure for the preparation and sanction of Budget of a Panchayat.

A document titled Kerala Municipal Budget Manual contains the procedures to be followed while preparing a budget by the Municipalities/

Corporations. The Municipalities/ Corporations are preparing the Budget following the guidelines of this document for the last couple of years.

As per GO (Rt) No 3291/2016/ LSGD dated 02.12.2016, Government have issued orders approving a document titled "Manual on Finance Management: Budget for Gram Panchayats in Kerala" prepared by KILA under the KLGSDP. All Gram Panchayats, Block Panchayats and District Panchayats are expected to prepare their Budgets for 2017-18 onwards as per this document.

Preparation of Annual Financial Statement (AFS) by the LGs

There are well-defined rules and procedures for the preparation of AFS by a LG As already mentioned in Section1, from 2007 onwards the urban local government and from 2011 onwards the rural local governments have been following the accrual based double entry system of accounting. This supplants the old cash-based single entry system.

Kerala Municipality (Accounts) Rules, 2007: As per GO (P) No.100/07/ LSGD dated 30th March 2007, Government of Kerala had issued **Kerala Municipality (Accounts) Rules, 2007**, which was made applicable to all municipalities in Kerala with effect from 1st April 2007. As per clause 3 the Municipalities shall maintain their books of account on 'Accrual' basis under the double entry system of book-keeping. Accordingly, the municipalities have adopted the Accrual Accounting System, whereby all the financial transactions are expected to be recorded based on accruals, i.e., on occurrence of claims and obligations in respect of incomes or expenditures, assets or liabilities.

Kerala Panchayat Raj (Accounts) Rules, 2011: As per GO (Ms) No.83/11/ LSGD dated 28th March 2011, Government of Kerala had issued Kerala Panchayat Raj (Accounts) Rules, 2011, which was made applicable to all Panchayat Raj Institutions in Kerala with effect from 1st April 2011. As per clause 3 of the Accounts Rules, the Panchayats shall maintain their books of account on accrual basis under the double entry system of book-keeping. As per GO (Rt) No 3291/2016/ LSGD dated 02.12.2016, Government have issued orders approving a document titled "Manual on Finance Management: Budget for Gram Panchayats in Kerala" prepared by KILA under the KLGSDP. All Gram Panchayats, Block Panchayats and District Panchayats re-expected to prepare their Budgets for 2017-18 onwards as per this document.

Kerala Panchayat Raj (Accounts) Manual: Even though Clause 3 (2) of the Kerala Panchayat Raj (Accounts) Rules 2011 stipulates that the Panchayats shall follow the Accounting Policies prescribed in the Kerala Panchayat Raj Accounts Manual, the Government have not so far prescribed separate

Accounts Manual for the Panchayats. The Panchayats are now following the procedures given in Kerala Municipal Accounts Manual for preparing its Accounts.

To complete the story a word about the coding structure is in order. The `Coding Structure' stipulated in Chapter 4 of the Kerala Municipal Accounts Manual applies uniformly to all the Municipalities of Kerala. The coding structure contains the following main groups, viz. (1) Fund, (2) Function, (3) Functionary, (4) Field, and (5) Account Head. In addition, there is a secondary account code for each Account head, and a Municipality code for each municipality. Changes to the codes can be made only as per the Guidelines/ Rules prescribed in this regard.

The coding structure for panchayats slightly differs from that for municipalities. As per Clause 14 of the Kerala Panchayat Raj (Accounts) Rules, the accounting entries shall be recorded using a uniform codification structure consisting of (1) Fund, (2) Function, (3) Functionary, and (4) Account Head. There is no provision at present for capturing data at field (ie ward) level as required for municipalities. Changes to the codes shall be made as per the guidelines/ rules prescribed in this regard.

It is important to underline the fact that as per GO (Ms) No 23/10/ LSGD dated 4th February 2010, the Accounts of all Municipalities in the State have been fully computerized from 1st April 2010, using "Saankhya", which is a dedicated software application developed by Information Kerala Mission (IKM). All accounting processes from preparation of vouchers to preparation of Annual Finance Statements are handled by "Saankhya". In the same manner, as per GO (Ms) No 128/2011/LSGD dated 6th July 2011, the Accounts of all Panchayats in the State also have been fully computerized from 1st April 2011.

Now that the Budget and the AFS stand apart, in order to enable a meaningful comparison between the Budget and the AFS, the following conditions should be fulfilled.

a) Budget document should be prepared in the same format in which the AFS is prepared.
b) The coding structure used for AFS and that for Budget should be the same.
c) The classification of head of account should be same for the Budget and the AFS.
d) The principle of accrual accounting should be strictly followed in preparing the AFS.

In this study we try to examine whether these logical and necessary pre-requisites are followed in practice.

Major Objectives of the Study

The major objectives of the study are:

(i) To empirically investigate whether the LG budget-making in Kerala is the outcome of a due process of law and financial propriety;

(ii) To examine whether budgets provide a set of consistent, comparable and credible fiscal data that will help in efficient decision-making, monitoring and accountability;

(iii) To examine whether the budget, revised budget and annual financial statements submitted for audit purposes and before the panchayat committee/municipal committee are duly integrated and consistent; and

(iv) To make preliminary suggestions/recommendations for evolving a reliable financial reporting system for local governments in Kerala in the light of the findings.

Methodology

This study is largely based on a few case studies supplemented by consultations with experts and focus group discussions with stakeholders. For case studies the corporation of Thiruvananthapuram, the Pallichal and Kalliyoor Gram Panchayats, the Nemom and Pothencode block panchayats and Thiruvananthapuram district panchayat were chosen. We concentrate mostly on the latest budget year / years for which budget actuals are available from the panchayat records. We thought that a large sample is perhaps not required for two reasons. One, as the rules, governing budget-making and accounting do not differ from unit to unit, one can come to reasonable inferences based on case studies. Two, this study is exploratory and is meant to raise and identify issues rather than come up with firm inferences and strong recommendations.

What the Case Studies Reveal?

The Thiruvananthapuram Corporation

We start with the Thiruvananthapuram Corporation with a population of 7.45 lakhs transacting a budget of over Rs.1000 crore per annum. The deputy mayor who is the Chairperson of the Standing Committee on Finance presents the budget prepared by the Committee and gets it duly passed before March 31st every year. The corporation has been following the accrual based double entry system of accounting during the last six years. Headed by a Secretary of the rank of an IAS officer the Corporation has a good administrative support system. With no intention to make any invidious comparison, only the corporation displays some travesty of truth with reference to budget and budget making.

The standard practice in budget presentation is to give the budget estimates (BE) of income and expenditure for the budget year (next financial year), budget estimate for the current year, revised budget estimate (RE) for the current year and the actual for the previous year. Annexure A Table 1 presents a comparison of the budget estimate, revised budget estimate and actuals for the major items of income and expenditure with reference to 2015-16. We also show in Table 1A, a comparison of budget actual with the AFS which logically should be the same. It is evident from the two Tables that the budgetary process and budget system of the corporation leave many things to be desired. Even a 10% slippage one way or the other may be considered on the high side[1]. On the revenue receipt side there is huge overestimates which ranges from over 31% in regard to fees and user charges to 97.86% in regard to income from investments. A near doubling be it above or below is not a prudent or reasonable estimate by any reckoning. By and large there is an unusually high margin of inflated figure in regard to receipts. The only item of receipts that agrees completely with the actual and the revised estimate is the opening balance. It is evident after looking into the budgets of earlier years that the opening balance numbers in the previous revised budgets (RE) and actuals match. In all probability the RE figures are taken from the trial balance of the ledger used in preparing the AFS. It seems the entries in several other items are adjusted to agree with this and this exercise lands the budgetary process in unjustifiable inaccuracies.

It is clear from Annexure A Table 1 that the expenditure items also show high variability and the amplitude certainly more sharper than in regard to receipts. In three items viz., programme expenses, loans, advances, deposits and investments we see gross under-estimate. For example in regard to loans, advances and deposits the actual is 3.72 times higher than the budget estimates. Estimates are wild guesstimates. When we go to disaggregated items there is sharp divergences which do not display any pattern. There is not much amiss in concluding that the budget estimates and actual diverge widely and display no rhyme or reason.

Are the actuals reported in the budget papers represent the true or actual numbers when we compare them with the AFS data? Table 1A compares the budget actuals with the AFS actuals. Normally both should be the same. Although the divergence has been narrowing over the years, the situation in 2015-16 continues to remain inexplicable if not untenable. It is clear from Table 1A that the actuals of revenue receipts in the AFS which is officially accepted for audit purposes is higher than the budget actual by over Rs. 107 crore. This is clearly unacceptable. That the slipshod manner of budget making can go to fictitious extreme is well exemplified in the case of income from investments where the AFS actual diverges from the budget actuals by 10338.83%. There is no pattern on the expenditure side. For example the actuals of administrative and establishment expenses which are pretty well known diverge by big margins the establishment expenses by nearly 431% and administrative expenses by 35.23%. It is not clear why establishment and administrative expenses which are fairly predictable diverge so widely. There is no need to labour the point any further to infer that the budget making follows no systematic procedures leave alone any principles. Under such a regime financial reporting using budget-based numbers becomes a farce and building fiscal data base an illusion.

The Pallichal Gram Panchayat

Pallichal Gram Panchayat in the Nemom block of the Thiruvananthapuram district is a large panchayat with nearly 54 lakh population and has an expenditure of over Rs. 20 crore per annum. Strange as it may appear, the budget for 2015-16 was not available in the usual format, although the revised budget is prepared in this manner. Soft copies are also not available. Many items shown in the revised budget estimates are missing in Budget Estimate and many in Budget Estimate do not appear in the Revised Estimate. This shows the lack of seriousness in the preparation of the budget and certainly the reliability of the data, becomes dubious. This is somewhat surprising given the size and tradition of the panchayat which surprisingly does not have a good office building or even good furniture. Appendix B presents the percentage change with reference to budget actual, from budget estimate and revised budget estimate. Appendix B shows the sharp difference between budget actual and AFS actual. It is easy to establish that the budget document is an indifferent exercise of doubtful consequence.

That the budget actual for 2015-16 (as reported in 2017-18 budget) and the budget estimate as well as the revised BE, diverge very high is evident from Appendix B. The budget estimate of own fund, for which predictable estimates are possible is Rs. 3.13 crore, the revised estimate is Rs. 1.27 crore which is nearly 60% lower and when it comes to actual it is a little over Rs. 1 crore or less than one third of the budget estimates. Mookunnimala the famous quarrying site is located in the panchayat and is a potential source of non-tax revenue. While the estimated non-tax revenue is 2.12 crore, the actual collection was only Rs. 31 lakhs or about 14.7% of the estimate. The real figure could not be culled out due to confusion in the account head and codes. This could be a case of over-estimate or a grave instance of laxity in revenue administration or brazen corruption or combination of all these. The budgeted total income for 2015-16 is Rs. 49.79 crore as against a reported budget actual of Rs. 22.36 crore which is only 45% of the budgeted estimate. Interestingly the real number reported in the AFS is still lower at 20.62 crore. Most budget estimates except capital expenditure are overestimates. Actual capital expenditure for loan repayments for 2015-16 (as reported in the 2017-18 budget) is over four times larger than what was given in the Budget estimate. This is the only item which reportedly shows an underestimate. The amplitude of slippages violates all canons of prudence and accounting principles.

The Kalliyoor Gram Panchayat[2]

This GP is not far away from Pallichal and falls within the Nemom block. Compared with Pallicahl GP, it is slightly smaller in size with a population of over 40,000 but has a budgeted expenditure of the order of Rs. 19 crore. In regard to maintenance of records Kalliyoor is certainly better than Pallichal and could supply a time series data. Appendix C, presents the BE, BE actual and AFS actuals on selected items (difficult to present a regular set as we have done in Appendix A Table 1 and 1A). Even on the basis of the few items it is evident that the budget data and AFS actual vary very widely. Take the tax revenue estimate for 2015-16 (Appendix C) where the collection has to be seen against the demand for revenue. As against an estimated tax revenue of Rs. 92.97 lakh the actual collection as per AFS data was only Rs. 21.14 lakh which means an uncollected balance of Rs. 71.83 lakhs. The famous DCB (Demand, Collection and balance) becomes a fiction. Here you make a mockery of budgeting or what? If you have a very weak tax administration you have to moderate your demand. In short what sanctity can you attach to a budget where the figures diverge six or seven times the actual (see for e.g see other grants, total capital income and closing balance in Appendix C).

For Kalliyoor GP we have more refined accounts for 2017-18. Appendix D gives comparative details of income and expenditure, assets and liabilities as per Budget and as per AFS. This is done using the coding structure followed. We have added a remarks column to explain the difficulties and *lacuna*, in the process of comparison. In some cases suggestions for improvements are also indicated. Appendix D clearly shows that it is very difficult to compare budget numbers with AFS because the heads of account are not always given under the same title. We have taken 26 items from Income and Expenditure account and 16 items relating to Assets and liabilities to illustrate the difficulties in comparing the budget and the relevant AFS accounting. Even where they are comparable the amplitude of variation is very wide. It is also possible to point out that the principles of accrual-based double entry system of accounting are not followed strictly even in the preparation of the AFS, not to speak of budget-making.

The Story of Block and District Panchayat

The panchayats at the intermediate level and at district level with no taxing powers has only a slender own source revenue base which is confined largely to rental income and other non-tax revenue sources which are negligible. Even so, the budget system, and the rules governing them are basically the same. In this section we document only very general findings based on the budget and AFS document of the Nemom block panchayat, the Pothencode block panchayat and the Thiruvananthapuram district panchayat. Given our broad findings that these upper tier panchayats do not consider budget as a serious tool of fiscal management and governance except as a necessary statutory evil we treat them only very briefly. The standard practice of presenting the revised budget of the current year and the actual of the previous year along with the budget estimate for the fiscal year is followed in its breach except in the Thiruvananthapuram District Panchayat.

The budget document of Nemom block which has an estimated expenditure of Rs. 54.8 crore for 2015-16 has a population of over 264000 depends heavily on plan and non-plan grants from state and central governments. The budget paper for 2015-16 shows only estimates. We are told that revised budgets are prepared for individual projects in December and are not part of an integrated budgetary exercise. The actual expenditure forms part of the Annual financial statement and does not appear in the Budget. In order to ascertain whether Nemom was an exception or part of a general pattern we examined the budget documents of Pothencode block Panchayat. In a way it is better in that the Pothencode block panchayat has been presenting a revised BE of the current year along the with the BE of the coming fiscal year in all the years since 2015-16. But in both cases the actual is missing and a meaningful comparison with AFS is rendered difficult. Further even this has no real meaning as could be seen from the abstract given under Appendix E. In a way these presentations have no meaning or purpose.

In short, block panchayats are not following any guidelines and abandon all standard principles of budget preparation. There is no actual in the budget which makes any worthwhile comparison difficult. Estimates are done and presented for meeting statutory requirements.

The Thiruvananthapuram district panchayat with an expenditure of over Rs. 100 crore per annum has a fairly regular system of record keeping. Budgets are duly prepared and statutory formalities are also followed. Even so, all the short comings of budget-making we have outlined holds true in this case as well (See Appendix F). It is instructive to note that for an estimated budget receipt of Rs. 152.54 crore, the reported actual is only Rs. 70.2 crore, less than half, as against the AFS actual of Rs. 97.9 crore.

Major Findings

It is useful at this stage to sum-up the important findings and present the suggestions that follow from this.

i. The sanctity and significance attached to budget preparation, presentation and its use as a tool for monitoring fiscal management research analysis and public scrutiny are notably absent in the case of local government budgeting in Kerala and most probably in other states in the country. Budget is not a serious instrument of financial management in Kerala, and I venture to say that LG budgeting is an exercise in self-deception. Honesty demands that we abandon the exercise or reform it radically to make it functional.
ii. The AFS and Budget stand poles apart. Why should this happen? How can this happen? An integration of both is long overdue.
iii. The budget is prepared manually whereas the AFS is system generated.
iv. True, it is possible to compare receipts and expenditure of Budget and expenditure not in any natural fashion, but with considerable difficulty. The heads of account of various items are not easily comparable as we have illustrated.
v. In budgeting revenue/capital differentiation is very basic. There is no relationship between budget and AFS in regard to capital receipts and capital expenditure and any comparison is virtually impossible.

Some Suggestions

We may briefly mention some suggestions for improving the situation.

i. Two reviews and reexamination are immediately needed. One, review the AFS practice and coding structure to ascertain its adequacy to meet with all the current requirements and suggest modifications in the software. This means instituting a study on the capability of the Saankhya software to meet with all the requirements and improvements needed. If any change in coding structure is required to bring out any additional information or statement it should be carried out. In short a requirement analysis must be made.

1.i.1. Two, review the "Kerala Municipal Budget Manual" and "Manual on Finance Management: Budget for Gram Panchayats in Kerala" and make modifications where necessary. This is immediately needed.

ii. Budget is admittedly a very comprehensive document as well exemplified in the theory and practice of Union and state budgets. Unless and until a budget goes into the details of development, project, reflect the priorities of the people and make it an integral component of accountability mechanism, we consciously create an institution that signify nothing. Every transaction should be linked to the functionary, function and the fund and should match with the AFS. If possible, a module similar to Saankhya software may be got developed to prepare the budget by all the LGs.

iii. The accounts staff in all the LGs should be given intensive training on the present Accounts Manual. They should also be trained on the preparation of Budget when the Budget Manual is ready.

To conclude, the budget-making by LGs is not strictly rule-based and does not seem to follow standard practices. It can never be the basis of a reliable financial reporting system. At any rate one can firmly say that the fiscal data generated in budget documents do not provide a consistent and reliable data for research, analysis and policy not to speak of theory. No meaningful decision-making monitoring and management is possible based on the type or data furnished.

* I have benefited from help received and discussions held with M Ganesan, Consultant, Price Water House Coopers, Dr. Thomas Thoomkuzhy, Gulati Institute of Finance and Taxation and Mr. Gireesh Kumara IAS (Retd). Dr. Mohan Kumar helped in the collection and organization of data from Pallichal GP as well as from the block panchayats. I thank them all. Originally published as occasional paper, 2018 by the Centre for Development Studies, Thiruvananthapuram.

Endnotes

1 That the estimates of union and state government budgets are scrutinized by an estimate committee of Parliament/Assembly is proof of the seriousness attached to making estimates of items of revenues and expenditure.

2 We have chosen another neighborhood GP to see if the budget data set reveals the same pattern as the Pallichal GP.

Appendix A

Table 1: Budget Estimate Revised Budget Estimate and Actuals for the Year 2015-16: A Comparative Account of Selected Items of Thiruvananthapuram Corporation

Sl.No.	*Particulars*	*Budget estimatesfor the year*	*Revised Budget Estimate for 2015-16*	*Actual for2015-2016*	*Percentage Change withBudget Estimate and Actual*	*Percentage Change with Revised Budget Esti-mate and Actual*
	OPENING BALANCE	**1,625,931,975**	**2,725,277,856**	**2,725,277,856**	**67.61**	**0**
	REVENUE RECEIPTS					
1	Tax Receipts	1,440,070,000	1,440,040,000	878,135,012	**-39.02**	**-39.02**
2	Rental Income from Municipal Properties	63,500,000	42,200,000	41,104,899	**-35.27**	**-2.6**
3	Fees and User Charges	206,615,000	259,226,150	142,422,169	**-31.07**	**-45.06**
4	Sales and Hire Charges	16,235,000	24,112,000	8,263,607	**-49.1**	**-65.73**
5	Revenue Grants, Contributions and Compensation	1,635,275,928	1,555,323,303	677,551,058	**-58.57**	**-56.44**
6	Income from investments	1,000,000	700,000	21,450	**-97.86**	**-96.94**
7	Interest from Bank	10,000,000	15,000,000	19,617,633	**96.18**	**30.78**
8	Other Income	623,750,000	674,120,000	23,328,180	**-96.26**	**-96.54**
	TOTAL REVENUE RECEIPTS	**3,996,445,928**	**4,010,721,453**	**1,790,444,008**	**-55.2**	**-55.36**
	CAPITAL RECEIPTS					
9	Grants, Contribution for Specific purpose	5,801,917,000	3,414,175,000	598,329,988	**-89.69**	**-82.48**
10	Secured Loans	625,000,000	607,000,000	17,243,611	**-97.24**	**-97.16**
11	Deposits received	35,000,000	25,000,000	30,342,792	**-13.31**	**21.37**
12	Earmarked Fund			1944903		

13	Other liabilites			142,065,164		
	TOTAL CAPITAL RECEIPTS	**6,461,917,000**	**4,046,175,000**	**789,926,458**	**-87.78**	**-80.48**
	Total Receipts including Opening Balance	**12,084,294,903**	**10,782,174,309**	**5,305,648,322**	**-56.09**	**-50.79**
	REVENUE EXPENDITURE					
15	Establishment Expenses	1,353,054,500	1,473,080,000	703,785,953	**-47.99**	**-52.22**
16	Administrative Expenses	82,230,000	34,014,000	21,595,313	**-73.74**	**-36.51**
17	Operation & Maintenance	1,296,835,000	684,953,000	310,193,638	**-76.08**	**-54.71**
18	Interest and Finance Charges	150,000	150,000	102,127	**-31.92**	**-31.92**
19	Programme Expenses	828,273,125	732,909,303	1,103,180,936	**33.19**	**50.52**
20	Revenue Grants, Contributions	3,700,000	3,845,000	40,310	**-98.91**	**-98.95**
21	Transfer to Reserve Fund	79,928,919	80,214,429	-		
22	Depreciation					
	Total Revenue Expenditure	**3,664,171,544**	**3,009,165,732**	**2,138,898,277**	**-41.63**	**-28.92**
	CAPITAL EXPENDITURE					
22	Fixed Assets	1,039,550,000	543,680,000	342,798,243	**-67.02**	**-36.95**
23	Capital Work in Progress	7,099,947,000	3,298,645,000	55,602,544	**-99.22**	**-98.31**
24	Stock in Hand	600,000	100,000	-		
25	Loans, Advances and Deposits	5,250,000	5,500,000	19,578,375	**272.92**	**255.97**
26	Investments	5,000,000	5,000,000	6,557,291	**31.15**	**31.15**
27	Period Period Items			3,699,391		
28	Pension fund for Contingent staff			180,680,622	-	-
29	Grants & Contribution specific purpose			716,488,792	-	-
30	Other liabilities			325,256,202		
	Total Capital Expenditure	**8,197,567,000**	**3,852,925,000**	**1,650,661,460**	**-79.86**	**-57.16**
	TOTAL EXPENDITURE	**11,841,738,544**	**6,862,090,732**	**3,789,559,737**	**-68**	**-44.78**
	CLOSING BALANCE	**242,556,359**	**3,920,083,577**	**1,516,088,585**		

Table 1A
Comparison of Actuals as Revealed in Budget Documents and AFS (2015-16) of Thiruvananthapuram Corporation

Sl.No	*Head of Account Code*	*Particulars*	*Actuals in Budget Document 2015-2016*	*AFS data 2015-16*	*Difference (Column 4-3)*	% to difference between AFS andbudget Actuals (col 5/3%)
	1	*2*	*3*	*4*	*5*	
		OPENING BALANCE	**2,725,277,856**	**2,725,277,856**	**Nil**	
I	**REVENUE RECEIPTS**					
1	110	Tax Receipts	878,135,012	994,264,458	116,129,446	***13.22***
2	130	Rental Income from Municipal Properties	41,104,899	43,678,678	2,573,779	***6.26***
3	140	Fees and User Charges	142,422,169	146,787,125	4,364,956	***3.06***
4	150	Sales and Hire Charges	8,263,607	9,048,175	784,568	***9.49***
5	160	Revenue Grants, Contributions and Compensation	677,551,058	1,641,569,342	964,018,284	***142.28***
6	170	Income from investments	21,450	2,239,129	2,217,679	***10,338.83***
7	171	Interest from Bank	19,617,633	20,602,576	984,943	***5.02***
8	180	Other Income	23,328,180	439,507.50	-22,888,673	***-98.12***
		Total Revenue Receipts	**1,790,444,008**	**2,861,205,434.53**	1,070,761,427	***59.80***
II	**CAPITAL RECEIPTS**					
9	320	Grants, Contribution for Specific purpose	598,329,988	1643261542	1,044,931,554	***174.64***
10		Secured Loans	17,243,611	0		***0.00***
11	340 &341	Deposits received	30,342,792	24354613	-5,988,179	***-19.74***
12	311	Earmarked Fund	1944903	1944903	Nil	

13	350	Other liabilities	142,065,164	33441636	-108,623,528	*-76.46*
		Total Capital Receipts	**789,926,458**	**1703002694**	913076236	***115.59***
		Total Receipts including OpeningBalance	**5,305,648,322**	4,564,208,128.53		
14	210	Establishment Expenses	703,785,953	951,719,422	247,933,469	***35.23***
15	220	Administrative Expenses	21,595,313	114,631,845	93,036,532	***430.82***
16	230	Operation & Maintenance	310,193,638	376,296,899	66,103,261	***21.31***
17	240	Interest and Finance Charges	102,127	102,127	Nil	
18	250 to 253	Programme Expenses	1,103,180,936	1,037,951,490	-65,229,446	***-5.91***
19	260	Revenue Grants, Contributions	40,310	40,310	Nil	
		Total Revenue Expenditure	**2,138,898,277**	**2,600,181,221**	461,282,944	***21.57***
IV	CAPITAL EXPENDITURE					
21	410	Fixed Assets	342,798,243	342,839,531	41,288	***0.01***
22	412	Capital Work in Progress	55,602,544	55,602,544	Nil	
23	460	Loans, Advances and Deposits	19,578,375	263477	-19,314,898	***-98.65***
24	420 &421	Investments	6,557,291	2,217,679	-4,339,612	***-66.18***
	350	Other liabilities	325,256,202	33441636	-291,814,566	***-89.72***
25	280	Prior period Items	3,699,391	3,699,891	500	***0.01***
	Fund Creation			0		
26	311	Pension fund for Contingent staff	180,680,622	180,680,622	Nil	
29	320	Grants & Contribution specific purpose	716,488,792	716,488,792	Nil	
		Total Capital Expenditure	**1,650,661,460**	**1,335,234,172**	**-315427288**	***-19.11***
		TOTAL EXPENDITURE (III+IV)	**3,789,559,737**	**3935415393**	145855656	***3.85***
		CLOSING BALANCE	**1,516,088,585**	**1,516,088,585**	**NIL**	

Appendix B
Comparison of Budget Estimate, Revised Budget and Actuals of 2015-16 - Pallichal Gram Panchayat

	PARTICULARS	*Budget Estimate 2015-2016*	*Revised Budget 2015-2016*	*Actual 2015-16*	*(Actuals-BE)/BE x 100*	*(Actuals-RE)/REx100*
A	Opening balance (net)	24,319,000.00	19,148,000.00	4,199,876.00	-82.73	-78.07
B	a)Tax revenue	10,142,000.00	7,350,000.00	7,634,358.00	-24.73	3.87
C	b)Non tax revenue	21,216,000.00	5,372,000.00	3,117,499.00	-85.31	-41.97
D	**Total Own Fund**	**31,358,000.00**	**12,722,000.00**	**10,751,857.00**	-65.71	-15.49
E	c)General Purpose Fund	0	13,245,000.00	13,761,187.00	0.00	3.90
F	**Total**		**25,967,000.00**	**24,513,044.00**	0.00	-5.60
G	d)Other Grants (Plan)	0	209,377,000.00	126,379,609.00	0.00	-39.64
H	e)Other Grants (Non-Plan)	0	42,000,000.00	52,141,000.00	0.00	24.15
	Grant in aid and Contributions (E+G+H)	**403,717,000.00**	**264,622,000.00**	**19,22,81,796**	#VALUE!	#VALUE!
I	**Total Revenue Income**		**277,344,000.00**	**203,033,653.00**	0.00	-26.79
J	Capital Income-Loans	12,110,000.00			0.00	0.00
K	Income other than loans *(which includesDepositsand Advances Inter Panchayat Payments)*	23,286,000.00	35,880,000.00	16,404,728.00	-29.55	-54.28
L	**Total Capital Income**	**35,396,000.00**	**35,880,000.00**	**16,404,728.00**	-53.65	-54.28
M	**Total Income**	**470,471,000.00**	**313,224,000.00**	**219,438,381.00**	-53.36	-29.94
N	**Total Income+Net opening balance**	**494,790,000.00**	**332,372,000.00**	**223,638,257.00**	-54.80	-32.71
O	Revenue Expenditure-Statutory functions		35,499,000.00	11,872,354.00	0.00	-66.56
P	Revenue Expenditure-Plan	235,188,000.00	195,720,000.00	94,236,640.00	-59.93	-51.85
Q	Revenue Expenditure-Non-Plan	134,022,000.00	46,255,000.00	52,741,000.00	-60.65	14.02
R	**Total Revenue Expenditure**	**369,210,000.00**	**277,474,000.00**	**158,849,994.00**	-56.98	-42.75
S	Capital Expenditure-Loan repayments	1,210,000.00	2,500,000.00	4,827,300.00	298.95	93.09
T	Capital expenditure other than loan repayments	76,275,000.00	32,150,000.00	46,327,202.00	-39.26	44.10
U	**Total Capital Expenditure**	**77,485,000.00**	**34,650,000.00**	**51,154,502.00**	-33.98	47.63
V	**Total Expenditure**	**446,695,000.00**	**312,124,000.00**	**210,004,496.00**	-52.99	-32.72
W	**Closing Balance**	**48,095,000.00**	**20,248,000.00**	**13,633,761.00**	-71.65	-32.67

Appendix C
Comparison of Budget Estimate and Budget Actuals of 2015-16
Kalliyoor Gram Panchayat

	PARTICULARS	*Budget Estimate* 2015-2016	*Budget Actual* 2015-16	*(Actuals-BE)/ BE x 100*	AFS	**Percentage change with budget estimate and AFS**	**Percentage change with budget actual and AFS**
A	Opening balance (net)	7,914,725.00	12,150,139.00	53.51			
B	a)Tax revenue	9,297,887.00	5,482,767.00	-41.03	2114836	-77.25	-61.43
C	b)Non tax revenue	3,001,000.00	1,153,948.00	-61.55			
D	**Total Own Fund**	**12,298,887.00**	**6,636,715.00**	-46.04			
E	c)General Purpose Fund	108666000	10,866,000.00	-90.00			
F	**Total**	**120,964,887.00**	**17,502,715.00**	-85.53			
G	d)Other Grants (Plan)		62,414,512.00				
H	e)Other Grants (Non-Plan)	1734700	12,958,868.00	647.04			
	Grant-in-aid and Contributions (E+G+H)		**86,239,380.00**				
I	**Total Revenue Income**	**183801587**	**92,876,095.00**	-49.47			
J	Capital Income-Loans	16,800,000.00					
K	Income other than loans *(which includes Deposits and Advances Inter Panchayat Payments)*		37,668,288.00				
L	**Total Capital Income**	**6,272,600.00**	37,668,288.00	500.52			
M	**Total Income**	**190,074,187.00**	**130,544,383.00**	-31.32	127243443	-33.06	-2.53
N	**Total Income+Net opening balance**	**197,988,912.00**	**142,694,522.00**	-27.93			
O	Revenue Expenditure-Statutory functions		12,606,206.00				
P	Establishment Expenses	8238805	7,883,979.00		2754904	-66.56	-65.06
Q	Administrative expenses	2016500	1,209,263.00		1209263	-40.03	0.00
R	Revenue Expenditure-Plan		38,181,432.00				
S	Revenue Expenditure-Non-Plan		1,849,702.00				
T	**Total Revenue Expenditure**	**174,611,508.00**	**52,637,340.00**	-69.85			
U	Capital Expenditure-Loan repayments	3,819,600.00	3,819,600.00	0.00			
V	Capital expenditure other than loan repayments	10,357,804.00	18,171,752.00	75.44			
W	**Total Capital Expenditure**	**14,177,404.00**	**21,991,352.00**	55.12			
X	**Total Expenditure**	**188,788,912.00**	**74,628,692.00**	-60.47	132582457	-29.77	77.66
Y	**ClosingBalance**	**9,200,000.00**	**68,065,830.00**	639.85			

Appendix D
Comparative details of Income, Expenditrue, Assets and Liabilities as per Budet and AFS of Kalliyoor GP (2016-17)

Head of Account	Budget 2016-17 (Rs lakhs)	AFS 2016-17 (Rs lakhs)	Remarks
INCOME			
Property Tax – residential building	22.00	27.15	The codes for Head of account used for Budget and AFS are the same. There is also a function code in the Budget. But no function code is seen in the AFS. It is to be verified whether the AFS is also prepared function wise. It is not certain whether the accrual accounting procedure is followed, where required.
Property Tax – non-residential building	8.00	14.70	
Profession Tax – Institutions	2.00	2.40	
Profession Tax – Employees	30.00	21.09	
Advertisement Tax	1.00	-	
Entertainment Tax	0.15	0.16	
Rental Income	0.25	0.03	-Do-
Fees & user charges	30.01	15.66	The coding structure and codes used for Budget and AFS are the same. However, in the Budget, all the heads of accounts are shown under Non-tax revenue. Hence comparison becomes difficult
Sale & hire charges		0.09	
Receipt from transferred institutions	-	2.00	There is no provision for this head in the Budget. It would be desirable if the Budget contains this head of account with a target of Rs Nil.
Revenue Grants, contributions & subsidies	123.56 425.66 10.35 400.00	1289.76	In the Budget, the amounts are shown under (i) General Purpose Fund, (ii) Various State sponsored schemes (iii) Various non-plan grants and (iv) Centrally Sponsored schemes, respectively. In the AFS all these receipts are shown in different heads under Revenue Grants and contributions, making it difficult to compare budget with actuals.
Housing Loan from Bank	67.20	-	This is a capital receipt and shown in AFS under Capital Receipt

<table>
<tr><th>Head of Account</th><th>Budget 2016-17 (Rs lakhs)</th><th>AFS 2016-17 (Rs lakhs)</th><th>Remarks</th></tr>
<tr><td>Interest Earned</td><td>-</td><td>2.57</td><td>In the Budget, this item is included under Non-tax revenue, whereas in the AFS the same is shown separately making it difficult to make a comparison</td></tr>
<tr><td>Other Income</td><td>-</td><td>0.44</td><td>-Do-</td></tr>
<tr><td>EXPENDITURE</td><td></td><td></td><td></td></tr>
<tr><td>Establishment Expenditure</td><td>131.20</td><td>99.60</td><td>The codes for Head of account used for Budget and AFS are generally the same. Whether the accrual accounting procedure is followed, where required, is also to be checked.
One apparent mistake noticed is that Rs 30.66 lakhs shown as Honorarium to anganwadi workers in the Budget, whereas the same is not included under this head in the AFS. It seems that this kind of expenditure is included in expenditure relating to decentralised plan program. Where exactly this expenditure is booked is not clear from the AFS.</td></tr>
<tr><td>Administrative Expenditure</td><td>17.82</td><td>11.82</td><td>Mistakes of above nature are seen here also</td></tr>
<tr><td>Operation & Maintenance Expenses</td><td rowspan="2">37.84</td><td>32.73</td><td rowspan="2">In the Budget both these heads are shown as Expenditure on Mandatory functions. A sum of Rs 17.35 lakhs is shown in AFS as Interest on loans from Co-operative Banks, but there is no provision for this anywhere in the Budget.</td></tr>
<tr><td>Interest & Finance Charges</td><td>17.95</td></tr>
<tr><td>Decentralised plan program – productive sector</td><td rowspan="6">425.66
10.35
3.56
400.00</td><td>80.93</td><td rowspan="6">In the Budget, the amounts are shown under (i) Non-plan revenue expenditure from state sponsored scheme funds (ii) Non-plan revenue expenditure from other grants, (iii) Plan expenditure on development and maintenance – included in projects and (iv) Plan expenditure on development and maintenance – not included in projects respectively. All these expenditures are shown under different schedules in the AFS as shown here, making it difficult to compare budget with actuals.</td></tr>
<tr><td>Decentralised plan program – Service sector</td><td>555.53</td></tr>
<tr><td>Decentralised plan program – Infrastructure sector</td><td>36.80</td></tr>
<tr><td>Decentralised plan program – Project not included in sector division</td><td>2.73</td></tr>
<tr><td>Expenditure of Transferred Institutions and state sponsored schemes</td><td>432.80</td></tr>
<tr><td>Maintenance Projects</td><td>80.05</td></tr>
</table>

<table>
<tr><th>Head of Account</th><th>Budget 2016-17 (Rs lakhs)</th><th>AFS 2016-17 (Rs lakhs)</th><th>Remarks</th></tr>
<tr><td>Depreciation</td><td></td><td>36.95</td><td>There is no provision in Budget for this expenditure</td></tr>
<tr><td>Prior period items (Net)</td><td></td><td>-19.78</td><td>- Do -</td></tr>
<tr><td>CAPITAL RECEIPTS (LIABILITIES)</td><td></td><td></td><td></td></tr>
<tr><td>Opening Balance</td><td>79.15</td><td></td><td></td></tr>
<tr><td>Surplus of Income over expenditure brought down</td><td>29.85</td><td>148.73</td><td></td></tr>
<tr><td>Panchayat Fund – General Fund</td><td>-</td><td>37.38</td><td></td></tr>
<tr><td>Special Fund/ Sinking Fund</td><td>2.00</td><td>0.37</td><td rowspan="6">In the Budget, the amounts are shown under (i) Liabilities to be discharged (ii) Housing Loan from Banks, (iii) Grants , Funds and contributions for Non-plan expenditure (iv) Centrally sponsored scheme funds and (v) Devolution of funds from State Government for Development and Maintenance (Less transfers to revenue income) respectively. All these expenditures are shown under different schedules in the AFS as shown here, making it difficult to compare budget with actuals.</td></tr>
<tr><td>Reserves</td><td></td><td>651.69</td></tr>
<tr><td>Grants & Contributions for specific purposes (320)</td><td rowspan="4">21.88
67.20
15.35
400.00
500.92</td><td>39.61</td></tr>
<tr><td>Secured Loans from Co-operative Banks (330)</td><td>134.40</td></tr>
<tr><td>Deposits received (340)</td><td>9.98</td></tr>
<tr><td>Sundry creditors (350)</td><td>9.62</td></tr>
<tr><td>CAPITAL EXPENDITURE (ASSETS)</td><td></td><td></td><td></td></tr>
<tr><td>Fixed Assets</td><td rowspan="8">28.80
220.45</td><td>635.19</td><td rowspan="8">The Budget figures represent (i) EMS total housing program (loan repayment) and (ii) Capital expenditure on development plan projects respectively. These figures and the AFS figures are not at all comparable as AFS figures contain opening balances also, whereas the budget contains the actual payment during the year</td></tr>
<tr><td>Capital Work in progress</td><td>21.42</td></tr>
<tr><td>Stock in Hand</td><td>-</td></tr>
<tr><td>Sundry debtors</td><td>48.10</td></tr>
<tr><td>Prepaid expenses (440)</td><td>134.40</td></tr>
<tr><td>Closing Balances (Cash & Bank) 450</td><td>174.67</td></tr>
<tr><td>Loans, Advances & Deposits (460)</td><td>18.01</td></tr>
</table>

Appendix E
Pothencode Block Panchayat – Revised Budget (2015-16)

Items	Closing Balance	Budget Income	Total	Budget Expenditure (till ***31/03/2016*** Expenditure limit)	Balance
Category (A) Fund (General)	1235070	28024000	29259070	29259070	0
Category (A) Fund (SCP)	2603761	14318000	16921761	16921761	0
Category (A) Fund (TSP)	0	93000	93000	93000	0
Maintenance Grant	334888	4081000	4415888	4415888	0
Indira Awass Yojana	0	150000000	150000000	150000000	0
Indira Awass Yojana (IAY)	4487250	37323500	41810750	41810750	0
Stable Income Project	2636	402421	405057	405057	0
Total sanitation Programme	0	4000000	4000000	4000000	0
M.P., M.L.A, Local Development Fund	0	40000000	40000000	40000000	0
General Purpose Grant	631807	3000000	3631807	2905990	725817
Sports, Tourism, Keralatosavam, etc	0	100000	100000	100000	0
Education	0	200000	200000	200000	0
Sales of Forms, Tender, Auction etc.,	0	200000	200000	200000	0
IAY State Fund	0		0	0	0
IWMP	94911	1080000	1174911	1174911	0
Income tax, Sales Tax, Construction Employees welfare fund	0	700000	700000	700000	0
Internal transfers of District Panchayats	0	11004010	11004010	11004010	0
Other Income	0	250000	250000	250000	0
Own Fund	3045625	465000	3510625	1671442	1839183
Total	**12435948**	**295240931**	**307676879**	**305111879**	**2565000**

Source: Budget Document 2016-17, Pothencode Block Panchayat

Appendix F
Budget Actual (2015-16) Vs Budget Estimate of Thiruvananthapuram District Panchayat

Sl. No.	*Particulars*	Budget Estimate 2015-16 (Rs. In thousands)	Actual for 2015- 2016 (Rs. In thousandas)	*Percentage Change with Budget Actual and Budget Estimate 15-16*	AFS 2015-16
	OPENING BALANCE	**55089.53**	**530,449**	**862.89**	
	PANCHAYAT FUND INCOME				
1	Revenue Account -Tax Receipts	0.00	0		
2	Revenue Account-Non Tax revenue	49627.76	53,446	**7.69**	
3	Grants-in -aid, and Contributions	1394935.39	640,426	**-54.09**	
4	Capital Account-Income	0.00	0		
5	Loans and Advances	2500.00	0		
	TOTAL PANCHAYAT FUND	**1447063.16**	**693,872**	-52	
	DEBT HEAD ACCOUNTS INCOME				
6	PF & Others		0		
7	FD & Advances	78406.258	8,518	**-89**	
8	Inter-panchayts remittances		0		
9	**TOTAL DEBT HEAD ACCOUNTS**	**78406.258**	**8,518**	**-89**	
10	**TOTAL INCOME**	**1525469.41**	**702,390**	**-54**	**979913725.00**
11	**Total Receipts including Opening Balance**	**1580558.94**	**1,232,839**	-22	
	EXPENDITURE				
	PANCHAYAT FUND				
12	**Total Revenue Expenditure**	**1,143,872**	**851,101**	-25.59	
13	**Total Capital Expenditure**	**333,764**	**225,541**	-32.42	
14	**Loans and Advances**	**12,075**	**12,316**	2.00	
15	**TOTAL REVENUE EXPENDITURE (I)**	**1,489,711**	**1,088,958**	-26.90	
	DEBT HEAD ACCOUNTS				
16	**FD & Advances**	**57713.929**	**20648.481**	-64.22	
17	**TOTAL DEBT HEAD ACCOUNTS EXPENDITURE**	**57713.929**	**20648.481**	-64.22	
18	**TOTAL EXPENDITURES (I + II)**	**1,547,425**	**1,109,606**	-28.29	
19	**CLOSING BALANCE**	**33,134**	**123232.932**	271.92	
	Total	**1,580,559**	**1,232,839**	-22.00	

CHAPTER 11

Local Governments in the Fiscal Space of Indian Federalism: Towards More Rational Arrangements*

The 73rd/74th Constitutional Amendments (CAs) that gave local governments, notably the Panchayati Raj Institutions (PRIs) a respectable place in Indian federal polity is a watershed in Indian democracy. Although many make romantic references to the panchayats of the past, it was the British administration that brought local governments first into the governance apparatus of the country. Despite Gandhiji's strong preference for local governance and village swaraj, the Indian constitution went for a dual federation comprising only the Union and the States. The 73rd/74th Amendments that ushered in a multi-tiered federal system in India and gave constitutional status to local governments (LGs) and mandated the Union and States to make them 'institutions of self-governments' endowed with the vital task of delivering 'economic development and social justice' at the local level (Article 243G and 243W). The creation of the District Planning Committee (DPC) (Article 243ZD) for facilitating bottom-up district planning and the State Finance Commission (SFC) (243I and 243Y) to rationalize state sub-state level fiscal relations is but complementary institutional arrangements to promote these mandates bestowed on them. The task of making LGs in particular the rural local governments (PRIs) active agents of socio-economic transformation at the local level depends a great deal on the direction and quality of the process of fiscal decentralization. The purpose of this paper is to make out a case for assigning local governments a viable fiscal space in Indian federal system as an integral strategy towards building sustainable local democracy.

Local Governments in India's Fiscal Federalism

It is important to place local governments in India's fiscal federal map from a wider theoretical backdrop and comparative perspective. Before the two CAs, India was a dual federation where LG was a subject under the state list and enjoyed no constitutional status. The Indian federation, sometimes characterized as a case of 'co-operative federalism' is different from similar patterns elsewhere in the world. For example, it is different from that of Germany or South Africa where the federal governments decide major polices and where the different levels of government are at best implementing agencies. It is also different from the Brazilian model where all the three tiers of government enjoy autonomous and equal status and coordinate their policies horizontally and vertically. India cannot also be called the 'marble cake model' of cooperative federalism where the various levels of government have shared and overlapping responsibilities and treated as equal partners. This is because Indian federation has a built-in bias in favour of the Union with great vertical imbalances in the resources and responsibilities at the state level and a local government with an amorphous functional domain and weak fiscal space. The problem is considerably confounded by the multi-layered character of the federation (comprising the three-tier Panchayati Raj Institutions, the municipalities and corporations besides the Union and States) with its multi-tiered public finance and multiple channels of transfer arrangements. The recent dismantling of the Planning Commission which provided investible grants to states can only compound the confusion.

In a federation the responsibilities for economic activities, policy, resource mobilization, transfers and so on are divided among multiple levels of government ostensibly to enhance efficiency and improve the quality of delivery of public services. Functional mapping which tells who should do what in a federal setup ideally is done on the basis of the principle of subsidiarity according to which what can be done best at a particular level should be done at that level and not at a higher level. Local governments will have to provide local public goods like street lighting, drinking water, sanitation, primary health care, primary education, waste management, link road connectivity and the like. Revenue assignments especially the marking of taxation responsibilities viz., who should tax what and where quite often follow convenience for collection besides the demands of equity and efficiency. The Indian federation under the British evolved more in an adhoc manner rather than on any scientific basis, and the Indian constitution spells out a union list, state list and concurrent list (Schedule VII) and after the 73rd/74th CAs two lists were added, one for PRIs (Schedule XI) and the other for urban local governments (Schedule XII)[1]. The subjects given under schedules XI and XII culled mostly from state list or concurrent list where the state and union have joint jurisdiction. Indeed, there is a *prima facie* case for a separate local list which of course calls for an amendment of the Constitution. This is particularly important because the constitution nowhere spells out the tax domain or fiscal space of local governments.

There is a rich body of literature on the structure and working of multi-level governments, referred to as 'fiscal federalism'[2]. Broadly speaking the policy theoretical framework underlying the fiscal federalism literature is in a neo-liberal mode whose efficiency and equity norms have a Pareto optimality basis[3]. But the basic rationale of decentralization in a federal polity is equity. Otherwise what is the basis for coming together and working together of very diverse entities as equal partners to achieve common goals. The Tiebout (1956) model which is one of the very early contributions to the theory of fiscal federalism literature assumes the existence of mobile households that select a residential location/jurisdiction based on their preferences for local public services which in turn is governed by a rational cost-benefit calculus. Admittedly this is irrelevant for India on many grounds. A sizeable proportion of families in India are landless, houseless or those who cannot afford to move around and buy a house in an environment where you have all the basic goods and services to live in reasonable comfort. While, the macro-economic stabilization and redistribution functions are outside the ken of a local government, given the institutional framework comprising gram sabha, ward sabha, Union Finance Commission (UFC), which is organically related to the State Finance Commission (SFC), District Planning Committee (DPC) and so on, the goal of providing every citizen a minimum level of basic local public goods irrespective of his or her choice of residence is certainly a desirable development goal. The decentralization framework envisaged in the fiscal federalism literature emanating from western scholars does not easily fit into this approach. To be sure, it cannot provide the theoretical underpinning or philosophical rationale for the democratic decentralization currently underway in India.

Measuring the fiscal space

The economic significance of LGs in a federal system.is generally measured by two parameters: (1) the share of local government expenditure to total public sector expenditure (the centre, states and local governments), and (2) the share of local governments' own source revenue (OSR) to total public sector OSR. One can also gauge these variables with reference to gross domestic product (GDP). The willingness to transfer resources to LGs and the readiness to take enabling measures by the higher level governments to finance the expenditure responsibilities assigned to them or to enhance investible resources to them especially in a system of considerable vertical and horizontal imbalances assigned to them (indeed an expression of political will) are also important in investigating LG fiscal space. Table 1 shows the share of LG expenditure and OSR in India's public sector expenditure and OSR disaggregated into PRIs and Urban Local Governments (ULGs). Fig. 1. shows the graphical presentation of the share of local expenditure in the public sector expenditure of PRIs, ULGs and LGs from 2002-03 to 2007-08.

Table 1
Trend in the Percentage Share of LGs in the Total Public Sector Expenditure, and Public Sector OSR (2002-03 – 2007-08)

Items	2002-03	2003-04	2004-05	2005-06	2006-07	2007-08
PRIs						
Share of Public Sector Expenditure	2.5	2.9	3.1	3.7	3.9	3.7
Share of Public Sector OSR	0.4	0.4	0.4	0.4	0.3	0.3
ULGs						
Share of Public Sector Expenditure	3.0	2.2	2.5	2.7	2.8	3.0
Share of Public Sector OSR	3.2	3.1	2.9	2.9	2.7	2.5
LGs						
Share of Public Sector Expenditure	5.5	5.1	5.6	6.4	6.7	6.7
Share of Public Sector OSR	3.6	3.5	3.3	3.3	3.0	2.8

Source: (See Chapter 8)

Figure 1
Trend in the Share of Expenditure of PRIs, ULGs and LGs in Total Public Sector Expenditure

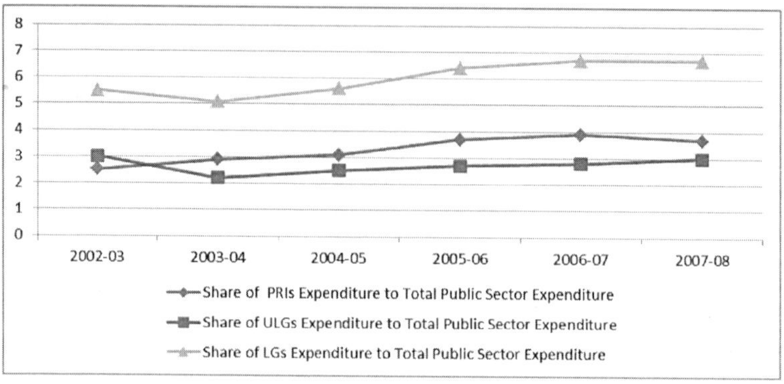

It is significant that the share of local governments' expenditure in the total public sector expenditure has increased almost steadily from 5.5% in 2002-03 to 6.7% in 2007-08. This is obviously because of the stepping up of PRIs' share which increased from 2.5% to 3.7% during this period. Actually, the share of ULGs stagnated around 3% and even declined in some years. The increasing trend of LGs has to be understood subject to the qualification that this increase is due to the step up in agency functions such as the centrally-sponsored schemes and several state sponsored programmes routed through PRIs and ULGs in recent years. This does not go well with the avowed goal of the Constitution to create 'institutions of self-government' at the third stratum of Indian federal governance.

At this point it is instructive to compare the LGs in India with other countries to see where India stands. Tables 2 and 3 help to facilitate this comparison.

It is clear from Table 2 that India is way below most countries and continents except Middle East and West Asia which are not known for their democratic decentralisation. While the European average is 23.9%, the actual expenditure share is 35% in Norway, Sweden and Finland and goes to 55% in Denmark (See World Bank (2008): 296). Enjoying considerable autonomy even under monarchic rule, as far back as 15th century LGs in Nordic countries "served their residents from cradle to grave", a really inclusive system [Boadway and Shah (2009): 267). Many countries notably India does not have such a decentralized past. But the two CAs of India are indeed great steps towards democratic decentralization.

Table 2
The Comparative Role of Local Government

Countries	Local expenditure as percentage of total expenditures
Africa	7.9
Asia	
South Asia	16.0
East Asia	40.0
South–East Asia	15.5
Eurasia	26.5
Europe (2008)	23.9
Latin America	11.1
Middle East & Western Asia	4.6
North America	26.8

Source: Second Global Report on Decentralization and Local Democracy. 2010, p.337

Table 3
Relative Size of Local Government Expenditure with Reference to GDP in the Asia Pacific Region

Countries	Local Public Expenditure (local and meso level only) % GDP
Australia	2%
China	22%
India	2.42%
Indonesia	6%
Japan	12.3%
Malayasia	4%
New Zealand	3.9%
Pakistan	2.6%
Korea, Rep. of	16%
Thailand	2%
Vietnam	11%

Source: First Global Report on Decentralization and Local Democracy in the World, 2008 p. 68. For India M See Chapter 8.

A comparison of local expenditure share reckoned in terms of GDP for Asia Pacific region given in Table 3 also corroborates the relatively poor position of India. Only Australia and Thailand stand below India. For China the percentage of local expenditure share goes as high as 22% and demonstrates a high degree of decentralization. But decentralization in India which statutorily gives a substantial role to the citizens forum of gram sabha and promotes several institutional arrangements for people's participation is qualitatively different from most other countries.

The yawning gap between the exponential expansion of LG expenditure, notably that of PRIs on the one hand and the near stagnation in the share of OSR on the other noted in Table 1 is a matter of concern. This is broughtout in bold relief in Figure 2 based on Appendix A. Appendix A presents the state-wise distribution of per capita tax, per capita OSR and per capita expenditure of PRIs. ULGs are left out because in their case the emerging scenario although disturbing has a solid revenue base. It is important to record some concerns that rise most prominently from Appendix A. One, the per capita expenditure trend is certainly encouraging with all-states PRI expenditure increasing at a compound annual growth of 16.9% per annum. In 2002-03, it ranges from Rs. 18 in Bihar to Rs. 1364 in Maharashtra with an all-states average of Rs. 356; the minimum- maximum (mini-max) ratio works out to 75.7. There is a steady increase in expenditure in all the states. In 2007-08, the per capita expenditure ranges from Rs. 48 in Bihar to Rs. 2967 in Karnataka with an all-states average of Rs. 779 and a mini-max ratio of 61.8. The min-max ratio registers a pronounced decline. Ideally the ratio should go further down. Two, all the three variables present an extremely uneven and disturbing scenario. In 2002-03, four states report no PRI tax revenue (See Appendix A). For the others per capita tax ranges from Re. 1, in Uttar Pradesh to Rs. 64 in Maharashtra with an all-states' average of Rs. 11. Assam, Bihar, Orissa and Rajasthan continue to report zero taxing and in 2007-08, the per capita tax for the other states ranges from Re. 1 in Uttar Pradesh to Rs. 88 in Karnataka. While property tax constitutes the major source of revenue of LGs the world over, it is a matter of concern that some states like Punjab, Haryana and Rajasthan abolished the tax. Three, the per capita OSR which includes non-tax revenue shows a slightly altered picture again with the exception of Bihar. In 2002-03 the per capita OSR of PRIs ranges from Rs. 3 in Orissa and Rajasthan to Rs. 86 in Kerala with an all-states average of Rs. 24. In 2007-08 it ranges from Re. 1 in Bihar to Rs. 180 in Haryana with an all-states average of Rs. 37. It appears 73rd Amendment has had no visible impact in Bihar and the situation in Rajasthan, Punjab and Uttar Pradesh no better compared to several other states. This means over 39 crore people or 33% (based on 2011 census) of the population of the country report no notable impact as a result of democratic decentralization that has been underway for nearly two decades.

Figure 2
Per capita Own Tax, Per capita OSR and Per capita Expenditure of PRIs (All States)

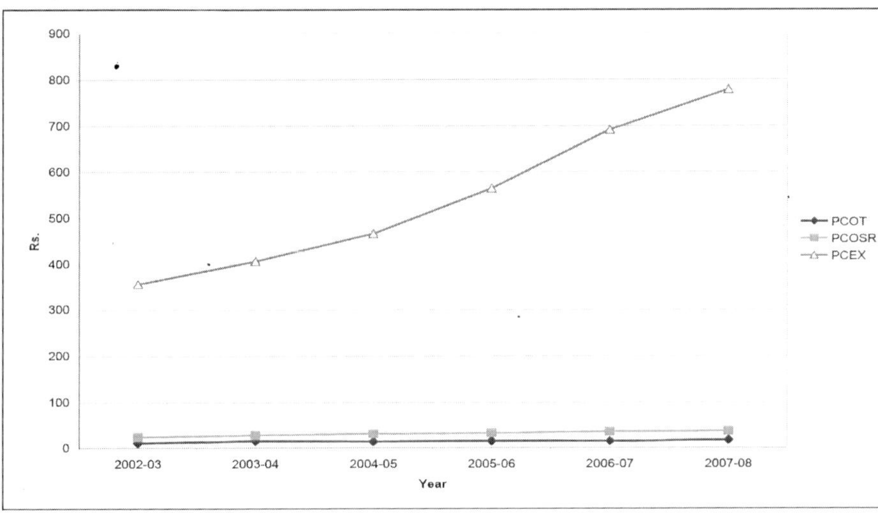

Source: Chapter 8 Note: PCOT: Per capita Own Tax, PCOSR: Per capita Own source Revenue PCEX: Per capita Expenditure

Fig. 2 which shows the widening trend in the per capita expenditure of all-states on the one-hand and per capita OSR and per capita tax on the other portrays a depressing scenario. The constitutional mandate to usher in 'institutions of self-government' at the local level seems to recede like the horizon. The magnitude of PRIs expenditure in absolute terms has increased and as a percentage of GDP from 1.17% to 1.36% in 2006-07 although slightly declined to 1.33% in 2007-08. It is only reasonable to infer that the growing expenditure might have generated a multiplier income effect in those states which have a critical level of per capita expenditure. In all probability with the state-wise allocation for MGNREGA and other flagship programmes steadily increasing the multiplier income effect could be higher. So long as local public goods and services are almost fully financed by grants from higher governments, it may create a fiscal illusion among the local people about the cost of such services and the distribution of its burden. This has to be addressed as a major fiscal problem.

Fiscal Decentralization: The Kerala Story

Given the language of the 73rd/74th CAs the success of democratic decentralization in India depends a great deal on the readiness of state governments to devolve relevant functions, required finance and the needed functionaries to the various LGs at the sub-state level. In other words, real devolution can happen only when the state parts with power and authority and virtually empowers the sub-state level governments. At best the two Amendments are only necessary conditions and much sufficient conditions remain to be realised. Kerala admittedly is one state that has taken measures to devolve more functions, finance and functionaries to the LGs. Almost the first step taken by the LDF (Left Democratic Front) government was to devolve 35-40% of the State Plan outlay to the LGs. This was no fictitious number as it was a rough estimate based on potential expenditure responsibilities that could be devolved to panchayats and municipalities. The decision was followed up by appointing a Committee (widely called the Sen Committee after the name of its first Chairman Subrato Sen) whose primary task was to map out functions (dividing into activities and sub-activities for the sake of functional clarity)[4] fiscal decentralization to facilitate financing of the assigned functions, deployment of required functionaries and creating appropriate legal framework to carry forward the process of democratic decentralisation. Table 4 gives the trend in devolution of resources to LGs by the Kerala state government from 1997-98 through 2012-13.

As already noted the readiness to transfer resources by the higher level governments to implement the expenditure responsibilities assigned to LGs and the creation of relevant statutory and administrative framework for autonomous decision-making by them is a necessary condition and indeed the first step towards democratic deepening at the local level. That Kerala has achieved this in a big way is well exemplified in Table 4. It is clear from Table 4, that the state has devolved nearly 24% of its investible resources (Development fund/plan outlay) to the local governments and the annual devolution ranges from 20.65% in 2009-10 to 33.33% in 2002-03. Figure 3 shows per capita transfers from 1997-98 through 2012-13. Although the nominal per capita transfers shows a CAGR of 7.55% per annum, the real per capita transfers using SDP deflators at 1993-94 prices increased only at the rate of 2.76%. The 16 years average of total resource transfers including non-plan transfers vis-a-vis the total state tax revenue (SOTR) works out to 17.61%. Although this is no small achievement in terms of the magnitude of devolution, the steady decline in the fund flow to LGs as a percentage of SOTR has to be noted.

While in 1998-99 it was as a high as 28.7% of SOTR it declined to 12.83% in 2012-13. The development funds (previously called plan grants) devolved were untied grants.

Table 4
Trends in Devolution of Resources to Local Governments by the Kerala State Government (1997-98 – 2012-13)
(Rs. in crore except per capita figures)

Year	State Plan outlay	SOTR	Devolution as per SFC Recommendation			Ratio of LG Plan Transfers to Plan outlay	Total Transfers as percentage of SOTR of State	Per capita Transfers
			Development Fund	Non Plan	Total	col. 4/col. 2	col. 6/col. 3	
1	2	3	4	5	6	7	8	9
1997-98	2855.00	4501.10	749.00	297.20	1046.20	26.23	23.24	337.07
1998-99	3100.00	4649.60	950.00	384.30	1334.30	30.65	28.70	429.89
1999-00	3250.00	5193.50	1020.00	405.40	1425.40	31.38	27.45	459.24
2000-01	3535.00	5870.30	1045.00	419.90	1464.90	29.56	24.95	471.97
2001-02	3015.00	5923.40	850.00	440.90	1290.90	28.19	21.79	415.91
2002-03	4026.00	7302.50	1342.00	472.20	1814.20	33.33	24.84	584.51
2003-04	4430.25	8088.80	1317.00	505.60	1822.60	29.73	22.53	587.22
2004-05	4800.00	8963.70	1350.00	531.10	1881.10	28.13	20.99	606.06
2005-06	5369.81	9778.60	1375.00	657.20	2032.20	25.61	20.78	654.75
2006-07	6210.00	11941.80	1400.00	650.00	2050.00	22.54	17.17	660.48
2007-08	6950.00	13669.00	1538.44	734.99	2273.43	22.14	16.63	732.47
2008-09	7700.47	15990.20	1670.23	786.43	2456.66	21.69	15.36	791.50
2009-10	8920.00	17403.50	1842.29	865.15	2707.44	20.65	15.56	872.30
2010-11	10025.00	21722.00	2277.72	951.67	3229.39	22.72	14.87	1040.46
2011-12	11030.00	25719.00	2563.76	1409.93	3973.69	23.24	15.45	1280.27
2012-13	14010.00	30077.00	2062.61	1797.34	3859.95	14.72	12.83	1150.88
16 Year Ratio	**99226.53**	**196794.00**	**23353.05**	**11309.31**	**34662.36**	**23.54**	**17.61**	**658.33**

Source: State Plan Outlay, Development Expenditure, Non plan expenditure etc., CAG Reports for various years and Government of Kerala (2011) SOTR:-State's Own Tax Revenue – Budget in Brief (various Years), Government of Kerala.

The major conditionality for the entitlement of plan grants was the preparation and implementation of annual LG plan based on a participatory decentralized planning methodology. The creation of a multi-stage process of planning with institutional mechanisms starting from calling the ward sabha to voice the felt needs of the citizens, to projectisation by the working groups and vetting by Technical Advisory Group and final clearance by the District Planning Committee has widened the avenues for consultation and participation by the people. While the decentralized planning initiative was a great participatory democratic project, over the years it got routinized and bureaucratic reassertion has become a reality, [see GoK (2009) for a documented evaluation upto 2009]. Even so, no one can gainsay the achievements made through greater fiscal space, which of course now needs reform and corrective action.

Figure 3
Per capita Transfers (1997-98 – 2012-13)

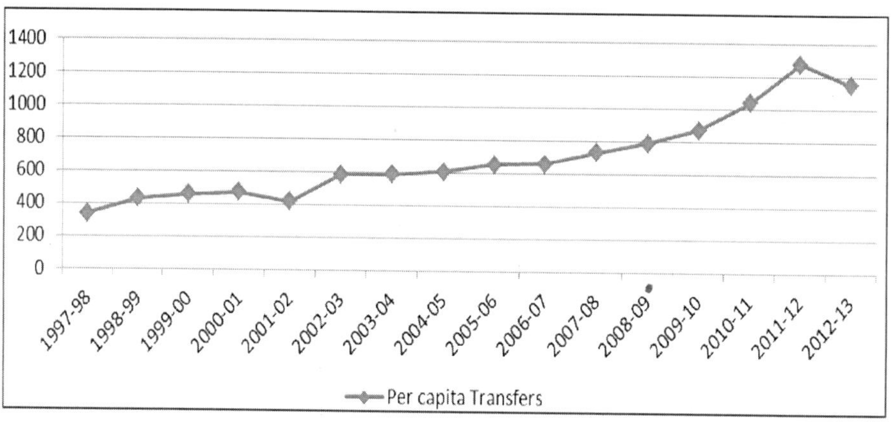

Table 5
Structure and Composition of LG Receipts by Major Sources from 2006-07 to 2012-13
(Rs. in crore)

Sl. No.	Sources of Resources	Year							
		2006-07	2007-08	2008-09	2009-10	2010-11*	2011-12	2012-13	CAGR
	Total Tax Revenue	357.41	334.42	385.36	450.76	--	561.79	661.01	
	Non Tax revenue	230.25	315.08	349.37	377.43	--	376.69	599.60	
	Non Tax revenue as %age to total Receipts	*6.21*	*7.20*	*7.29*	*7.17*	*0.00*	*4.94*	6.26	
1	**Total OSR (i+ii)**	**587.66**	**649.5**	**734.73**	**828.19**	**952.97**	**938.48**	**1260.61**	**12.45**
	Total OSR as %age to total Receipts	***15.85***	***14.84***	***15.33***	***15.73***	***12.80***	***12.32***	*13.16*	
	State Grant: General Purpose Grant	299.96	329.98	363.98	399.31	440.47	644.98	757.89	16.65
	State Grant: General Purpose Grant as% to total receipts	*8.09*	*7.54*	*7.59*	*7.59*	*5.92*	*8.46*	7.91	
	Development Fund	1400.36	1538.44	1670.23	1842.29	2277.12	2021.52	2062.61	7.47
	Development Funds % to Total receipts	*37.77*	*35.14*	*34.85*	*35.00*	*30.58*	*26.53*	*21.53*	
	Maintenance Expenditure (Road + Non Road) Assets	350	404.98	397.52	448.04	440.58	713.94	1039.45	17.44

Sl. No.	Sources of Resources	Year							
		2006-07	2007-08	2008-09	2009-10	2010-11*	2011-12	2012-13	CAGR
	Maintenance Expenditure (Road + Non Road assets)as % to Total Receipts	*9.44*	*9.25*	*8.29*	*8.51*	*5.92*	*9.37*	*10.85*	
	State sponsored Schemes & State Share of Centrally Sponsored Schemes	585.84	976.91	807.44	840.8	1358.24	1358.45	1865.73	18.09
	State sponsored Schemes & State Share of Centrally Sponsored Schemes as % to total Receipts	*15.80*	*22.32*	*16.85*	*15.97*	*18.24*	*17.83*	*19.48*	
2	**Total state Grant**	**2636.16**	**3250.31**	**3239.17**	**3530.44**	**4516.41**	**4738.89**	5725.68	12.97
	Total State Grant as % to total Receipts	***71.11***	***74.25***	***67.58***	***67.07***	***60.66***	***62.19***	***59.77***	
3	**Centrally sponsored schemes**	**323.09**	**454.68**	**811.12**	**832.49**	**1163.79**	**1903.56****	2582.77	40.20
	Total GoI Grants as %age to total Receipts	***8.71***	***10.39***	***16.92***	***15.82***	***15.63***	***24.98***	*26.96*	
	Receipts from loans and other sources	**160.42**	**23.14**	**7.81**	**72.35**	**812.36**	**39.16**	**10.27**	**18.19**
	Receipts from loans and other sources as % to total Receipts	***4.33***	***0.53***	***0.16***	***1.37***	***10.91***	***0.51***	*0.11*	
	Total Receipts	**3707.33**	**4377.63**	**4792.83**	**5263.47**	**7445.53**	**7620.09**	**9579.33**	**17.00**

Source: Comptroller and Auditor General Report for various years. Note: All the Ratios are worked out. *The break-up of OSR into tax and nontax revenue is not available for 2010-11. ** including Development expansion fund. CAGR-Compound Annual Growth Rate.

Receipts do not include MPLAD and MLALAD funds that pass through the LGs.

Table 5 presents the structure and composition of LG finance of Kerala for the period from 2006-07 through 2012-13 based on data for seven years provided by the Annual Reports of the Comptroller and Audit General of India since 2006-07. Such a macro trend is not available for earlier years. The pie-diagrams for 2006-07 and 2012-13 [figure 4 (a), and 4 (b)] help to compare two periods and the changes that occurred in the structure and composition of the funds at the LG level in the State in recent years. Unfortunately CAG does not provide separate figures for panchayats and municipalities. The total receipts of LGs in 2006-07 was over Rs. 3707 crore and rose to Rs. 9579 crore with a compound annual growth rate (CAGR) of 17% per annum. The per LG number works out to Rs. 3.07 crore in 2006-07 and Rs. 7.92 crore in 2012-13. That several gram panchayats in Kerala today spend over Rs.10 crore per annum is certainly an enviable record compared to their counterparts in the rest of the country.

Figure 4 (a)
Percentage Share of Receipts of LGs of Kerala (2006-07)

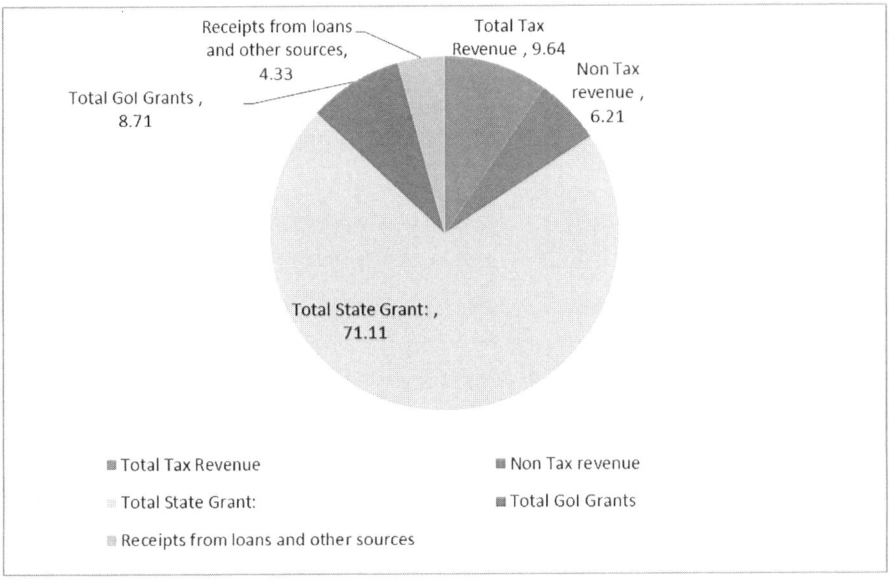

Figure 4 (b)
Percentage Share of Receipts of Local Governments of Kerala (2012-13)

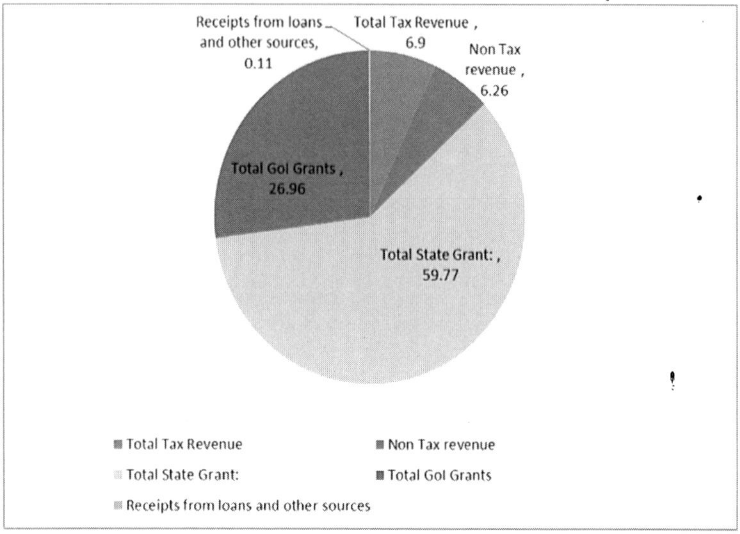

Table 5 clearly shows that state government grants constitute the major share. It ranges from around 60% in 2012-13 to over 74% in 2007-08. Of late, there is a tendency for GoI grants to increase and over the 7 year period their CAGR is over 40%. Probably the worst part is the decline in the share of OSR over the years. In 2006-07 the share of OSR was 15.85% and if loans are included it is well over 20%. The share of OSR declined to 13.16 in 2012-13 and that of loans to a negligible sum. But this does not mean a disturbing indication because the per capita OSR in 2006-07 which was Rs. 176 rose to Rs. 270 in 2011-12 and Rs. 363 in 2012-13, the latter more than double of that in 2006-07.

A moot question that arises at this stage is to investigate whether the increase in grants has adversely affected the revenue mobilisation efforts of gram panchayats. Appendix B gives the list of 24 gram panchayats and the correlation coefficient. The clear conclusion is that increase in grants has not adversely affected the tax efforts. There is no flypaper effect.

Working towards a Well-reasoned LG Space

To be sure, LGs notably the PRIs do not occupy a respectable space in the public finance of India. The 73rd/74th CAs offered a historical opportunity to restructure public finance and address the issue. However, the issue persists as an unfinished task. Barring the creation of several institutions like the gram sabha, SFC, DPC, State Election Commission, introduction of reservation of seats for women, and backward communities and so on, the onus of transferring power and authority through appropriate statutory changes was left to the State Legislative Assembly. While the conformity legislations were passed by all the states as scheduled by April 1994, the empowerment of LGs, particularly the fiscal decentralization exercise and fiscal empowerment of LGs have turned out to be a matter of relevant statutory support and political will. This explains the 'big bang' decentralization of Kerala compared to the snail-like progress in other states. The terms of reference of the XIth UFC as well as that of the XIIth UFC required these Commissions to make recommendations for restructuring public finance. However, both commissions submitted their recommendations without bringing LGs into the picture. The problem continues and has to be addressed by the decision-makers of the country.

We have already underlined the yawning gap between the growing expenditure and shrinking OSR of LGs. Two sets of reforms seem to be in order: one, at the macro level and the other at the level of the states in order to strengthen the process of fiscal empowerment of the LGs. Some general observations that will be helpful in working towards a reasonable fiscal space for LGs are discussed below.

First we may take up the macro reforms. The most compelling macro fiscal policy reform especially with the exit of the Planning Commission relates to the redesigning of the transfer arrangements. The real macro fiscal policy that needs attention is to rationalize the multiple channels of transfers keeping a well-defined space for LGs. Fiscal space and inter-governmental resources flow take place through assignments and transfers in India. As part of assignments we reiterate the suggestion already made to revisit Schedule VII of the Constitution and add a proper local list (in which case one can even drop schedules XI and XII) spelling out the fiscal space of LGs. Another assignment that needs reform is the scheme of Union tax sharing. An unambiguous clause to give a specific share to LGs through suitable constitutional amendments may be added. Till the dismantling of the Planning Commission, Indian federal system had three major channels of transfers (1) the Union Finance Commissions (ii) the Planning Commission, and (iii) the Centrally Sponsored Schemes of the central ministries. These agencies have multiple objectives and strategies and require suitable reforms. Needless to say, the overarching concern of all transfers should be towards delivering improved quality of life and social justice. It is not clear whether the Five Year Plan formulations are going to be dispensed with. Whatever be the possible outcome, there is a great need to work towards a comprehensive framework of transfers. The distinction between plan and non-plan certainly will have to be re-examined because even before the exit of the Planning Commission much confusion had crept in. For one, plan allocations are no longer investible resources meant to augment the productive capacity of the economy and the bulk of the so-called plan expenditure is now revenue expenditure [for details See GoI (2011)]. Moreover for any evaluation of the outlay vis-à-vis outcome, an integrated and holistic picture of expenditure is needed. In other words the transfer system needs to be redesigned. Although it is not the purpose of this paper to go into the design of transfer arrangements that should be considered, how the normal central assistance based on the modified Gadgil formula and all other central assistance to state plans (e.g. centrally sponsored schemes, additional central assistance, special central assistance, central sector schemes and so on) cannot be omitted in any scheme of rethinking. Surely no redesigning can afford to ignore the issues related to the fiscal space of LGs. CSSs assume particular significance in this respect. The state governments have all along been resisting the proliferation of CSSs, many of them being implemented through the LGs. If the various central ministries continue to execute the CSSs without quantitative and qualitative evaluation of delivery and outcome (and in substantial number of cases even transfers are treated as expenditure)[5] the transfer system of the country under the new regime without planning commission can only worsen the situation. Moreover, the growing presence of CSSs means the super imposition of people's preference by the central government preferences. The most compelling rationale for establishing local governments in a democracy is that they reflect the preferences of the local people.

While admittedly the LGs in several states have a poor record of resource mobilization, it is important to point out that several moves and measures taken by the Union and State governments have also harmed the process of creating autonomous LG institutions. The Member of Parliament Local Area Development Scheme (MPLADS) introduced almost simultaneously with the inauguration of the decentralised process of governance, the MLALAD copied by most states for their MLAs as constituency development fund, several Chief Minister's funds (e.g. Janmabhoomi fund in Andhra Pradesh) the centrally-sponsored and state-sponsored schemes and other parallel projects and parallel bodies have aggressively encroached into the functional and fiscal domains of local governments constraining their operational fiscal domain and jeopardizing the process of autonomous local governments and the project of local democracy itself in the country. The Sansad Adarsh Gram Yojana released by the Prime Minister on October 11, 2014 requires MPs to identify one village with a population of 3000-5000 in the plains and 1000-3000 in the hills within a month for convergence of existing schemes for socio-economic development. Being initiated and going to be coordinated and monitored by the Centre, we are on the threshold of a centralization process that seemingly neglects the role of PRIs in the economic transformation of the country. It is widely documented that the central ministries and the Planning Commission (till its recent exit) have been widening their areas of discretion in the use of central resources even after constitutional amendments and the passing of the conformity legislations by the states in 1994. Out of the total centrally sponsored schemes (CSSs) of Rs. 6.6 lakh crore during the XIth Plan, the nine flagship CSSs alone constituted 79.4%. The share of all CSSs as percentage of GBS (Gross Budgetary Support) has continuously increased during the last four plan periods. [For more details see GoI (2011 (a) (also called Chaturvedi Committee Report].

Given the primary focus of this paper we may have to indicate also the underlying principle that should govern all transfers at the Union government level (whatever be the channel) as well as at the state sub-state level. It is acknowledged that even after 67 years of Independence there is acute disparities in the availability of primary services (including toilet coverage) in the country. A necessary condition of all transfers (grants, tax-sharing etc.,) should be to ensure equalization of fiscal capacity of all LGs. In brief, all LGs should have the fiscal capacity to provide comparable levels of public services at reasonably comparable levels of taxation so that no citizen should suffer deprivation due to their choice of residential location. Making tax effort is very important. Of course, this is easily said than done [See Table 1 and Fig. 2). Even so, considerable progress can be achieved if the UFC and SFCs which are organically linked, work towards a common goal.

So far we have discussed some macro reforms to be considered in providing a viable fiscal space to LGs. In those panchayats where the size is very small the question of building a viable size needs to be examined. This is an issue which the country has skirted around. Along with that it is very important to take steps to have a working financial reporting system based on proper annual budgets, accounting practices and audit reports. For this, building a reliable consistent and historical data set is a prime requisite. To build such a data base the practice of budget making and accounting has to be streamlined. This is the major drawback of local governance in India. Even in Kerala known for its advance in democratic decentralisation the situation leaves many things to be desired. A senior IAS officer of Kerala with a firm commitment to the cause of decentralisation famously remarked: "At the local government level, the data given on Monday will be different from that provided on Tuesday." While this is a fact, it is equally important to note that the revenue and expenditure of the LGs after the 73rd/74th CAs expanded on an unprecedented scale. The union, state and parallel agencies started pumping in money via LGs to be utilized for multifarious purposes. The old accounting system and certainly the administrative system were inadequate to tackle the growing challenges. As this situation suited a corrupt regime demand for reforms was slow and actions remains slower. Of course, the needed reforms cannot be handled at the LG level.

FC-11 realized the seriousness of the problem. They recommended that (a) the Comptroller and Auditor General (CAG) should help the Department of Local Fund Audit (DLFA) to improve the situation. Technical Guidance and Supervision (TGS-later renamed as Technical Guidance and Support) and (b) the CAG should prescribe the formats for budgeting and accounting. The CAG has taken steps at the local level including capacity building of the Department of Local Fund Audit. After long deliberations the CAG has prescribed the accrual-based double entry system for municipalities and the cash based single entry system of accounting for the panchayats.[6] Kerala not only adopted this accounting format first for municipalities, but later on adopted it for panchayats. At the instance of the Principal Accountant General (Audit) Kerala, reform measures were instituted from 2003 onwards. Kerala can now boast that it has fully implemented the accrual-based accounting for both panchayats and municipalities. Unless and until this is done in all the states, the case for building more fiscal space will remain weak.

To conclude, the panchayats and municipalities are now constitutionally endowed with the vital task of providing primary services and delivering 'economic development and social justice' at the local level. This is also envisaged as a way for deepening participatory democracy in the context of a representative democracy that failed the people in ushering in an inclusive society. Without assigning a respectable fiscal space for LGs in India's federal polity, all the grandiose objectives regarding local democracy would be empty rhetoric. The rich body of fiscal federalism literature handed down from the West does not offer the policy-theoretic required for developing local democracy in India. The task of fiscal empowerment depends on assignments and transfers. This paper argues the case for reforms in assignments and transfers from the perspective of LGs that are required for a restructuring of public finance in realising these objectives. There is a strong case for a comprehensive, holistic and integrated transfer system based on territorial equity. The overarching goal should be to equalize the fiscal capacity of local governments given their genuine tax effort so that all citizens should have basic needs irrespective of their choice of residential location. Even so, building OSR is the best and sure way to create institutions of local self-government in the country.

* Published as occasional paper No. 2, 2015, RULSG Centre for Development Studies, Thiruvananthapuram.

Endnotes

1 Item No. 5 in the State list (given below) which gives a subordinate status to local government is a relic of the past and needs to be abolished.

> Local government, that is to say, the constitution and powers of municipal corporations, improvement trusts, districts boards, mining settlement authorities and other local authorities for the purpose of local self-government or village administration.[The constitution of India, Schedule 7, List II-State List] Keeping this clause in the Constitution is certainly an anachronism.

2 For a brief review of literature see Oates (2005) and also chapter 2

3 An economic activity or fiscal intervention with reference to its outcome in a society is considered Pareto-optimal when no one can be made better off, without making someone else worse off. Under such a regime when Rome is burning, the fiddling Nero cannot be disturbed because that will make him worse off. This offends all canons of ethics and social justice.

4 The idea of activity mapping was later followed by several other states and the MOPR (Ministry of Panchayati Raj) in 2004 pushed it even by entering into MOUs with individual states by the then MoPR Minister Mani Shankar Aiyar.

5 According to GoI (2011) (Rangarajan Committee Report), 31% of Union government expenditure treats allotment (transfers) as expenditure.

6 It is to be recalled here that in the Regulation on Audit and Accounts, 2007, issued by the Comptroller and Auditor General of India, on the authority of the powers vested in him/her under Article 150 of the Constitution and Section 23 of the CAG's (DPC)Act,1971, CAG has mandated that , within a short period, the accounts of the Union and States shall be switched over from the cash based single entry system to the accrual based double entry system of accounting. Nothing happened.

References

Boadway Robin and Anwar Shah (2009), *Fiscal Federalism: Principles and Practice of Multi-order Governance,* Cambridge University Press.

Government of India (2011) , *Report of the High Level Expert Committee on Efficient Management of Public Expenditure,* (Rangarajan Committee Report) Planning Commission, New Delhi.

--- **(2011)** (a) ; *Report of The Committee on Restructuring Of Centrally Sponsored Schemes (CSS)*, (B K Chaturvedi Report), Planning Commission, New Delhi.

--- Report of the Eleventh Finance Commission (2000-2005).

--- Report of the Twelfth Finance Commission (2005-2010).

Government of Kerala (2009), *Report on Committee for Evaluation of Decentralised Planning and Development, (*M A Oommen Committee Report), Thiruvananthapuram.

--- **(2011)**, *Report of the Comptroller and Auditor General of India,* for various years.

--- State Planning Board, *Economic review* (for various years).

Oates, Wallace (2005), "Toward A Second-Generation Theory of Fiscal Federalism", *International Tax and Public Finance,* Springer, vol. 12 (4), pages 349-373, August.

Tiebout Charles (1956), 'A Pure Theory of Local Expenditure', *Journal of Political Economy,* October.

World Bank (2010), *Local Government Finance: The Challenges of the 21st Century,* Second Global Report on Decentralisation and Local Democracy, United Cities and Local Governments.

--- **(2008),** *Decentralisation and Local Democracy in the World,* A co-publication of the World Bank and United Cities and Local Governments.

Appendix A
Per capita Own Tax, Per capita OSR and Per capita Expenditure of PRIs (in Rs.)

States	2002-03			2003-04			2004-05			2005-06			2006-07			2007-08		
	PCOT	PCOSR	PCEX	PCOT	PCOSR	PCEX	PCOT	PCOSR	PCEX	PCOT	PCOSR	PCEX	PCOT	PCOSR	PCEX	PCOT	PCOSR	PCEX
Andhra Pradesh	20	51	187	22	52	192	25	60	216	28	66	263	31	70	281	33	89	371
Assam	0	4	272	0	4	489	0	4	555	0	4	863	0	6	1257	0	7	866
Bihar	0	0	18	0	0	18	0	0	1	0	0	44	0	1	45	0	1	48
Gujarat	7	22	1342	7	22	1387	14	39	1507	7	27	1718	12	34	2013	26	45	2080
Haryana	3	74	177	1	73	201	5	134	234	4	173	451	4	187	469	4	180	637
Karnataka	19	19	1199	33	33	1335	24	24	1409	36	36	2057	46	46	2391	88	88	2967
Kerala	49	86	351	48	94	600	52	107	674	66	127	760	66	133	820	63	112	874
Madhya Pradesh	5	11	77	6	12	69	7	13	341	7	15	468	3	11	868	3	13	1153
Maharashtra	64	85	1364	106	127	1531	85	109	1687	70	96	1872	73	103	2067	80	114	2268
Orissa	0	3	268	0	3	295	0	3	291	0	3	326	0	3	568	0	3	576
Punjab	2	77	175	2	70	193	11	95	235	11	95	267	12	111	520	8	29	136
Rajasthan	0	3	50	0	3	51	0	4	81	1	3	90	1	4	84	0	3	75
Tamil Nadu	14	65	686	22	55	715	24	65	828	27	70	838	29	78	979	34	74	1229
Uttar Pradesh	1	5	93	1	5	129	1	6	146	1	7	169	1	6	196	1	7	186
West Bengal	2	7	181	3	9	209	2	12	254	3	13	267	4	17	433	0	0	581
All States	**11**	**24**	**356**	**15**	**28**	**406**	**14**	**31**	**466**	**15**	**33**	**564**	**15**	**36**	**692**	**18**	**37**	**779**

PCOT: Per capita Own Tax, PCOSR: Per capita Own source Revenue PCEX: Per capita Expenditure

Source: 13th Finance Commission website Note: State-wise rural populations as per 2001 census is used for per capita computation. No Projection is made.

Appendix B
Correlation between Tax and Grants

	2012-13		2013-14
Correlation	0.252		0.435

LG Code	2012-13		2013-14	
	Per capita Grants	Per capita Tax	Per capita Grants	Per capita Tax
GP103	2,456	138	2,620	153
GP12	2,014	80	1,956	90
GP26	1,942	120	2,230	121
GP29	1,272	87	1,431	93
GP35	2,980	293	2,922	348
GP42	3,583	472	3,729	466
GP44	4,529	346	3,904	179
GP45	3,673	290	3,542	208
GP46	2,757	233	3,015	214
GP47	1,585	123	3,245	98
GP54	2,019	126	2,343	149
GP58	3,435	105	3,579	107
GP60	3,320	520	4,826	565
GP64	2,635	209	2,864	212
GP65	2,518	179	2,719	179
GP75	3,251	553	3,290	608
GP83	2,437	199	2,348	237
GP87	2,788	277	2,835	417
GP90	3,153	157	2,349	186
GP91	4,109	162	3,600	156
GP93	5,140	134	3,962	180
GP94	5,174	191	4,822	232
GP95	4,494	149	3,790	211
GP96	3,277	81	2,425	98

INDEX